The Opioid Crisis

The Opioid Crisis

A Policy Case Study

GAIL UKOCKIS

OXFORD
UNIVERSITY PRESS

Oxford University Press is a department of the University of Oxford. It furthers
the University's objective of excellence in research, scholarship, and education
by publishing worldwide. Oxford is a registered trade mark of Oxford University
Press in the UK and certain other countries.

Published in the United States of America by Oxford University Press
198 Madison Avenue, New York, NY 10016, United States of America.

© Oxford University Press 2024

All rights reserved. No part of this publication may be reproduced, stored in
a retrieval system, or transmitted, in any form or by any means, without the
prior permission in writing of Oxford University Press, or as expressly permitted
by law, by license, or under terms agreed with the appropriate reproduction
rights organization. Inquiries concerning reproduction outside the scope of the
above should be sent to the Rights Department, Oxford University Press, at the
address above.

You must not circulate this work in any other form
and you must impose this same condition on any acquirer.

Library of Congress Cataloging-in-Publication Data
Names: Ukockis, Gail L., 1962– author.
Title: The opioid crisis : a policy case study / Gail Ukockis.
Includes Description: New York, NY : Oxford University Press, [2024] |
bibliographical references and index.
Identifiers: LCCN 2023058746 (print) | LCCN 2023058747 (ebook) |
ISBN 9780197585207 (hardback) | ISBN 9780197585221 (epub) |
ISBN 9780197585238
Subjects: LCSH: Opioid abuse—United States. |
Opioids—Government policy—United States.
Classification: LCC HV5822.O45 U46 2024 (print) | LCC HV5822.O45 (ebook) |
DDC 362.29/30973—dc23/eng/20240125
LC record available at https://lccn.loc.gov/2023058746
LC ebook record available at https://lccn.loc.gov/2023058747

DOI: 10.1093/oso/9780197585207.001.0001

Printed by Sheridan Books, Inc., United States of America

Contents

Preface	ix
Note	xiii

1. **The importance of policy in the opioid crisis** — 1
   - Why study policy? — 1
   - What is policy? — 2
   - The power of stigma — 3
   - Opioid addiction is nothing new — 6
   - Structure of the book — 9

2. **The causes of the opioid crisis** — 14
   - Introduction — 14
   - Self-reflection exercise — 15
   - Background of the current opioid crisis — 15
     - Pharmaceutical companies — 16
     - Drug cartels — 19
     - Despair — 20
     - Government health care — 21
     - Pain — 22
   - Applying the Framework of Addiction to the opioid crisis — 23
   - Socio-ecological framework of the opioid crisis — 23
     - Sociodemographic factors — 23
     - Stress and trauma exposure — 24
     - Physical and mental health — 24
     - Biological and genetic susceptibility — 25
     - Pain — 25
     - Self-determination — 25
     - Self-stigma — 26
   - Social determinants of health — 27
   - Policy case study: The homeless population in Seattle — 28
     - Problem description — 28
     - Problem solutions (policy ideas) — 32

3. **The political context of the opioid crisis** — 37
   - Introduction — 37
   - Rise of political violence — 37
   - Impact of President Trump on political discourse — 40

- The political spectrum ... 41
  - Centrists ... 42
  - Conservatives ... 43
  - Far right ... 44
  - Liberals ... 45
  - Far left ... 46
- The political spectrum and the opioid crisis ... 48
- Thoughtful activism ... 49
- Rules for radicals: Is being radical such a bad thing? ... 51
- Frederick Douglass ... 55

4. The punishing effects of poverty ... 59
   - Introduction ... 59
   - The concept of poverty ... 60
   - The power of hierarchy ... 62
   - The power of capitalism ... 70
   - Policy analysis: Poverty Bill of Rights (2020) ... 73
   - Role of Medicaid in the opioid crisis ... 76

5. Child welfare and the opioid crisis ... 81
   - Introduction ... 81
   - Impact of the opioid crisis on the child welfare system ... 82
     - Racial and ethnic aspects ... 84
     - Parents in recovery ... 86
   - Permanency planning ... 88
   - Grandparents and other kinship providers ... 89
   - Fathers' rights and responsibilities ... 94
     - Who's the daddy? ... 94
     - Deadbeat dads ... 95
   - Adverse childhood experiences ... 96

6. Women and OUD ... 99
   - Introduction ... 99
   - The criminalization of pregnancy ... 100
   - Human trafficking ... 106
     - Intersection of SUD and human trafficking ... 111
     - The international picture of drugs and human trafficking ... 113
     - Intersection of the opioid crisis and human trafficking ... 113
   - Women in prison ... 119

7. Special populations ... 123
   - Introduction ... 123
   - Blacks/AA ... 123
   - Case study: Washington, DC ... 128
   - Hispanic/Latinx ... 129

- ▹ Native Americans — 133
- ▹ Older adults — 137
- ▹ Successful aging — 137
- ▹ Veterans and active military personnel — 141
- ▹ OUD and transgender/nonbinary persons — 145

8. The role of criminal justice in the opioid crisis — 148
   - ▹ Introduction — 148
   - ▹ The era of mass incarceration — 150
   - ▹ The War on Drugs — 153
   - ▹ Drug use and treatment in prisons/jails — 158
   - ▹ Social costs of mass incarceration — 160
   - ▹ Impact of mass incarceration on justice-involved persons — 162
   - ▹ Fixing a broken system — 165
   - ▹ Second look laws — 166

9. Ongoing challenges — 171
   - ▹ Introduction — 171
   - ▹ The impact of COVID-19 — 171
   - ▹ Co-use of methamphetamine — 177
   - ▹ Fentanyl — 182
   - ▹ Stigma of SUD — 187

10. Advocacy and the opioid crisis — 193
    - ▹ Introduction — 193
    - ▹ A community fights back — 194
    - ▹ Innovation: Linking the legal and medical systems — 196
    - ▹ Policy case study one: Good Samaritan laws — 197
    - ▹ Policy case study two: Drug-induced homicide laws — 201
    - ▹ Homelessness and SUD: One advocate's view — 204
    - ▹ More policy suggestions for homelessness in Denver — 206
    - ▹ Harm reduction — 209
    - ▹ Jobs and sober housing — 210
    - ▹ Conclusion — 212

References — 215
Index — 245

Preface

Can you remember where you were when you realized that COVID-19 was going to be such a big deal? In March 2020, I was sitting in a community center with several other people. A woman looked at her cell phone and announced, "WHO has just declared COVID to be a pandemic." Huh, I thought. What happens next? I had no idea of what to do at the beginning of a natural disaster that was invisible but deadlier than any hurricane or earthquake.

If the lockdown and its severe impact on people and businesses were not enough trauma for everyone, the virus itself is even worse. Two months after getting this book contract, I found myself inexplicably exhausted after taking a shower. Then I ended up in the ER with the diagnosis of severe COVID-19. The term "long covid" now applies to me, with fatigue affecting me daily. Considering that over one million Americans have died of COVID-19, though, I consider myself fortunate (covid.cdc.gov/covid-data-tracker).

Inevitably, the shadow of COVID-19 has influenced this book because society is still grappling with its impact. Not surprisingly, COVID-19 worsened the opioid crisis due to factors such as interrupted services and social isolation. One medical article title states it succinctly: "An epidemic in the midst of a pandemic: Opioid use disorder and COVID-19" (Alexander, Stoller, Haffajee, & Saloner, 2020).

Hope, though, arises from this darkness caused by mass deaths, disabling conditions, and economic turmoil. Although we may feel exhausted by COVID-19 and its aftermath, our determination will overpower any barriers to helping persons with substance use disorder (SUD). The vaccination success story in 2021, for example, indicates the power of policy to change lives for the better. To get my own vaccine, I had entered a large building filled with hundreds of people and my heart had lifted at the sight. Policy was evident in the needles going into arms, the staff guiding the patients, and the organizers who handled the logistics of vaccinating thousands a day. Indeed, policy is as solid as the number of vaccinated persons worldwide—71 percent of the world's population has received at least one vaccine dose by 2022 (Holder, 2022). Despite the anti-vaccine resistance that arose after my hopeful experience, I still posit that the development and implementation of the COVID-19 vaccines were a great policy achievement.

If hope has emerged during the COVID-19 pandemic, it also appears during the opioid crisis. Scientific research continues to help us understand the biological basis of SUD, especially regarding the brain. Dedicated professionals confront the multiple challenges related to SUD, while community activists try to make treatment and other services more accessible.

Thus, social workers and others who are committed to helping persons with SUD are not alone in this opioid crisis. In March 2021, Congress passed the American Rescue Act of 2021 (called the "COVID relief bill") that designated 4.25 billion dollars for SUD and mental health treatment (www.samhsa.gov). As President Joe Biden continued to push for more social spending, advocates in the SUD field will have an advantage.

Discussion question

Look up the grant allocations on SAMHSA's website for the COVID-19 Relief Bill (www.samhsa.gov/sites/default/files/covid19-programs-funded-samhsa-fy21.pdf). Find your state on the list and review the agencies who received funds. Do you think that these funds had an impact on your community? Why or why not?

The background of this book started in 2018, when I was about to start my new job as a drug counselor at a medication assisted therapy (MAT) clinic. My diverse social work experiences had included some exposure to substance misuse, but I was certainly no expert. However, I had pitched a book about applying policy to a specific social problem, and my editor had suggested that the opioid crisis could be a good fit. In the United States, many social workers encounter the opioid epidemic even if they are not in the alcohol and other drugs (AOD) field. My home state of Ohio is especially hard-hit by drug trafficking. As a counselor, I have worked with family members grieving the deaths of an overdose victim. Parents who have children on the streets or in recovery also carry a difficult burden. As a professor, I had also encountered students who had to attend funerals of an overdose victim or witness a person's fatal overdose.

The first MAT clinic I worked at was in Lancaster, Ohio, which was one of the epicenters of opioid misuse because it is on the edge of Appalachia. Driving down Route 33 ("Heroin Highway") to Lancaster, I had no idea of what to expect. The news about the opioid epidemic had been relentlessly grim, with over 70,000 overdose deaths in 2019 (www.cdc.gov/opioids/basics/epidemic.html). Media images of distraught parents and desperate drug users flooded the news cycle.

What I did not expect was to stand at my office window with a mother and her toddler, gazing at the groundhog outside. While some of my clients have lost custody of their kids, many parents had come to the clinic with their kids because they cannot find daycare. As somebody who used to volunteer with foster children, I was now trying to keep kids out of foster and kinship care.

Some clients would travel a four-hour round trip to the clinic, a weekly pilgrimage that entailed a urine drug screen and a large waiting room. On busy days, the clients overflowed from the waiting room into the hallways and outside. These persons showed a resilient determination to live without opioid use disorder (OUD) so they now longer felt like they were living in a fog. They said that they wanted to feel awake and alive again.

The second MAT clinic I worked at had fewer clients, so I had more time to connect with them about their recovery goals. For most of my clients, their opioid misuse was but one of their many challenges: chronic pain, domestic violence, housing crisis, unemployment, and simply being cash poor. Many clients experienced stigma as they struggled to rebuild their lives. Barriers to getting jobs and housing sometimes seemed insurmountable. Although the impact of the opioid crisis could appear overwhelming and complicated, I felt confident in the recovery of many of my clients. Treatment works, especially if social workers continue to help both individuals and communities with the healing process.

If I did not believe in the power of social workers and other activists to fight against the opioid crisis, I would not be writing this book. It is critical, though, for us to have a clear grasp of policy making to become effective. Fortunately, we have been toughened by the pandemic and other stressors. We understand the need for critical thinking and thoughtful activism. I am writing this book in a spirit of hope—hope not just for the persons affected by the opioid crisis but for all persons who may feel disheartened about current events. May optimism crowd out any discouragement, as we consider the next chapter in our lives.

Note

During the book, I use the term "white" reluctantly, but I have stopped using the term "Caucasian" after finding out that this term was coined by a white supremacist (see Mukhopadhyay, 2016). Instead of using the term "Black/African American", I have shortened it to "Black/AA" for easier reading.

1
The importance of policy in the opioid crisis

Why study policy?

"But policy is so boring! Why do I have to take this class? I only want to do case management or clinical!"

When I first heard my classmates complain about policy classes, I was shocked. As a history buff and news enthusiast, I loved talking about how Medicare legislation passed in 1965. Who wouldn't be intrigued by the difference between SSI and SSDI?

Later when I accepted the offer to teach my first policy class, I feared that some students would dismiss it as a waste of time. I spent weeks finding material that would grab their attention and make them love policy as much as I do. Shortly before the fall quarter started, I spent a week in Florida.

My flight back to Ohio was scheduled at 5 a.m. on Tuesday, September 11, 2001.

A few days later, I took the bus home because the airports were still closed. From town to town, flags flew in defiance of the terrorist attacks. It was an eerie time.

Then I stood before a classroom filled with shell-shocked faces. Several questions swirled in our heads: Who was Osama bin Laden? What was al-Qaeda? What did Afghanistan have to do with these attacks?

"Do you want me to prepare a lecture about what happened?" I asked. The students nodded, appearing grateful and relieved. Obviously, that year I had no need to explain the importance of policy.

Through the years, many of my students have demonstrated that they can connect how policy affects their practices. Some told me that they had started advocating against injustice, while one said that she might even run for office one day. These anecdotes are not hard data, but they make me hopeful that I was not wasting their time in class.

This book is not primarily about the opioid crisis but about how policy knowledge is essential for social workers confronting crises such as the drug epidemic. No matter the crisis, social workers must know how policy works, or they will fail their clients. Good intentions are not enough, because clients need competent workers with policy expertise. Just focusing on one's caseload and billable hours are not enough for social work professionals, since advocacy is a key aspect of practice.

What is policy?

What is "policy" really? The Oxford English Dictionary defines it as "A principle or course of action adopted or proposed as desirable, advantageous, or expedient; esp. one formally advocated by a government, political party, etc. Also as a mass noun: method of acting on matters of principle, settled practice" (Oxford English Dictionary, n.d.). Using the Socratic approach, let us probe these concepts as they relate to you as a person and future social worker:

What is desirable for society? For example, reducing the rate of child hunger might be a desirable goal for those who want to diminish the suffering of others.

Why would reducing child hunger be advantageous? On the individual level, a well-fed child would probably do better in school and enjoy better health. On the social level, a school with well-fed children might have better retention rates and fewer behavior problems. These children would be more likely to grow up to be self-sufficient adults instead of struggling to get by.

Is reducing child hunger an expedient (useful) course of action? During the Great Depression of the 1930s, many children were malnourished. When the U.S. started drafting men for World War II, the government found that many were not suitable for service because they had grown up hungry. In 1946 (the year after World War II ended), the government established the National School Lunch Program because it was expedient (School Food Programs, n.d.).

How does the term matter of principle apply to reducing child hunger? Those who care about social justice are probably outraged by the idea of such a prosperous country as the U.S. allowing children to go hungry. Persons who want to restrict government spending and the role of the "nanny state," though, may object to the school lunch program and other policies intended to reduce child hunger.

Policy, then, is about values. Social work students usually value helping others besides their own educational goals. If you are not sure about what values you have, review your checking account. What do you spend money on? A person who values their pets more than vacations, for example, may spend more money on veterinarian bills than plane tickets.

On the government level, the budget is the clearest statement of the lawmakers' values. When a budget reduces taxes that cause cuts in social services, such as Medicaid, then lawmakers show that they value business interests more than the low-income persons who need medical care. Another budget may increase spending on solar and wind power, which shows that environmental concerns are valued.

If policy is about values, then it is also about money. To be blunt, social workers can do little without proper funding of their programs. Occasionally, a sympathetic lawmaker may help an advocacy group achieve their goals of being heard and getting funding. Usually, though, an advocacy group has to fight for years to be heard. As Box 1.1 indicates, secondary trauma is another aspect of policy.

The power of stigma

One tragic example of an urgent but ignored crisis occurred in the 1980s. During the early days of the HIV/AIDS epidemic, President Reagan remained mute about it while thousands of Americans died. Medical research and other desperately needed services remained underfunded. The recent documentary called "When AIDS was funny" includes tapes of the press secretary repeatedly laughing off AIDS-related questions from journalists (Wong, 2017). AIDS Coalition to Unleash Power (ACT UP), founded in 1987, was only one group to fight the indifference of both the government and the mainstream society (Rimmerman, 1998).

Not until 1990 did Congress pass the Ryan White Act to create an organized response (Health Resources and Services Administration, n.d.). While doing my field placement at the state health agency that provided HIV-related services, I heard many clients complain about how the Act was named after this hemophiliac boy who was "innocent" of sexual behavior or drug use. They were understandably bitter that when the epidemic was first called the "gay plague," the mentality of "let them die" dominated the policy discussions.

Box 1.1 Secondary trauma

Like most drug overdose victims, first responders must endure wrenching pain. Police officers, for example, have seen some rough stuff. One officer in Huntington, West Virginia described the daily occurrence of overdoses in their city: "You name it, he's seen it: Moms passed out with their kids still seat-belted. Dads sprawled on floors, their toddlers within an arm's reach of heroin. Never once has a heroin user thanked McClure for saving his or her life. Sometimes they complain about the interruption of their high" (Drash & Blau, 2016).

Ambulance crews are also first responders who must cope with the emotional impact of this crisis. One emergency medical technician (EMT) in south Jersey discussed how she would worry about the persons she had resuscitated. "I can save the same person over and over again, but when I don't see them out there for a while, I think, 'Did they get help, or did they overdose another time in another area when I wasn't working and when I wasn't able to save them?'" (Leonard, 2018).

In some communities, teachers find themselves on the front line when dealing with their students' traumas. "Teachers console children whose parents have died, gone to jail, or disappeared as foster care rates increase, often resulting from drug abuse. Sleep-deprived youngsters come to school hungry and dirty, describing drug busts in their homes. Sometimes, the abusers are the students themselves. Overloaded school counselors struggle to assist hundreds of kids and parents" (Hefling, 2018).

Drug counselors, of course, are not immune to secondary trauma (Bride, 2009). Lack of training, besides lack of support from employers, can lead to burnout and staff simply leaving the their jobs. On a personal note, one of my new coworkers told me that he had worked as a drug counselor in Columbus, Ohio for eight months. He suffered from such a bad sleep disorder that he had to quit and take some time off before being hired as a general counselor.

> How much research has been done on drug counselors and secondary trauma? (Hint: the Google Scholar website can be handy.) Should there be more research? How would secondary trauma affect the quality of addiction services if there is too much turnover?

> Prepare a proposal to lawmakers noting that secondary trauma is a factor in policy planning. What should we do about it?

This "let them die" mentality is related to the current public health emergency presented by the opioid crisis. The parallels between the two crises are striking. Both first appeared in marginalized populations: gay/bisexual men for HIV/AIDS and hardcore addicts for the drug crisis. Then the "normal" people became identified as the victims. Ryan White became the new face of AIDS patients while the soccer moms and other "respectable" persons are getting more public support for fighting the opioid crisis than would a lower-income group or persons of color.

For marginalized populations, the theme of "stigma" resonates in many policy debates. Stigma, defined as a "spoiled identity" by Erving Goffman (1963), determines who should be excluded from a social group. For example, a thief would face rejection because their stealing would endanger the tribe's survival. Social workers, of course, often work with stigmatized persons and may even be stigmatized themselves for their jobs. Language can amplify or decrease stigma—consider the difference between the terms "whore" and "sex worker." The term "addict" implies a person who is destructive to both self and others, so professionals have shifted the language from "addiction" to the term "SUD" for substance use disorder (Partnership for Drug-free Kids, 2017) Depending on the context, this book will use the term "SUD" instead of "addiction"; if a person is in treatment, the term "person in recovery" will be used instead of "recovering addict."

Discussion questions

- Besides persons coping with HIV/AIDS and/or addiction, are there other groups that people might be callous about?
- One social work value stresses the dignity and worth of each person. How does that relate to the "let them die" attitude?
- In the preface, the author's brief description of working at a suboxone clinic includes observations about the clients. Do these anecdotes represent hard data? Why or why not would they be effective to use when advocating for these clients? Box 1.2, a case study, provides another example of anecdotal data.

> **Box 1.2 Case study**
>
> Brandy was arrested several times for selling drugs and other drug-related offenses. As a self-professed "junkie," she had open sores on her face from picking at imaginary insects crawling on it. Her teeth were rotten, and she was severely underweight. Then she went through a "miracle" of giving up addiction and has abstained from drugs for over 10 years. Her career path as a substance abuse counselor and later as the director for a re-entry program shows her strong commitment to helping others. "I am the first convicted felon to be sworn in as a deputy in the history of the . . . Sheriff's Office. It just goes to show that no matter if you have tattoos or a felony number behind your name, if you work hard and prove yourself, you can change your life" (Morris-Hafner, 2019, p. 146). She has also regained custody of her children.
>
> Discussion questions
> Brandy narrates her recovery journey by calling herself a "junkie." In my practice experience as a drug counselor, I have also encountered persons who used this term about themselves. Why do you think that this self-labeling happens? Do you consider it harmless, or does it add to the stigma of SUD?

Opioid addiction is nothing new

Opium is derived from the poppy plant. Since Neolithic times, "God's own medicine" (opioids) have been used by humans to alleviate pain and experience euphoria (Halpern & Blistein, 2019, p. 3). Opium dens, the age-old precursor to crackhouses, allowed users to smoke in peaceful bliss. Anti-Asian sentiments resulted when lawmakers associated the Chinese immigrants with these opium dens, as seen in Illustration 1.1. In the 19th and early 20th centuries, opium was also sold over the counter for a variety of medical complaints.

Modern chemists came into the picture in 1898, when they developed heroin as a medical treatment. Heroin, of course, created a new path to drug misuse. In World War II, when Germany lost its source of opium supply, another synthetic was created—methadone. In the 1960s, methadone treatment presented a new way for heroin users to stop using without experiencing the

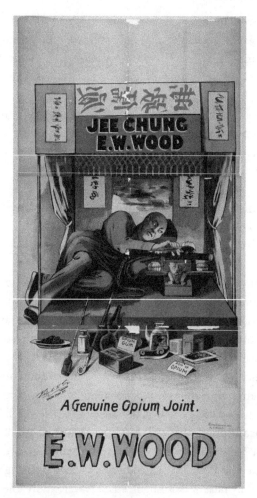

Illustration 1.1 Media portrayal of opium den.
Library of Congress website—https://www.loc.gov/pictures/item/2014637451/

brutal effects of withdrawal such as "cold turkey" symptoms (e.g., shivering and goosebumps). Methadone, which has been proven as an effective treatment, decreases the withdrawal symptoms and cravings that are barriers to quitting opioids. It provides a "narcotic blockade" that keeps a person from getting high with more opioids (Strang & Tober, 2003, p. 7). Daily doses are usually required, with clinics usually situated in cities.

For decades, methadone has been called both a "panacea and a poison" because it can heal or harm a person (Strang & Tober, 2003, p. 12). The debate over medication assisted treatment (MAT) expanded when other medications became available, including suboxone/buprenorphine in 2002. Several challenges regarding the proper use of such medications exist, especially the lack of access in underserved areas, such as rural counties (Calcetterra et al., 2019).

MAT remains a controversial issue in the recovery community and the general public. Based on my professional experience working in suboxone clinics, the concerns about persons in recovery using these medications include the following:

- possible misuse that could lead to overdoses and even deaths;
- possible diversion to the streets so suboxone is traded or sold;
- physical dependence on this medication for years.

Steven Scanlan, a medical expert who has used suboxone himself, states that "There's no way your brain chemistry can heal while on buprenorphine .... You're continuing to give someone a narcotic." Scanlan says patients who want to get off the 8 to 16 mg levels physicians typically prescribe must taper very slowly because of the drug's half-life (Matesa, 2011).

Another concern is that "Big Pharma" (pharmaceutical companies) do not have a stellar reputation after the scandals related to Oxycontin as described in Chapter 2. In an article titled "Capitalism gone wrong: how big pharma created America's opioid carnage," McGreal (2019) writes of a British company paying a $1.4 billion civil settlement regarding its sales tactics for suboxone. "A Reckitt Benckiser subsidiary had been pressing doctors to prescribe its opioid by falsely claiming it was safer and more effective than similar medicines on the market." Another journalist also accuses "Big Pharma" of overpricing its products such as suboxone and naloxone (Narcan kits). "Pharmaceutical companies have proven, after all, that they are opportunistic if nothing else."

MAT is related to harm reduction, which "accepts, for better and or worse, that licit and illicit drug use is part of our world and chooses to work to minimize its harmful effects rather than simply ignore or condemn them" (www.harmreduction.org). The social work profession supports this perspective, as stated in the Encyclopedia of Social Work: "Harm reduction is a helping strategy that attempts to alleviate the social, legal, and medical consequences associated with unmanaged addiction, and in so doing, limit the harms, such as infectious disease (HIV, hepatitis), violence, criminal activity, and early death, without necessarily attempting to 'cure' the addiction" (Davis, 2013).

As evident in this book, the harm reduction philosophy remains a strong component of the opioid issue. Its focus on "reducing the negative consequences of substance use for individuals, communities and societies... rather than focusing on decreasing or eliminating substance use" (Pauly et al., 2007, p. 19). A social worker might state is as: "starting where the client is." Examples of harm reduction include needle exchange programs and syringe cleaning kits (Smye et al., 2011). Chapter 10 discusses harm reduction in more depth.

Methadone and other MAT options, then, are complicated responses to an even more complicated problem. The opioid crisis has generated many ethical dilemmas for social workers and other professionals, especially regarding harm reduction.

Discussion question

The article title "You're nothing but a junkie: Multiple experiences of stigma in an aging methadone maintenance population" (Connor & Rosen, 2008) describes the impact of stigma on those using methadone. This stigma is not only about SUD but also about poverty and race. A more recent article about stigma stresses the risk to continuing methadone or buprenorphine treatment (Enos, 2021). Design a public awareness campaign to decrease the stigma of using MAT. (Box 1.3 provides a glossary of the book's terms.)

Structure of the book

The opioid crisis presents several complicated questions that defy easy answers. This book's purpose is to both educate on the policy aspects of the opioid crisis and provide points for in-depth discussion. Also, the book will apply the concepts to the real-life challenges of the opioid crisis. Each chapter will stress critical thinking skills, besides suggesting Action Steps for concrete actions.

This book concentrates on the macro level of social work, defined here as working for policy changes to decrease a social problem. I have worked at the micro level by providing direct care for clients with SUD. Agency-level work

> **Box 1.3 What the heck does that mean?**
>
> Opioid: a class of drugs that affect the opioid receptors in the brain. Because opioids often cause euphoria, addiction can occur even if a person was properly taking a prescribed medication. The term "opioid" includes both opiates (natural drugs, such as heroin, derived from the poppy plant) and synthetics (e.g., fentanyl).
>
> OUD: specifically refers to the misuse of prescription drugs, heroin, and synthetics, such as fentanyl, etc. This term is used instead of "opioid addiction."
>
> SUD: refers to substances such as alcohol and street drugs. If a person uses more than one drug, this is called "polysubstance use." This term is used instead of "addiction."
>
> MAT: is evidence-based treatment that uses buprenorphine, naloxone, methadone, and other medications. Patients find relief from cravings and withdrawal symptoms as they work on their recovery. Per SAMHSA, counseling and/or group treatment are mandatory for MAT patients (www.samhsa.gov/medication-assisted-treatment).
>
> Narcan: the brand name for the nasal spray that administers naloxone to an overdose victim. Opioids can slow down a person's breathing so much that they could die. Naloxone reverses the opioid's effects so that a person wakes up and breathes normally again. Once only available to first responders, now Narcan is widely distributed to the public according to the manufacturer's website (www.narcan.com).

is called the mezzo level, which is also a valuable component of social work. All three levels intertwine and truly cannot be separated from each other.

Chapter 2 focuses on the causes of the opioid crisis, including the overprescribing of opioid painkillers. The chapter introduces the reader to two tools of analysis, the Framework of Addiction and the Social Determinants of Health. A policy case study of the homeless population in Seattle includes both a problem description and problem solutions (policy ideas).

Chapter 3 describes the opioid crisis in the context of U.S. politics. Readers will learn how the political spectrum (liberal, conservative, etc.) affects the decisions that will stimulate or stymie the efforts to fight the crisis. It ends

THE IMPORTANCE OF POLICY IN THE OPIOID CRISIS 11

> **Box 1.4 A drug counselor's perspective**
>
> A drug counselor in Lancaster, Ohio recently stated that "People don't realize that addiction can happen to anybody. It doesn't discriminate. It just takes one bad event to make somebody an addict—an accident where they get injured or emotional trauma. We need to pay now or pay later. Pay a lot more later, I should say. Don't brush it under the rug—we need to address it now" (Blackford, 2019).

with a discussion of thoughtful activism and whether being a "radical is such a bad thing" in the context of Saul Alinsky and Frederick Douglass.

Chapter 4 first presents a holistic view of poverty beyond the financial aspects, including time poverty. The power of hierarchy (i.e., race-based classism) argument is discussed alongside the power of capitalism section, which stresses the "white trash" concept. A policy analysis of the Poverty Bill of Rights follows, besides a discussion of Medicaid.

One of the most tragic aspects of the opioid crisis is its impact on children, as described in Chapter 5. Social workers need a solid understanding of the child welfare system such as foster care. Policy decisions on permanency planning are controversial since it is difficult to determine when an addicted parent should be given more chances to recover while a child is still in limbo. At what point should a child be returned home or be considered for adoption? The challenges faced by grandparents and others who provide kinship care are also discussed. Adverse childhood experience (ACE) is another child welfare topic that deserves attention.

Chapter 6 focuses on women affected by the opioid crisis, especially those who become pregnant while using drugs. The criminalization of pregnancy has emerged as a reproductive justice issue because women who need treatment are arrested instead. Human trafficking is also linked to drug use. The last section, "Women in prison," discusses how the War on Drugs has resulted in the mass incarceration of women.

Special populations are the focus in Chapter 7 because the opioid crisis affects them differently. Despite the popular perception that mostly whites are using opioids, persons of color are also struggling with opioid use disorder (OUD), including Blacks/African Americans. A case study of Washington, DC, where most overdose victims are Black/AA, shows the dilemma faced

Box 1.5 The question of bias

While writing this book, I was working in a suboxone clinic, so I am definitely biased on this topic. Although I am aware of the disadvantages of suboxone, I consider it to be essential for addressing the opioid crisis. Without suboxone, my clients would have a much lower chance of abstaining from street drugs—especially fentanyl. Recently, 10 people died of fentanyl overdoses in a 24-hour period, and the Columbus Health Department had to issue an advisory (Cooley, 2020).

By emphasizing the MAT approach instead of the abstinence only approach, this book's bias is supported by health authorities, such as SAMHSA. This federal agency oversees SUD treatment facilities and issues waivers to medical providers with strict guidelines. The website states that buprenorphine "is safe and effective. Buprenorphine has unique pharmacological properties that help: diminish the effects of physical dependency to opioids, such as withdrawal symptoms and cravings; increase safety in cases of overdose; and lower the potential for misuse" (www.samhsa.gov/medication-assisted-treatment/medications-counseling-related-conditions/buprenorphine). Numerous scientific studies also confirm the efficacy of MAT (e.g., Ma et al., 2019).

---

by local officials. Hispanic/Latinx and Native Americans are also discussed, besides older adults and veterans/active service members.

Chapter 8 exposes the problematic intersection of the criminal justice system with the opioid crisis, especially the impact of mass incarceration. The War on Drugs, which prioritizes punishment over treatment, has had a decisive influence on the opioid crisis. Drug use and treatment in prisons/jails are also discussed, besides the social costs of mass incarceration. The impact of mass incarceration on the justice-involved persons includes the barriers to successful re-entry into society. The section titled "Fixing a broken system" describes criminal justice reforms, such as "second look" laws.

COVID-19 is one of the ongoing challenges in Chapter 9, especially since social isolation and limited treatment access contributed to a shocking rise in overdose deaths. The co-use of methamphetamine has emerged as another challenge. Also, fentanyl (synthetic heroin) is proving to be a deadly risk for all persons who use any street drugs because of widespread contamination of cocaine and other substances. Lastly, a discussion of stigma and SUD presents another ongoing challenge.

Building on the framework in the previous chapters, Chapter 10 provides examples of successful activism regarding the opioid crisis. A case study of homelessness in Denver, besides a discussion of harm reduction, also present the reader with concrete ways to advocate for persons with OUD.

Action steps: So, what do we do now?

- Educate yourself about OUD and its related issues. Although this book is a good start, its focus is on community activism. Resources for in-depth information about addiction include the following:
  o SAMHSA (Substance Abuse and Mental Health Services Administration) is the federal agency that provides resources for those affected by addiction and/or mental illness (www.samhsa.gov).
  o Another excellent website to explore is the National Institute on Drug Abuse (www.drugabuse.gov).
  o Books by medical experts can be helpful not only for those directly affected by the opioid crisis but also for community activists and include the following:
- *Overcoming Opioid Addiction: The Authoritative Medical Guide for Patients, Families, Doctors, and Therapists* by Adam Bisaga and Karen Chenyaev. (New York, NY: The Experiment, 2018).
- *The Opioid Epidemic: What Everyone Needs to Know* by Yngvild Olsen and Joshua M. Sharfstein (New York, NY: Oxford University Press, 2019)
- *The Addiction Solution: Treating Our Dependence on Opioids and Other Drugs* by Lloyd I. Sederer. (New York, NY: Scribner, 2018).

Start a conversation about the opioid crisis with your social circles (neighbors, coworkers, etc.) Grassroots efforts often start with small groups in living rooms who then create a united effort. Although addiction is a painful topic, constructive conversations all over the nation are necessary to address it. Box 1.4 provides an example of a productive discussion of the topic, while Box 1.5 analyzes the importance of knowing one's biases.

2
The causes of the opioid crisis

Introduction

America's 1 million overdose-death count is predicted to double by this decade's end. It is already as if a city the size of San Jose has vanished, and by 2029, those deaths will be Houston-sized.

But such disappearances are quiet and geographically dispersed as the epidemic remains hidden in plain sight, buried in a fierce, century-old battle between shaming drug users as criminals or treating them as patients worthy of medical care.

At this point, too much attention is focused on stemming the oversupply of prescription opioids. A quarter century into the crisis, many people with OUD have long since transitioned from painkillers to heroin, methamphetamine, and fentanyl, the ultra-potent synthetic opioid. And we now have a generation of drug users that *started* with heroin and fentanyl. (Macy, 2022, p. xiv)

How did things get so dire with so many overdose deaths from substance use disorder (SUD), especially from opioid misuse? This chapter will explore different perspectives about the causes of the opioid crisis, including the social determinants of health framework (Healthy People 2030 initiative) and an analysis of the social-ecological factors. A policy case study about homelessness in Seattle will enable readers to examine the complexities of this social issue.

The first priority, though, is to consider the reader's self-reflection about SUD, not just opioid use disorder (OUD). What is your attitude regarding the causes of SUD? Knowing one's bias can motivate the reader to open themselves to new concepts. For instance, a person who has had ten years' sobriety may be more optimistic about the issue than a person who has only been exposed to media images of drug users hiding in alleys.

Self-reflection exercise

What do you think are the causes of SUD? In one research study, respondents were asked about these possible causes:

- Lacking willpower;
- Lacking good moral values;
- Social pressure to take drugs;
- Living in a situation where family members are taking drugs;
- Having a psychological illness, such as depression or anxiety;
- Having major personal, family, financial, or job problems;
- Genetic background (adapted from Murphy, 2017).

After reviewing this list, think of other possible causes to add to this list. Childhood trauma, for example, could be a separate item from the "psychological illness" item. Then rank these items in the order of importance—which one is the most likely to cause SUD?

Next, sort out the causes into two categories: SUD as a disease (medical-social framework) and as a moral failing (moral framework). This dichotomy influences how the public regards SUD, especially regarding how society should address the issue. Simply put, jail or treatment? Write down your responses to these statements:

- "We need a more stable society, and these addicts are ruining our cities. Stop throwing money at the problem!"
- "It's a disease, so we need more government funding such as Medicaid to provide treatment."

Background of the current opioid crisis

Imagine if the news headlines on the date of this book's publication proclaimed: "Opioid crisis is over. Addiction rate is zero!" This unlikely scenario would not concern me about the book's topic being obsolete. First, the aftermath of this disaster could be as devastating as a Category-5 hurricane hitting an island. From 1999 to 2020, the number of Americans who died of drug overdose was 932,000, with 75 percent being opioid-related (CDC, Death Rate & Maps, available at cdc.gov). The structural damage will take years to rebuild. For example, thousands of children are orphaned or separated from parents who are trying to restore their levels of functioning. In 2017, Substance Abuse and Mental Health Services Administration (SAMHSA) issued a report that around 8.7 million children were directly affected by opioids, other street drugs, and alcohol (SAMHSA, 2017).

Secondly and most importantly, the opioid crisis provides an excellent case study of the best and worst of policy making. The debate over the causes of this crisis is political because any social problem is inherently political. Vergano (2018) provides a list of causes that outlines a useful framework for this discussion.

Pharmaceutical companies

In 2003, New York Times reporter Barry Meier was one of the first writers to cover the story of how companies such as Purdue Pharmaceuticals were heavily promoting opioid-based medications despite their known risk. Fifteen years later, he updated his book titled *Pain Killer: An Empire of Deceit and the Origin of America's Opioid Epidemic*. He writes that "OxyContin became the centerpiece of the most aggressive marketing campaign for a powerful and potentially addicting narcotic ever undertaken by the pharmaceutical industry" (Meier, 2018, p. xi) because so many doctors did not use their critical thinking to determine the potential harm of prescribing this drug. First marketed in 1996, OxyContin had a modified time release of four to 12 hours. This was a blessing for cancer patients, and others in severe pain, but a curse for thousands who did not need such a strong drug. Only a year later, Purdue's internal memos indicated that the company knew that OxyContin could be easily crushed or dissolved for a quick high.

The American Pain Society and other entities hosted seminars that criticized doctors for being "opiophobic" (Meier, 2018, p. 29) and not recognizing the problem of untreated pain. Patients who repeatedly requested opioids were not drug-dependent but "pseudo-addicts" who should get the prescription—an assertion that had no research to back it up (Meier, 2018, p. 49). As the pharmaceutical companies paid millions to doctors for expensive gifts and trips, they also gave away free coupons for OxyContin for seven to 30 days—enough to hook somebody into addiction. Of course, OxyContin was only the beginning of this crisis. By the time this "hillbilly heroin" was produced with tamper-proof protections in 2010, other opioids emerged as public health threats.

In her provocatively titled book *Drug Dealer, MD*, Anna Lembke (2016) describes how she was feeling pressure to prescribe opioids. Once she encountered a patient who had been prescribed over 1,000 opioid pills from several different doctors.

> I went to see the patient. I heard her before I met her, her demands for more painkillers ricocheting off the walls of the hospital hallway. Her nurses hovered outside her door, afraid to enter, a look of panic in their eyes. When I walked in, the patient saw my white coat and seemed relieved. She launched into her story of unbearable pain. She also freely admitted to being addicted to opioids in any form, from prescription painkillers to intravenous heroin. But to her this presented no obstacle to obtaining more pain medication: "I know I'm addicted, Doc, but if you don't give me the pills I want, I'll sue you for leaving me in pain."
>
> I realized then that we—I and my fellow health care providers—had become trapped in a system gone mad. (Lembke, 2016, p. 3)

Besides the stress on doctors to overprescribe, "pill mills" enabled doctors to prescribe opioids to hundreds of "patients" a day. For example, two young men started the American Pain clinics in Florida. They kept on wondering why the authorities were not stopping them when the clinics were obviously a front for drug dealing.

> Being inside the waiting room was like being inside the fevered skull of a junkie: conniving, scheming, desperate, delirious. It was loud in there, the babble of the zombie horde, and it stank. Ceiling fans stirred the air, but nothing could dispel the funk of 150 people who'd spent the night squeezed into the back seats of shitbox clunkers rolling south from Kentucky and West Virginia. (Temple, 2015, p x)

Once when a drug wholesaler brought in the drugs in boxes, one manager realized the truth. "And that's when it really hit home for Derik, what they had here. They had a license to deal drugs. No one was watching" (Temple, 2015, p 35). Florida's lax laws allowed the business to prosper, but the DEA (Drug Enforcement Agency) finally shut it down and sent the men to prison. Several overdose deaths have been attributed to pill mills, besides the spread of opioid use across state lines.

18   THE OPIOID CRISIS

These pill mills would not have existed if not for the pharmaceutical companies providing millions of opioid pills without question. One small town in West Virginia, for example, had a population of only 3,000, but in 2006 over 30 million opioid pills were sent "just to those three pharmacies, in one of the poorest counties in America. Ballengee and the other drug store owners kept escalating the orders, and the distributors filled them without flinching" (McGreal, 2019a).

By 2019, nearly every state has filed lawsuits against Purdue Pharmaceuticals and other companies for their allegedly Ideceptive practices. By marketing OxyContin and other opioids as safe for long-term use of chronic pain, the companies are possibly liable for the financial costs to the child welfare, health care, and other systems affected by the opioid epidemic.

Discussion questions

Government regulation remains a controversial topic in politics. Should the government regulate how many opioids are prescribed? The Prescription Drug Monitoring Program (PDMP) is one tool used by many states

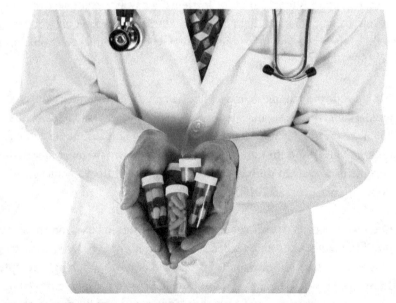

Illustration 2.1 Doctors' role in overprescribing.
Credit: © tab62/Shutterstock

to keep track of how many controlled substances, such as opioids and benzodiazepines, are prescribed per doctor. Look up your state's PDMP and review its website. What are the pros and cons of the PDMP monitoring the use of controlled substances?

Drug cartels

This book uses the term "opioid crisis" with the understanding that it is actually a "drug crisis" because many addicts use more than one type of drug (e.g., benzodiazepines, such as Valium). Also, fentanyl has emerged as the new threat because it has appeared in cocaine and other non-opioids. As discussed in Chapter 8, this synthetic opioid is cheap, easily available from China via the mail, and hard to detect for the average user (Vergano, 2017).

When prescription opioids became less available, many addicts turned to heroin to avoid withdrawal symptoms and continue to get high. Mexican cartels provide 80 percent of the heroin supply (Vergano, 2018). Even areas as far north as Duluth, Minnesota are affected by the flow of heroin and methamphetamine from Mexico. "(Duluth) Police had little question about where the heroin was coming from. It was 'caballo'—brown heroin. The bricks of powder still bore the stamp of the Mexican cartels" (Mannix, 2019).

The Mexican cartel issue became entangled with the U.S.–Mexico border wall proposal as promoted by President Trump, who had used the drug trade as partial justification for the strict measures on immigration from the south. When he announced his candidacy for president in 2015, for example, he stated that "When Mexico sends its people, they're not sending their best. They're sending people that have lots of problems, and they're bringing those problems with us [sic]. They're bringing drugs, they're bringing crime, they're rapists. And some, I assume, are good people" (quoted in Gabbatt, 2019).

Discussion question

How can we have an in-depth discussion about the Mexican cartels without demonizing all Mexican nationals? If you had a client who said that they despised Mexican immigrants because they bring drugs into this country, how would you respond?

Despair

Case and Deaton (2015) first proposed the "deaths of despair" that occur among middle-aged, less-educated whites: alcohol, drugs, and suicide. Simply put, economic despair increases the self-destructiveness of persons who feel defeated.

Lancaster, Ohio exemplifies the theory that economic despair has driven the opioid epidemic. Alexander (2017) links the decline of the glass industry in this factory town with the 1 percent of the American population with an overaccumulation of wealth. Once labeled a model town, Lancaster slipped into an economic slump in which most jobs were low-paying and dead-end. One police official noted that the drug issue was economic in nature.

> (It) had to do with the economy, of course—with the decimation of downtown, with the fact that, every morning, Route 33 was packed with cars making the hour commute to Columbus because there weren't any good jobs in Lancaster. Sometimes it seemed that the only adult males left during the day were heavily tattooed and skinny, hoodies drawn up over their heads (Alexander, 2017, p. 1).

Another Ohio city featured in a book about this issue is Quinones' *Dreamland: The True Tale of America's Opiate Epidemic* (2015). Portsmouth, located on the southern border of Ohio, once prospered as an "all-American town" until factory closures and long-term unemployment dragged the city down. By the late 1990s, it had become populated with pill mills staffed by doctors willing to prescribe to hundreds of "patients" a day. When a person went into treatment, though, they found barriers to reclaiming their lives: housing, jobs, childcare, and transportation. "Addicts usually had no car, no driver's license, and no gas money. (Some) people go back to drugs because they hadn't been able to get to a court date or an appointment with a doctor or a probation officer" (Quinones, 2015, p. 147).

Big cities, such as Philadelphia, are also hit hard by the opioid epidemic. Although the Kensington area is notorious for its homeless camps and overdose rates, other parts of the city are also struggling with this issue (Whelan, 2018). Boston's Methadone Mile is also famous for its drug problems (Bedford, 2016).

Despite these examples of hard-hit areas, some researchers have questioned the "deaths of despair" concept. Ruhm (2018) concludes that only 10 percent of the opioid crisis is related to economic decline. He raises three significant questions:

- Why are the areas that are more prosperous also experiencing a steep rise in drug overdoses?
- Why are persons of color less affected by the opioid epidemic despite their lower economic status?
- Why are persons in other countries also facing economic decline not experiencing these "deaths of despair"?

Discussion question

Review Case and Deaton's proposal and Ruhm's counterargument. Is there anything in their academic backgrounds or institutional support to affect your opinion of them? Review the data and methodology used. Using your critical thinking and determine who has the better argument.

Government health care

Did Obamacare do it? In 2018, Representative Ron Johnson, chairman of the Senate Homeland Security and Governmental Affairs Committee, released a report titled: "Drugs for Dollars: How Medicaid Helps Fuel the Opioid Epidemic." The report asserts that because of the Medicaid expansion under Obamacare (Affordable Care Act), the epidemic has worsened. Medicaid fraud, for example, has resulted in more prescription drugs hitting the streets (Homeland Security and Governmental Affairs, 2018).

The report also links the rates of drug abuse with the states that had accepted Medicaid expansion. This linkage prompts the question of whether correlation is the same as causation. What are other causes for this rise in Medicaid spending for addiction services? In the first case, the addiction rate could have been high before the Medicaid expansion. Also, the rise in fentanyl use is more associated with street drugs than with misuse of prescriptions drug (Vergano, 2018).

Discussion question

Consider the concept that "correlation is not causation." For example, a state may have a high number of donkeys and college-educated persons. The prevalence of donkeys, though, is probably not the cause of more college-educated persons. Does this "correlation is not causation" concept apply to the correlation of Medicaid expansion and opioid crisis in some states? Why or why not?

Pain

Although the United States has only 4.4 percent of the world's population, its citizens use 80 percent of the world's opioid prescriptions and 99 percent of the hydrocodone supply (Minnesota Department of Health, n.d.). Why do Americans take so many opioids compared to other countries? One factor, of course, would be the doctors' willingness to prescribe opioids. In one study of eight countries (Burden, et al., 2019), researchers found that U.S. doctors were far more likely than their international counterparts to prescribe opioids to hospital patients both during and after their stay. One major reason was that U.S. patients were reporting a higher level of pain than the others. Patients' expectations of pain control, then, was a crucial factor in this study.

"The number of people who suffer from severe and chronic pain is striking," states the director of the National Institutes of Health's National Center for Complementary and Integrative Health (NCCIH). In their 2015 study, the researchers found that over 25 million Americans experience chronic pain and nearly 40 million Americans suffer from severe pain (NIH, 2015). As the population ages, and conditions such as arthritis worsen, these numbers will probably rise.

The policy question regarding pain management is whether the government should set limits on opioid prescriptions. Public funding of Medicare, for example, enables the government to restrict use of opioids by refusing to pay for them.

Discussion question

The author used a nonacademic source (writer for *Buzzfeed*) for the list of causes. In your opinion, was this appropriate? Research the *Buzzfeed* website to determine the credibility of this source.

Figure 2.1 Socio-Ecological Framework of Opioid Crisis (adapted from Jalali, Botticelli, Hwang, Koh, & McHugh, 2020).

Applying the Framework of Addiction to the opioid crisis

Another method for exploring the causes of the opioid crisis is the Framework of Addiction (Jalali, et al., 2020). Several discussion questions are bolded to provide an interactive exercise.

Socio-Ecological Framework of the opioid crisis

Considering the complex and interrelated factors of opioid abuse from this perspective, it is easy to see how many of them overlap with poverty. The first circle in Figure 2.1, Individual, includes the factors discussed below.

Sociodemographic factors

These factors include the following:

- Age. Younger persons are at higher risk for OUD. "Adolescence and young adulthood are key risk periods for opioid misuse" because they are more likely to be exposed to opioids (Jalali, et al., 2020, p. 4).
- Race/ethnicity. The CDC states that "OUD is a medical condition that can affect anyone—regardless of race, gender, income level, or social class" (www.cdc.gov/dotw/opioid-use-disorder/). The Special Populations chapter provides further information about the racial/ethnic breakdowns.

- Geography. Appalachia and other geographic areas are more heavily affected by the opioid crisis than others (East Tennessee State University and NORC at the University of Chicago, 2019). Geography also affects the quality of social services because some states are more generous than others.
- Socioeconomic status (SES), as defined by income, education, and occupation (source: www.thoughtco.com). In 2018, the U.S. poverty rate was 11.8 percent. For Native Americans it was 25.4 percent, Blacks/AA was 20.8 percent, and Latinos was 17.6 percent. However, for whites it was only 10.1 percent (source: www.povertyusa.org).
- What other sociodemographic factors would you add to this list?

Stress and trauma exposure

- What are some stressors caused by poverty that make opioid use more likely?
- Trauma exposure can include economic trauma (i.e., the long-term stress of being cash-poor) and living in high-crime areas where violence is common (Resler, 2019). What protective factors would decrease the impact of these sociodemographic factors?
- What protective factors would you suggest for persons growing up in impoverished neighborhoods? For example, would a free gym be helpful because of the beneficial effects of exercise?

Physical and mental health

- One doctor who has served low-income families for years states: "Poverty is a negative, independent factor that influences lifelong health. Through the science of toxic stress, we understand that early childhood adversity and poverty is a factor that affects not only brain architecture and [neurologic and endocrine] function, but affects the probability of lifelong illness, including cardiac disease and diabetes" (Esposito, 2016).
- Poor mental health, especially depression, is also strongly associated with poverty. Parents who are depressed are less likely to interact with their children. The abovementioned doctor also described how a father was

complaining about his son's behavior. The mother then told him that this family of five was homeless and living a tiny hotel room (Esposito, 2016).

Biological and genetic susceptibility

Since 1960, researchers have linked SUD with genetics. Genetic susceptibility to OUD, however, is much more complex because it involves multiple neurological factors such as opioid receptors and brain reward circuits. One study notes that "many genes have been linked to opioid addiction; thus, opioid addiction is more likely a complex disease rather than a single gene disorder" (Wang, et al., 2019). Polygenic risk score analysis, a tool used for conditions such as arthritis and Alzheimer's, is a cutting-edge method that involves gene editing.

Neurobiology also plays a role. One framework for OUD is a "3-stage cycle—binge/intoxication, withdrawal/negative affect, and preoccupation/anticipation—that represents dysregulation in 3 functional domains . . . and is mediated by 3 major neurocircuitry elements (basal ganglia, extended amygdala, and prefrontal cortex, respectively)" (Koob, 2020). Euphoria is followed by dysphoria, while hypersensitivity to pain can also result from opioids. Patients with chronic pain, then, often experience even more pain if they are taking opioids on a regular basis because their bodies' tolerance increases. How should society ensure that persons with increased risk of SUD get preventive services?

Pain

As stated earlier, low-income persons are more likely to have physical problems. In some cases, then, pain could be related to poverty. Since many low-wage jobs are physically demanding (e.g., housekeeping), workers are more likely to be injured and thus require pain medication. When I met a client with OUD who was a manual laborer, the first question I asked was whether they were in any physical pain. The answer was usually "yes," even for clients in their twenties.

Self-determination

Defined here as the internal motivation to act in a positive manner (e.g., the motivation to exercise more), self-determination can be inhibited by poverty (Buckner, Mezzacappa, & Beardslee, 2003). How would you design a program to increase the self-determination of low-income youth so they will feel resilient enough to avoid drug use?

Self-stigma

Both poverty and SUD can cause persons to internalize their stigmas, as indicated in the article title " 'Who do they think we are, anyway?': Perceptions of and responses to poverty stigma" (Reutter, et al., 2009). Self-stigma may result from being rejected by society, thus leading to distorted thinking (e.g., "I'm no good") and diminishing a person's sense of worth. (Matthews, Dwyer, & Snoek, 2017). How would you decrease the self-stigma of a client who is both low-income and dealing with OUD?

Now that the first circle (Individual) has been reviewed, the second circle (Interpersonal) deserves consideration. The Interpersonal factors include:

- Family history of substance abuse. A child growing up in a family affected by substance abuse may have a genetic predisposition for SUD. Poverty is also related to this factor because it is linked to parental distress and the increased likelihood of an adverse childhood experience (ACE) affecting their child(ren). (Steele, et al., 2016).
- Opioid access via family, friends, and coworkers. If a person is living in a drug-saturated area, the availability of street drugs is obviously an environmental factor. Based on my practice experience, I posit that some work environments are more conducive to drug use than others. For example, clients in recovery have told me about co-workers who would "party" after a shift and endanger the client's sobriety.
- Influence of family, friends, and coworkers. This influence may encourage or discourage drug use. Do you think that poverty is related to this factor?

The third circle, Community, lists even more factors related to poverty:

- Geographic variations. As discussed elsewhere in the book, non-urban areas, such as Appalachia have been hard hit by the opioid crisis. Rural patients were more likely to be prescribed opioids because of their older age or their physically demanding jobs.
- Community norms regarding substance use (including tobacco and alcohol) also play a role in OUD rates. What is the norm in your community toward legal and illegal drug use?

In the fourth circle titled Social, factors such as the economy and government programs overlap with the book's topics. Overall, the Framework of

Addiction provides a useful tool for analysis because it makes it impossible to claim that SUD is simply a matter of an individual's willpower.

Social determinants of health

Another framework for considering the causes of the opioid crisis is the Social Determinants of Health, the basis of the Healthy People 2030 initiative (available at https://health.gov/healthypeople/priority-areas/social-determinants-health). The five social determinants are:

- Economic stability, with the goal to "Help people earn steady incomes that allow them to meet their health needs" and three policy ideas: "employment programs, career counseling, and high-quality child care." Pick one idea and make an argument about how it would (or would not) decrease the impact of the opioid crisis.
- Education access and quality, which recognizes the impact of poverty and bullying on a child's education. Do you think this determinant is related to the opioid crisis? Defend your answer.
- Health care access and quality. This book focuses on the need for more SUD treatment, especially medication assisted treatment. What other aspects of health care would impact persons affected by the opioid crisis?
- Neighborhoods and built environments. Safe neighborhoods are considered important to health. For example, a person living in a high-crime area with multiple shootings may experience more stress symptoms than normal. What other factors could be related to the opioid crisis?
- Social and community context. Food insecurity (defined here as often being worried about obtaining enough food) is one factor, besides the bullying of transgender students. In your city, which factors would you add to this list?

Discussion questions

- Pick one of these five determinants that you consider to be the most pressing. Make an argument for how improving that determinant could decrease the opioid crisis.

➤ Pick the determinant that you consider to be the most "doable" in terms of policy change. Suggest a policy change and how you would implement it. For example, how would you make a neighborhood safer for children?

Policy case study: The homeless population in Seattle

While browsing YouTube looking for a kitten or hedgehog video, I came across a Fox News clip about the homeless encampments in Seattle's parks and other open spaces. Although this topic was much more depressing than watching a hedgehog sneeze, I knew that the clip could be instructive because the link between SUD and homelessness is well documented (e.g., McVicar, Moschion, & Van Ours, 2015). The homeless encampments provide a case study of how media, policymakers, and social workers can confront a difficult problem.

Problem description

Before considering the social problem, let us first consider the sources. Fox News is famous for its conservative viewpoints, as evidenced by its featuring of several Republican commentators and its $1,000,000 donation to the Republican Governors' Association in 2010 (Ray, n.d.). One academic noted that "Fox's appeal lies in the network's willingness to explicitly entwine reporting and opinion in the service of Republican, and white identity" (Kreiss cited in Nelson, 2019). Despite Fox's record for bias, though, the news story "Seattle residents speak out on homeless crisis" is worth analyzing.

First, challenge the story title using the term "homeless crisis"—is it really a "crisis" or just an ongoing problem? A review of other online sources, including government publications, confirms that homeless encampments (some even appearing as miniature tent cities) have proliferated around Seattle. In 2015, the mayor had issued a proclamation declaring a civil emergency regarding homelessness (http://murray.seattle.gov/wp-content/uploads/2015/10/Proclamation-of-Civil-Emergency.pdf). First, consider the story title using the term "homeless crisis"—is it really a "crisis" or just an ongoing problem? A review of other online sources, including government publications, confirms that homeless encampments (some even appearing as miniature tent cities) have proliferated around Seattle as the number of homeless persons has risen five percent in the past year to 11,751 in 2020. King County, home to Seattle, has an annual Point in Time count that uses "volunteers (who) spread out across King County on a single night to count persons experiencing unsheltered homelessness. The one-night count is supplemented by surveys and shelter data to inform the final report" (King County, 2020). Because this count had occurred in January 2020 (before COVID-19), the 2021 count would probably be higher due to the economic distress. Since the mayor had declared the civil emergency on homelessness in 2015, and the homeless count has only continued to rise, the word "crisis" thus appears fitting and not media hype.

Another key point about the news story is the content, especially the interviewees. The reporter states that "residents are reaching a breaking point" as he interviews a dog walker who is afraid of her dog stepping on needles. A group of school-age children states that they are unable to use a playing field due to its proximity to an encampment. The camera sweeps over the encampment in the park, focusing on the trash. The reporter points out that "You see the needles, you see the caps to the needles, you see the tin cans."

The third point is the portrayal of the street people, who are seen as huddled and pathetic beings. One man is digging through the dumpster while sad music plays in the background (video retrieved from www.youtube.com/watch?v=yxpueF7XJ44). This three-minute clip presents only the social problem but no possible answers.

In 2019, Fox News aired a longer clip titled "Left behind: Homeless crisis in Seattle" that mentioned mental illness and housing costs as two contributing factors. It also focused on drugs, especially persons openly using or selling drugs. In 2018, King County decriminalized the possession of hard drugs—a decision criticized in the news story. The 2019 homeless count stated that 32 percent of the respondents had some form of SUD.

Besides interviewing the "person on the street" like the 2021 clip, the reporter also talked to local experts from the Downtown Seattle Association, LEAD National Support Bureau, and the Union Gospel Mission. Seattle spent $78 million in 2018 for shelter, outreach, supportive housing, and other services. The implication appeared to be that Seattle was throwing away its money because the programs were failing (video retrieved from www.youtube.com/watch?v=N-7jAFYI4D4). See Illustration 2.2 for an image of Bread of Life Mission in Seattle.

Illustration 2.2 Homeless shelter in Seattle
Credit: © RUBEN M RAMOS/Shutterstock

Two documentaries have also described the homeless crisis: "Seattle is dying" (2019) and "The fight for the soul of Seattle" (2020). Produced by KOMO (a station owned by Sinclair Broadcasting, which is considered conservative), these documentaries present a grim picture of downtown Seattle. In the introduction of "Seattle is dying," the camera focuses on desperate-looking street persons as the narrator intones that they are "lost souls who wander our streets, untethered to home or family or reality, chasing a drug which in turn chases them. It is about the damage they inflict on themselves, to be sure, but also on the fabric of this place where we live" (retrieved from www.youtube.com/watch?v=bpAi70WWBlw&t=74s).

Discussion questions

In the films by Fox News and KOMO, the portrayals of persons living on the street (who are assumed to be homeless, but they could just be passersby) are extremely negative. For me, it was like a modern-day freak show so viewers could gape at somebody nodding off or having convulsions. What can be done to restore the dignity and worth of these people instead of dehumanizing them?

In "The fight for the soul of Seattle," business owners and other citizens speak out about their safety concerns. One business owner who had to close his bike shop due to multiple break-ins states, "Seattle has become a hellhole (with) no law or order.... Seattle has committed civilizational suicide." One scene shows two people talking on the sidewalk as the narrator stresses the "decay and desperation" of downtown.

This theme of doom resonates throughout the documentary, as it criticizes the city government for its "hands-off" approach. One fundamental policy question was posed by an expert about the persons who were openly using drugs or appeared impaired: "Do we intervene, or do we let them be?" The speaker claimed that the city de-emphasizes law enforcement and stresses social services that are not mandatory, which has generated much criticism (video retrieved from https://www.youtube.com/watch?v=WijoL3Hy_Bw&t=207s).

While the Fox News and KOMO films focus only on SUD as the cause of homelessness in Seattle, the city government has a more nuanced understanding. Besides the root causes listed below, "adverse life events such as a health issue, the loss of a job, or the need to escape a domestic violence situation" can be compounded by many factors. According to the City of Seattle's website, the root causes of homelessness are:

- Mental health and addiction, with "drug overdose the leading cause of death among people who are homeless.... Washington State ranks 47th in the nation for psychiatric beds per capita" (www.seattle.gov) and 46th for persons with unmet needs around SUD (https://wallethub.com/edu/drug-use-by-state/35150);
- Economic disparities and poverty, as many residents have been left out of the "booming economy and high-wage jobs" (www.seattle.gov);
- Lack of affordable housing, with almost half of the households spending over 30 percent on rent;
- Racial disparities;
- The criminal justice system that ignores "the historic and systemic issues of racial equity and social justice" (www.seattle.gov);
- A decentralized response to a regional crisis, which led to a fragmented approach;

- Lack of wraparound services for youth within and exiting the foster system (endhomelessness.org/blog/diverting-foster-youth-from-homelessness).

Discussion questions

- Besides the first root cause (mental health and addiction), which root cause do you consider to be the most important? Explain your answer.
- Have you ever encountered a decentralized system that was too fragmented to function properly? What would you do to coordinate services for the homeless in a major city such as Seattle?

Problem solutions (policy ideas)

According to its website Homelessness Response (https://performance.seattle.gov/stories/s/Homelessness-Response/w79s-qyv8/), the city of Seattle has instituted these steps to fight the homeless crisis:

- Prevention by the Seattle Rental Housing Assistance Pilot Program to assist 1,000 low-income families with housing and utility assistance;
- Increase in "bridge housing" (emergency shelters) of more than 500 beds;
- Removing trash and syringes;
- Providing day and hygiene centers so persons will have access to toilets and showers;
- "Permitted villages" that consist of 300 tiny houses for "people who have lived outside (who) need time to transition to indoor shelter" (www.seattle.gov/homelessness/city-permitted-villages).

Discussion questions

Research the scope of homelessness in your city or state and the community response.

- Is SUD considered to be the major cause or just one of many?

- Has your community implemented any steps like the Seattle model?
- Which steps (if any) would you recommend for your community? Does your community have any program ideas that a city like Seattle should consider?

Another step taken by Seattle was the Navigation Team program, which provides an example of the unintended consequences of well-meaning policies. These teams of police officers and outreach workers had provided outreach to the homeless, but this practice stirred controversy for two reasons. First, the presence of police traumatized those who had a troubled history with law enforcement. In 2020, a coalition comprised of Native Americans and homeless advocates wrote a letter to the mayor that the police presence was "contrary to trauma-informed principles and perpetuates harm" (cited in Savransky, 2020a).

Discussion questions

If you were an outreach worker visiting homeless encampments, would you consider yourself safer or more at risk if accompanied by a police officer? Would you prefer the police presence, or would you want to work without it?

The second objection to the Navigation Teams was their practice of removing settlements, which usually resulted in people just moving to another settlement. The city stated that these "sweeps" of the settlements only occurred after weeks of outreach efforts and shelter referrals. In 2020, the COVID-19 crisis made the "sweeps" even more problematic since they could increase the spread of the virus if not enough individual housing was available. The Centers for Disease Control and Prevention (CDC) recommended that because of COVID-19, "the risks associated with sleeping outdoors or in an encampment setting are different than from staying indoors in a congregate setting such as an emergency shelter or other congregate living facility. Outdoor settings may allow people to increase physical distance between themselves and others" although the risks of unhygienic conditions and the rigors of living outdoors also had to be weighed (CDC, 2020).

Besides these concerns, the budget problems caused by the pandemic resulted in Seattle suspending this program starting in 2021. The mayor still supported the program and another version of the Navigation Teams may emerge later (Savransky, 2020b). Box 2.1 gives a historical perspective on the homeless issue in Seattle.

Discussion questions

- If you were the mayor of Seattle, would you try to create a new version of the Navigation Team program or simply scrap the project? What other policy ideas would you suggest?
- A Facebook post from a Seattle resident reads: "I live in a townhouse on 154th Street. I find homeless people sleeping by my car constantly because we have a covered carport, so they find it a place to stay dry and sleep. Since living here, I have found numerous needles, our cars have been broken into, our storage doors broken, and things stolen. . . . I've called and reported this, but nothing gets done or changed." If you were a city official, what policy ideas would you suggest?
- On the city of Seattle's website, the terms "outreach worker" and "case manager" are often used when describing social services. Do you think that these roles should be filled only by licensed professionals, such as social workers? What are the pros and cons of allowing nonprofessionals to work with the homeless population?
- Does homelessness cause or increase substance use? The question came up when I was researching this section because if I were living in such rough circumstances, I would be sorely tempted to use substances. The Hooverville residents who drank their homemade liquor may have found comfort in alcohol. One Australian research team addresses this question (McVicar, Moschion, & Van Ours, 2015) and found that homelessness did not affect substance use. Do you think that further research should be done? Why or why not?

Box 2.1 Historical perspective: Hoovervilles

When the Great Depression hit the United States in the 1930s, mass unemployment and worsening poverty soon followed. People derided President Herbert Hoover for his inadequate response to the crisis. They called newspapers "Hoover blankets" and squatter settlements of thousands who could not afford rent "Hoovervilles." For roughly 10 years, Hoovervilles symbolized the devastating hardships of homelessness in an era when almost no government programs existed. Shacks and other makeshift buildings clustered together in these settlements all over the United States—an estimated 15,000 people lived in them.

Hooverville residents had nowhere else to go, and public sympathy, for the most part, was with them. Even when Hoovervilles were raided by order of parks departments or other authorities, the men who carried out the raids often expressed regret and guilt for their actions (History.com, 2018). Illustration 2.3 is a 1936 picture of a "Hooverville" shack in nearby Oregon.

Seattle hosted eight Hoovervilles, including one of the nation's largest on a nine-acre plot at the port. At first, the city government burned down the settlement, but the residents came back and rebuilt. In 1932, the new city administration decided to work with the settlement by negotiating rules, such as prohibiting women and children. Many residents rejected private charity because of its poor quality. One reporter noted that one man "had a distaste for organized charity-breadlines and flop-houses so he decided to build a shack of his own and be independent" (cited in Demirel, n.d.).

Despite the city mostly tolerating their Hoovervilles, the public still stigmatized the following traits of its residents:

Illustration 2.3 Hooverville shack in Portland, OR.

- Alcoholism, with an emphasis on illegal stills;
- Political radicalism, with the fear that they were communist agitators;
- Violent behavior, although most of the victims were other homeless persons;
- Being the "other"—immigrants and/or persons of color (Smith, n.d.).

Early on, though, Seattle's major Hooverville had organized its own town council and even had a mayor. Fighting against stigma and deprivation, residents advocated for themselves and maintained their dignity. One resident explained at a council meeting, "I live in a shack. I try to keep my shack as clean as possible. I don't love living in a place like that. But what can I do when I can't get any other place? They tell me I am too old when I ask for work" (cited in Smith, n.d.).

One example of advocacy appears in the archives of the Seattle city government. In 1938, a typewritten letter from the Hooverville committee of 25 residents requesting a hearing about a planned eviction.

A critical situation has arisen in Hooverville wherein unemployed and aged people with no source of income are being evicted. They have no place to go ... we are asking the Mayor and the City Council use police powers to stop homeless people from being evicted in the face of a housing shortage and in face of the coming winter (retrieved from www.seattle.gov/Documents/Departments/CityArchive/DDL/Hoovervilles/1938Oct10.pdf)

Discussion questions
- Consider the similarities between the Hoovervilles and today's homeless encampments. Does the historical perspective deepen your understanding of the issue?
- The Great Depression impoverished millions, while the 21st-century tech companies and other segments of Washington's economy have created thousands of good-paying jobs. What are the policy implications of this striking difference between the Hoovervilles and today's encampments?

3
The political context of the opioid crisis

Introduction

Politics can be messy, obnoxious, and more frustrating than being a one-legged man at a butt-kicking contest. In the past few years, being an informed citizen can be a daunting task—but we have to engage in the political process or we will lose our power. A few days before the 2020 election, I waited in heavy traffic so I could deliver my absentee ballot to the Board of Elections. Thank goodness I had requested one, since the line for early voting stretched out for blocks. The sight of so many determined voters heartened me because it shows that people have realized that voting is critical.

Despite this hopeful moment, one cannot dispute the high level of vitriol between persons who disagree. In 2020, opponents called each other "Antifa!," "Socialist!," and "Fascist!" and the red Make America Great Again (MAGA) hats and black Black Lives Matter (BLM) tee-shirts symbolized the ideological gap. Illustration 3.1 shows a MAGA hat.

This chapter will explicate the rise of political violence and the impact of President Trump on political discourse, which might influence any policy debate. Then a discussion of the political spectrum will delineate the basic terms used by citizens, leading to an exploration of thoughtful activism with two role models: Saul Alinsky and Frederick Douglass.

Rise of political violence

Sitting in a college classroom in the 1980s, I heard my professor reveal a key aspect of U.S. politics: the peaceful transfer of power. If a president loses an election, they must be willing to gracefully step down from power. Without this transfer of power, democracy would perish because dictatorship would prevail. No longer would the will of the people matter in the political system.

Through the decades since then, I had felt pride in this country's ability to maintain the peaceful transfer of power—until January 6, 2021. The attack on

Illustration 3.1 "MAGA" hat—symbol of Trump's followers.
Credit: © Fadziel Nor/Shutterstock

the U.S. Capitol, instigated by a president unwilling to accept the 2020 election results, created a maelstrom of shock and violence.

"Where is Nancy?" cried out the insurrectionists in search of Nancy Pelosi, who was the Democratic House Speaker at the time. Almost two years later, a home intruder would viciously attack her elderly husband with a hammer. He was also calling out "Where's Nancy?" (Schnell, 2022).

"Hang Mike Pence!" shouted out the insurrectionists who were angry at the then-vice president for not obeying President Trump's orders to stop the counting of electoral votes (NBC News, 2022).

According to the House January 6 Committee (report available on govinfo. gov website), the attack on the U.S. Capitol that day was not just a riot or protest but an insurrection—a real plan to overthrow the government. Anti-democracy forces had planned and implemented this event. A new term emerged in the political vocabulary: election denier, a person (sometimes even a candidate) who states that the 2020 presidential election was stolen and that other elections might be stolen in the future. One striking example of an election denier is Kari Lake, who unsuccessfully ran for governor in Arizona in 2022 and spent months denying the election results. In January 2023, she declared herself the "duly elected governor" despite court rulings against her lawsuits (Papenfuss, 2023).

Overall, the threats of violence have increased against political opponents. The Department of Homeland Security noted a disturbing trend in a 2022 advisory bulletin.

Several elected officials, candidates, and political organizations received threatening letters with suspicious powders, which, while found not to be dangerous or toxic, were likely intended to target the political process... some social media users have sought to justify the use of violence in response to perceptions that the midterm elections were fraudulent. (www.dhs.gov/ntas/advisory/national-terrorism-advisory-system-bulletin-november-30-2022)

Political violence has also erupted against people with whom the perpetrators disagree. Two examples that occurred in Ohio (my home state) were deeply disturbing. First, Doctor Amy Acton was the public health official in 2020 who had developed the "Stay Safe Ohio" program for COVID-19 lockdown restrictions. Armed with assault weapons, protesters showed up outside her house and said there would be no violence—"for now" (Justice, 2020). Antisemitic slurs also appeared in the criticisms against her, which drew worldwide attention. She resigned from the position a few months later (Zuckerman, 2021). Later in 2022, a drag queen story hour was planned in a Columbus, Ohio church. Proud Boys, a right-wing group, appeared wearing guns and uniforms to threaten the participants. The church had to cancel the event to avoid a violent confrontation (Romero, 2022).

In this context of current political violence, then, activists for any cause must be cautious about blowback from angry people. For example, opponents of BLM and other social movements have used the term "antifa" in a pejorative sense—although being called an "anti-fascist" sounds like a compliment to me. Although the "antifa" movement has caused only some property damage and limited violence (Allam & Urquhart, 2020), conservative commentators spread so much alarm about them that "'antifa' morphed into a phrase that was used to broadly paint liberal protest organizers as driven to destroy civilized society through extreme measures" (Nguyen, 2020).

This political turmoil can be contrasted to other, calmer times, in which presidential campaigns generated so little drama that people may have fallen asleep during the debates. The first debate in 2000, for example, featured Al Gore promising to put Medicare funds into a lockbox. George W. Bush later replied that he would put Social Security funds in a lockbox (Miller, 2000). This showdown over the "lockbox" idea did not excite voters at all—voter turnout was only 50.5 percent that year. In comparison, the voter turnout was 67 percent in 2020 when Joe Biden was elected (Washington Post graphic, 2020).

Impact of President Trump on political discourse

Besides the political violence of the recent past, another factor in politics is the current upheaval in the Republican Party. As an outsider to the Party and a nonpolitical businessman, Donald Trump disrupted the traditional Republican structure by winning the primaries in 2016. For decades, Republicans had represented certain ideals, but "(Trump) didn't talk about the need for limited government or for balancing the federal budget. He didn't talk about the United States as the guarantor of freedom worldwide. He didn't extoll free trade" (Lemann, 2020). Instead, he won votes by stressing anti-immigration sentiments (i.e., "Build the Wall!") and promising to promote "America First" over international cooperation (Seunagel, 2017). The subsequent withdrawal of the United States from international treaties such as the Iran nuclear deal and the Paris climate accord implemented this "America First" philosophy.

During Trump's term in office, Republicans had to choose between defending or defying their president. Most Republicans chose to defend him. In contrast was Senator Jeff Flake, whose defiance of Trump ended his political career. In his speech announcing his retirement from the Senate, Flake stated: "Because politics can make us silent when we should speak, and silence can equal complicity. I have children and grandchildren to answer to, and so, Mr. President, I will not be complicit" (Flake, 2017).

One crucial indicator of the party's instability appeared in August 2020, when the Republican National Committee decided not to construct a new platform. A party's platform is a policy statement that informs the voters about several issues. For example, the 2020 Democratic Party platform was 92 pages and covered such topics as COVID-19, job creation, and health care. In 2016, the Republican Party platform was 66 pages long and addressed issues such as trade, taxes, and foreign policy. The Republican Party issued a one-page statement in 2020, which stated little except for its support of Trump and opposition to Democrats. Many political observers expressed shock, including one British journalist who wrote that "The Republican Party is now the Party of Trump" (Zurther, 2020).

Under these circumstances, it is difficult for any critical thinker to consider the policies of the two major parties if one of them does not issue a clear statement. Informed citizens, though, still need to understand the basic political terms with the hope that the system will achieve equilibrium again. Without a common understanding of these terms, we cannot understand the system itself. A mechanic who lifts the car hood but does not understand the difference between a radiator and a battery will never be effective.

The political spectrum

The political spectrum is a good place to start if one is new to this topic. Picture a football field with goalposts (poles) on either side. The closer you are to one of these poles, the more extreme/radical you are. You may express your strong opinion in a *polemic*, and people may be *polarized* by the issue. Gun control, for example, is a polarizing issue because its opponents often claim that the government plans to confiscate all guns and tyrannize its citizens (e.g., "If Joe Biden can force a needle in your arm, he can take your gun" advertisement by Second Amendment Foundation—www.saf.org). On the other side, proponents of gun control stress the horrors of mass shootings (e.g., Newtown Action Alliance).

Many variations of the political spectrum exist, but this textbook will use the simplest version (adapted from Saylor Academy, no date):

In this context, consider this historical example of an editorial cartoon in 1961 by Hy Rosen that shows two vultures pecking away at the arm of the Statue of Liberty.

One vulture is labeled "Extreme Right Wing, John Birch Society, Neo Nazis, Klu Klux Klan"; the other, "Extreme Left Wing, Communist Party, Red Fronts." Suggests that damage is done to freedom by extremists at both ends

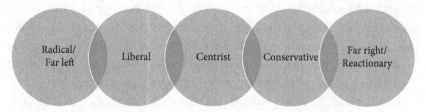

Figure 3.1 Political spectrum (adapted from Saylor Academy).

of the political spectrum. (Library of Congress, https://www.loc.gov/item/2016684063/)

In many cases, the terms "extremist" and "radical" are used interchangeably.

Are radical extremists really vultures out to destroy our country as that cartoon image suggests? The term "extremist" has negative connotations, especially when used to describe terrorists and others with whom one cannot reason. In contrast, the word "radical" implies that the root of a social issue needs to be uprooted and replaced. National crises may require radical actions, such as the U.S. government's response to the 9/11 attacks that exposed the weaknesses in its self-defense structure. The Department of Homeland Security (dhs.gov) appeared almost overnight, as several government agencies were created or shuffled about to develop more robust protections. Likewise, Immigration and Customs Enforcement (ICE) replaced Immigration and Naturalization Services (INS), as ICE's mission stressed the nation's security over expediting immigration (Rodriguez, 2008).

Another national crisis demanding a radical response was the COVID-19 pandemic, which caused overflowing morgues and other frightening realities. One government response was the CARES Act of 2020, which provided an unprecedented stimulus package to decrease the economic damage of the lockdowns (LaBrecque, 2020).

Centrists

Who is a radical, and who is a centrist? The answer may depend on one's opinion. For example, some social work instructors can be regarded as either flaming radicals or tame apologists for the system. In the early 1960s, conservatives, such as Ronald Reagan, warned that the proposed Medicare program would make Americans lose their freedoms under socialism (speech retrieved from www.americanrhetoric.com/speeches/ronaldreaganreagansocializedmedicine.htm). Liberals, though, did not regard Medicare as radical but only a step in the right direction to provide health care for older and disabled persons. Now Medicare is so popular that the idea of ending Medicare seems unthinkable to most Americans—in one study, 75 percent of Medicare recipients were satisfied with the program (Masterson, 2019).

Another "radical" policy was the Affordable Care Act (ACA) of 2009 (also called Obamacare), which terrified people as a possible government takeover of health care that would result in killing off grandma. (Fortunately, no grandmas were killed in the pursuit of this radical agenda.) Leftist progressives, though, regarded ACA as an inadequate reform that was not at all radical, because it left the health insurance industry intact and even flourishing (Roy, 2016).

Perhaps the biggest distinction between radicals and centrists (also called moderates) is that radicals are more likely to challenge the political system while moderates try to work within it. Unlike the radicals on either side, a centrist is a moderate who tries to work with both sides. The terms "cross the aisle" (in the House and Senate, an aisle separates the parties) and "bipartisan" apply to a centrist. As a "New Democrat" in the 1990s, Bill Clinton presented himself as a centrist leader because he supported many pro-business measures that are usually associated with the other party (Kane, 2018). John McCain (Republican) was also a centrist on some issues, such as campaign finance reform (Harwood, 2008).

Conservatives

The term "conservative" differs from country to country, but the foundation of U.S. conservatism is based on British history. As one writer notes, "The nature of a conservative is to be prudent, cautious, respectful, and opposed to radical change. Going back to its origins with Edmund Burke in the 18th century, it is to prefer stability and continuity to disruption and chaos" (Mazenko, 2021).

Edmund Burke may have started as a Whig who supported the American Revolution and Irish independence, but the French Revolution shifted his views. Disturbed by the political violence and complete rejection of the past, he wrote to the revolutionaries:

> Your constitution, it is true, whilst you were out of possession, suffered waste and dilapidation; but you possessed in some parts the walls and in all the foundations of a noble and venerable castle. You might have repaired those walls; you might have built on those old foundations.... You had all these advantages in your ancient states, but you chose to act as if you had never been molded into civil society and had everything to begin anew. You began ill, because you began by despising everything that belonged to you. You set up your trade without a capital. (Burke, 1790)

Repairing the walls of a castle instead of tearing them down—that image exemplifies conservatism with its stress on moderate change. One Burke expert writes that "To this day, Burkean conservatism is defined by a belief in the authority of tradition, the organic nature of society (that is to say, gradual rather than violent or radical political change), order, the Christian religion and private property" (Illingworth, 2020).

Burke also stressed the "harmony of the universe" (Burke, 1790), a key element for many conservative thinkers. In their view, a government runs well when it has the consensus (agreement) of the people. This idea is related to John Locke's Social Contract theory, which heavily influenced the Founding Fathers' work.

> Property is the linchpin of Locke's argument for the social contract and civil government because it is the protection of their property, including their property in their own bodies, that men seek when they decide to abandon the State of Nature (to make a social contract with the government). (Friend, no date)

In fact, property ownership was required in order for White males to vote in the first few decades of the Republic (Bump, 2016). Property ownership connotes stability both at the financial and social levels. Neighborhoods with a high percentage of renters such as college areas, for example, appear as more transitional and even "trashy." Another connotation is race-based, since Whites are more likely to be homeowners than persons of color. Homeowners are also more likely to vote Republican, which may have prompted a Trump adviser to contemplate reinstating the property requirement for voting (Bump, 2016).

Besides valuing property ownership, conservatives also attach great importance to the concept of limited government. Ronald Reagan, deemed as a conservative icon, expressed this well in his 1981 inauguration speech: "In this present crisis, government is not the solution to our problems—government is the problem. . . . It is my intention to curb the size and influence of the Federal establishment . . . (because of the) unnecessary and excessive growth of government" (cited in Hayward, 2013).

Far right

Further right on the political spectrum is the "far right," which consists of multiple groups who want to eliminate the government as much as possible.

The Libertarian Party, for example, opposes all taxes because it is "fundamentally opposed to the use of force to coerce people into doing anything. We think it is inherently wrong and should have no role in a civilized society" (Libertarian Party website: www.lp.org). Instead, citizens should donate to the government on a voluntary basis. Stressing individual freedom over the common good, Libertarians state that private charity is a better alternative to the "welfare state" (Tanner, 2019).

Simply calling them "conservatives" is problematic, though, because their support for abortion rights and LGBT+ rights are on the "liberal" side.

Besides Libertarians, the "far right" term also encompasses groups that are associated with white supremacy and even the violence that occurred at the U.S. Capitol on January 6, 2021. Once called the "alt right" (alternative right), groups such as the Proud Boys and Rise Above Movement had been advocating violence months before the Capitol riot (Zidan, 2020). Although the "far right" term once signified a non-violent and acceptable component of the political spectrum, it now represents nonsensical aspects, such as the Q-Anon conspiracy. It is beyond the scope of this text to discuss this issue in-depth, but social workers must stay informed about current events.

Liberals

On the political spectrum, left of center are the liberals (not to be confused with Libertarians—or Liberians or librarians, for that matter). Like conservatives, liberals work for incremental change because they are moderates.

President Barack Obama expressed his underlying motivation for liberal views in this passage from his 2006 book *The Audacity of Hope: Thoughts on Reclaiming the American Dream*:

> I was drawn to the power of the African American religious tradition to spur social change. Out of necessity, the black church had to minister to the whole person. Out of necessity, the black church rarely had the luxury of separating individual salvation from collective salvation. It had to serve as the center of the community's political, economic, and social as well as spiritual life; it understood in an intimate way the biblical call to feed the hungry and clothe the naked and challenge powers and municipalities. In the history of these struggles, I was able to see faith as more than a comfort

to the weary or a hedge against death; rather, it was an active, palpable agent in the world. (Obama, 2006, p. 207)

Senator Edward Kennedy also exemplifies the liberal perspective, especially since he tried for decades to create a universal health care program. At an event honoring his contributions to ending child poverty, one speaker noted:

> He (had) a comprehensive view about how you should end child poverty, but he knew you couldn't do it all at once and that you had to see the whole thing.... So he went at it in many, many pieces, but I think it was all within the context of a coherent, comprehensive whole. (Edelman, no date)

The "Lion of the Senate" and his staff effected over 300 bills that were passed, including:

- Civil Rights Bill of 1964, which banned segregation;
- Immigration and Naturalization Act of 1965, which ended discrimination against non-European persons;
- Voting Rights Act Extension of 1970, which lowered the voting age to 18;
- Americans with Disabilities Act of 1990, which prohibited discrimination against the disabled;
- State Children's Health Insurance Program, which expanded coverage to low-income children;
- Family Opportunity Act of 2006, which enabled children with special needs to obtain Medicaid coverage (Khan & Taylor, 2009).

Far left

Although a review of Kennedy's legislative career demonstrates how working within the system can be effective, the far left advocates for bigger and faster changes. One example of the far left emerged in 2011, when the Occupy Wall Street movement started in a small park in New York City. This leaderless movement focused on the "simple yet powerful point of unity: 'The one thing we all have in common is that we are the 99% that will no longer tolerate the greed and corruption of the 1%.'" (Gautney, 2011). This statistic referred to the top 1 percent of households owning most of the wealth in the United States. An updated statistic about wealth inequality shows that the top 1 percent still owns a huge chunk of assets—even more than the middle class (60 percent of households) in 2019 (Sawhill & Pulliam, 2019). The Declaration of the Occupation of New York City states that:

> As we gather together in solidarity to express a feeling of mass injustice, we must not lose sight of what brought us together. We write so that all people who feel wronged by the corporate forces of the world can know that we are your allies. (the full text is available on archive.org)

Besides protesting the influence of corporate money in politics, the activists also spoke out about student loans and workers' rights. Illustration 3.2 shows one example of the Occupy Wall Street activism.

Illustration 3.2   Occupy Wall Street (Shutterstock # is in picture).
Credit: © Glynnis Jones/Shutterstock

Although the Occupy Wall Street movement disbanded several years ago, its legacy still affects U.S. politics. The demands for a higher minimum wage, including the $15-an-hour option, have yielded some success. Also, many supporters for the presidential campaigns of Bernie Sanders and Elizabeth Warren were associated with this movement (Sanders, 2020). One former activist wrote that the struggle against the 1 percent with their concentrated wealth

> won't be easy. Wresting power from the ruling financial elites will be an ongoing challenge, and ending big money's grip on politics lies at the core of this effort. But business as usual must change because the planet can't wait, and the people can't, either. (Levitin, 2015)

The political spectrum and the opioid crisis

Not surprisingly, research shows that political ideology is one factor in the public's attitudes about substance used disorder (SUD) in general (Murphy, 2014). However, the opioid crisis has emerged as a nonideological issue in many ways. Based on the author's review of conservative and liberal websites, it is safe to say that a consensus has built up on this issue. The CATO Institute, for example, is a conservative think tank that has expressed opposition to the War on Drugs:

> This dominant abstinence-based policy model is grounded in the logic of prohibition, and it depends not upon healing but upon shame, isolation, prosecution, and penalty. The better model is "harm reduction," grounded in connection and care, reason and rights, and human dignity and worth. (Bowers & Abrahamson, 2020)

Republican governors have also made public stances to fight the crisis. For instance, Scott Walker of Wisconsin has promoted the Heroin, Opioid Prevention, and Education (HOPE) agenda that includes laws regarding treatment, law enforcement, and required training for medical professionals who prescribe controlled substances (American Security News Reports, 2018). In fact, governors from both parties have consistently advocated for adequate Medicaid funding for drug treatment (e.g., Malone, 2017).

Besides the state level, policymakers on the federal level are working across the aisle to fight the opioid crisis. Senator Rob Portman of Ohio, a Republican, has worked with his Democratic counterpart, Sherrod Brown, for both legislation and funding. Portman's website lists "fighting addiction" as one of his top priorities, and notes that he had authored the Comprehensive Addiction and Recovery Act (CARA) in 2016 (www.robportman.com).

Another example of bipartisan agreement focuses on expanding access to buprenorphine (e.g., suboxone) through medical providers. The Mainstream Act, proposed in 2019, would remove the requirement that these providers get certified by taking an eight-hour computer course. Both Democrats and Republicans (sometimes called "GOP"—Grand Old Party—in the media) supported this act (Wang, 2021). However, the Biden administration forestalled this act in 2021 by issuing new guidelines that removed this requirement (Mann, 2021).

Not all opioid-related issues are bipartisan, of course. Liberals such as Andrew Yang (2020 Democratic presidential candidate) have supported more drastic measures for harm reduction, including decriminalization of street drugs.

> We have to let the country know this [SUD] is not a personal failing. This was a systemic government failing. . . . Then we need to open up safe consumption and safe injection sites around the country because they save lives. (Dodge, 2019)

However, "more needs to be done" can mean many different things along the political spectrum.

A review of the political spectrum as related to ideology, then, reveals the wide range of opinions within the United States. Acquiring this knowledge base is an essential component of thoughtful activism, which is discussed in the next section. Thoughtful activism includes an understanding of responsibility and the common good, which is explicated in Box 3.1.

Thoughtful activism

Despite the recent turmoil, thoughtful activism requires self-reflection and focus on the long-term aspects of policy. A person may ask: who has time to sit down and contemplate when so much has happened recently? However, thoughtful activism should do more than put out fires in the immediate present. If activists are building a strong movement instead of a temporary task force, they must consider self-reflection as a foundation.

One topic for self-reflection is how one feels about the political process. A person may have tuned out the news because it is so depressing, while another may have spent countless hours "doom scrolling" and obsessing about recent events. Neither option is viable for a thoughtful activist because they both express despair over the political process. Despite the system's

---

Box 3.1 Responsibility and the Common Good

Collective responsibility—the philosophical assumption that a group could be morally blameworthy, not just individuals (Stanford Encyclopedia of Philosophy, 2005). A city, for instance, may neglect the needs of its older adults and be morally responsible for their suffering. Liberals on the left are more likely to stress collective responsibility.

Personal responsibility—the concept that every individual is responsible for their own economic well-being. "Personal responsibility, in a capitalist system, means individuals freely control their own money, and personally enjoy or suffer the consequences of their own choices" (Wall Street Journal Opinion, 2008). Encouraging somebody to get a job and not ask for any financial help, for example, would be congruent with this concept.

Common good—"As a philosophical concept, the common good is best understood as part of an encompassing model for practical reasoning among the members of a political community. The model takes for granted that citizens stand in a 'political' or 'civic' relationship with one another" so that they build libraries, parks, and other facilities for the public" (Stanford Encyclopedia of Philosophy, 2018).

Discussion questions
- How does the "personal responsibility" concept relate to a person with OUD? Would it differ based on the political spectrum or other variables?
- How much "collective responsibility" does our society have regarding the opioid crisis?
- What is the "common good" related to providing services for persons with OUD?

flaws and fumblings, it does function well at times. Compare the political process to a clunker car you drive to work every day—it is not a Mercedes, but it mostly works. As Winston Churchill once said, "Democracy is the worst form of government, except for all the others" (retrieved from www.goodreads.com).

Indeed, a thoughtful activist can concentrate on self-efficacy (i.e., one's belief that they can succeed) instead of cynical despair over the political process. If a person lacks faith in their ability to make significant changes, they are limiting themselves and their allies. This author, for example, could lack faith in her ability to write a policy book as a tool for advocacy. She could list several reasons for a possible failure: she is a lousy writer, nobody is going to read the book anyway, her ideas are stupid, and what is the point of trying to change anything because the political system is too corrupt for any reform. Instead of promoting self-efficacy, she could wallow in enough self-doubts to sink this writing project.

Any thoughtful activist, though, knows that they are not alone. This chapter draws on the wisdom of activists who exemplify the strengths that we need in our fight for social justice, whatever the issue chosen by the activist. Thinking about how to advocate in general will provide a foundation for advocating for the issues of the opioid crisis.

Rules for radicals: Is being radical such a bad thing?

When Saul Alinsky wrote *Rules for Radicals* in 1971, the United States was still in turmoil over the Vietnam War, civil rights, and other controversies. This influential book is only part of his legacy to the social justice movement because his remarkable life story also deserves attention. Having grown up in Chicago, Alinsky's first exposure to injustice was as a Jew who lived close to a Polish neighborhood that would instigate attacks. Both the Jews and Poles formed gangs. Later in his career, Alinsky's early experiences with these gangs enabled him to communicate well with criminal gangs.

At the University of Chicago, Alinsky became involved with the sociologists who worked to reform the city. One hypothesis, for example, stressed that cities had certain zones, such as the central business district and slums. A slum neighborhood went through cycles of immigrant groups that started out in poverty before moving to higher income areas.

The Chicago sociologists argued that social disorganization, not heredity, was the cause of disease, crime, and other characteristics of slum life. Thus, when members of an immigrant group became acculturated and prosperous enough to move out of a slum neighborhood, social disorganization and its consequences did not follow them to the new neighborhood. This recurring pattern . . . showed that it was the slum area itself, and not the particular group living there, with which behavior pathologies were associated. (Horwitt, 1992, p. 13)

Discussion question

How does the "person in environment" concept relate to the hypothesis of social disorganization?

Alinsky's career experiences also included work in the Joliet prison before he became the pioneer of community organizing (Horwitt, 1992). During the Depression, he worked with a Catholic leader to form the Back of the Yards Neighborhood Council in the stockyards area of Chicago. Catholic churches, workers unions, and small businesses joined together for a "multi-issue, nonpartisan, democratic populist 'voice of the people'" that overcame ethnic and political divisions (Miller, 2010). In the 1980s, Barack Obama worked as a community organizer in an agency founded by Alinsky. He wrote that "organizing begins with the premise that the problems facing inner-city communities do not result from a lack of effective solutions, but from a lack of power to implement these solutions" (Obama cited in Miller, 2010).

Alinsky's community organizing and close encounters with poverty, especially during the Great Depression, shaped his political beliefs and inspired him to write books. *Rules for Radicals* (1971) is his most famous work—or infamous, according to his conservative critics. The book "has done more to destructively transform America than any rampaging foreign army could hope to accomplish" (Adamo, 2019, p. iii). "At its core, the Alinsky strategy necessitates lying, intimidation, and exploiting the lowest and basest failings of human character" (Adamo, 2019, p. iv), and reading the book is an "extremely distasteful task" because of the "renewed focus of the sheer ugliness in the souls of those who ascribe to it" (Adamo, 2019, p. v).

Decades after his death, then, Alinsky can still evoke deep hostility. Although he was too much of an individualist to be a Communist (Horwitt, 1992), he self-identified as a radical without any apologies.

> The Radical believes that all peoples should have a high standard of food, housing, and health . . . . The Radical places human rights far above property rights. He is for universal, free public education and recognizes this as fundamental to the democratic way of life . . . . The Radical believes completely in real equality of opportunity for all peoples regardless of race, color, or creed. He insists on full employment for economic security but is just as insistent that man's work should not only provide economic security but also be such as to satisfy the creative desires within all men. (Alinsky, 1946, cited in Matthews, 2016)

While it is beyond the scope of this text for a full analysis of Alinsky's work, the critical reader should be aware that they may not agree with all of his actions or statements. However, the *Rules for Radicals* does provide key insights about community organizing that social workers should consider. For example,

> It is not enough just to elect your candidates. You must keep the pressure on. Radicals should keep in mind Franklin D. Roosevelt's response to a reform delegation, "Okay, you've convinced me. Now go on out and bring on me!" Action comes from keeping the heat on. No politician can sit on a hot issue if you make it hot enough. (Alinsky, 1971, p. xxiv)

For advocates, "keeping the heat on" does not have to involve confrontational tactics. Building and maintaining relationships with legislators and other influential people will always be critical. If a legislator has done something praiseworthy, commend them. For example, I occasionally contact my progressive senator when he does something noteworthy. Everybody loves to hear a "good job!" comment, especially politicians who must face constant criticism and complaints.

"Keeping the heat on" also means offering your expertise to legislators because the issues of SUD and mental health are so complex. Even if you disagree with a legislator about other issues, focus on the common ground regarding the opioid crisis. Unfortunately, politics (like social work) can pose ethical dilemmas on a regular basis. At what point do you refuse to work with a politician whose stances are antithetical to social work values? A politician who denigrates LGBTQ+ persons, for instance, may not be an acceptable ally for social justice advocates.

Another relevant idea from Alinsky's work is how to confront a policy debate head-on.

Pick the target, freeze it, personalize it, and polarize it. In conflict tactics there are certain rules that the organizer should always regard as universalities. One is that the opposition must be singled out as the target and "frozen." By this I mean that in a complex, interrelated, urban society, it becomes increasingly difficult to single out who is to blame for any particular evil. There is a constant, and somewhat legitimate, passing of the buck . . . . the problem that threatens to loom more and more is that of identifying the enemy. Obviously there is no point to tactics unless one has a target upon which to center the attacks. One big problem is a constant shifting of responsibility from one jurisdiction to another—individuals and bureaus one after another disclaim responsibility for particular conditions, attributing the authority for any change to some other force. (Alinsky, 1971, pp. 130–131)

Besides personalizing the target, Alinsky recommends polarization. However, U.S. politics became so painfully polarized during the Trump presidency and 2020 election (Bump, 2021) that the idea of creating any further polarization can be problematic.

One argument against polarization emerges in the climate change debate, which usually results in Democrats urging government action and Republicans denying the importance of environmental regulations. Jaffe (2017) advises climate change activists to avoid such political splits.

Tackling an unprecedented, overwhelming, global-scale problem like climate change will require sustaining pollution-reduction efforts for many decades . . . . As we work to execute this transformation, the political pendulum will continue to swing (between Democrats and Republicans). Environmentalists must embrace the goal of cultivating a working coalition regardless of who is in power. (Jaffe, 2017, p. 486)

Discussion questions

Social workers must consider when it is fitting to polarize an issue and when it is better to compromise with the other side. For example, the Black Lives Matter movement stressed the slogan "Defund the police!" in response to the police killings of George Floyd and other victims. This term "means reallocating or redirecting funding away from the police department to other government agencies funded by the local municipality" to increase social services (Ray, 2020). Advocates argue that providing more counselors and affordable housing, not riot gear and military-level weapons for the police, would decrease crime and benefit the community.

- ▷ Do you consider the "Defund the police" a polarizing issue, or is there a way to attract support from people across the political spectrum?
- ▷ Could it be possible to defund the police in an incremental fashion by small steps, or can it only be done by a bold action? How does this relate to polarization?

Frederick Douglass

The silver trump of freedom had aroused my soul to eternal wakefulness. Freedom now appeared, to disappear no more forever. It was heard in every sound, and seen in every thing. It was ever present to torment me with a

Illustration 3.3 Statue of Frederick Douglass in Harlem.
Credit: © Here Now/Shutterstock

sense of my wretched condition. I saw nothing without seeing it, I heard nothing without hearing it, and felt nothing without feeling it. It looked from every star, it smiled in every calm, breathed in every wind, and moved in every storm. (Douglass, *Narrative*, pp. 68–69)

Slavery, the "ownership" and exploitation of fellow humans, epitomizes the extreme of capitalism. For centuries, American slaveholders and their defenders used biblical quotes and historic precedents to uphold the moral imperative of "civilizing" the savages from Africa. For example, one defender of slavery wrote that "The intelligent, christian (sic) slave-holder at the South is the best friend of the negro" (no author, 1859). Douglass, an escaped slave who became an international sensation, wrote books and emerged as the spokesperson for the abolitionist movement. During his speeches, he displayed slave collars, whips, and sometimes even his scarred back (Blight, 2018).

One astonishing moment in the abolitionist movement occurred in 1848, the tenth anniversary of Douglass' escape from Thomas Auld. He wrote an open letter to Auld—a dramatic example of Alinsky's "Pick the target, freeze it, personalize it, and polarize it" credo.

Although he had previously referred to Auld in his speeches, this letter "is a masterpiece of antislavery propaganda as well as an expression of personal rage" (Blight, 2018, p. 198). He wrote of the absurdity of one person owning another: "I am myself; you are yourself; we are two distinct persons, equal persons. What you are I am . . . . God created both, and made us separate beings" (Douglass cited in Blight, 2018, p. 199). Now Douglass was a married father of four, a respectable man with a house and career. He speaks of his children in their beds, where

> There are no slaveholders here to rend my heart by snatching them from my arms, or blast a mother's dearest hopes by tearing them from her bosom. Oh! Sir, a slaveholder never appears to me so completely an agent of hell, as when I think of and look upon my dear children. It is then that my feelings rise above my control. (Douglass cited in Blight, 2018, p. 199)

He further personalizes the target by describing the time he had been arrested for attempting to escape.

> You well know that I wear stripes on my back inflicted by your direction; and that you, while we were brothers in the same church, caused this right

hand, with which I am now penning this letter, to be closely tied to my left, and my person dragged at the pistol's mouth, fifteen miles, from the Bay side to Easton to be sold like a beast in the market. (Douglass cited in Blight, 2018, p. 199)

Even today, these passionate words can evoke outrage. In the slavery debate, polarization became inevitable.

Besides this powerful letter, Douglass contributed to the abolition of slavery by "keeping the heat on" with one famous politician—Abraham Lincoln. Historians acknowledge that Lincoln has a mixed record regarding slavery and equality. When the Civil War began, he stressed the preservation of the union rather than the end of slavery. His support of the colonization of former slaves was justified by his belief that the races were too different for them to live together. Speaking to five black leaders in 1862, he said that racial equality was impossible and that "It is better for us both, therefore, to be separated" (White, 2009, p. 510). When he heard about this event, Douglass wrote in an editorial that Lincoln's "contempt for Negroes and his canting hypocrisy" made him a "genuine representative of American prejudice and Negro hatred and far more concerned for the preservation of slavery, and the favor of the Border Slave States, than for any sentiment of magnanimity or principles of justice and humanity" (White, 2009, p. 511).

As shown above, Douglass was not afraid to polarize the issue even if it meant confronting the president. Later they met and became allies. The military decision to arm black troops in 1863 was a significant step, which Douglass supported by encouraging blacks to enlist. By the time Lincoln gave his second inaugural address in 1865, he called slavery an evil that stained the country's history. Douglass' influence on Lincoln was not the only cause of the president's shift, but "keeping the heat on" did play a role.

Discussion question

In contrast to the United States, the fight to end slavery in Britain was a slow and incremental process. The British economy, especially its international trade with their colonies, derived tremendous profits from slavery. For decades, court cases regarding individual slaves and parliamentary motions by William Wilberforce tore down the edifice of slavery piece by piece. By 1833, the Parliament had abolished slavery in the British colonies—three days before Wilberforce died. Each law, including the 1833 one, was incomplete and needed more work (Brain, no date).

Can you think of a critical social problem that can be solved incrementally over decades, or do you believe that immediate and decisive actions are necessary?

4
The punishing effects of poverty

Introduction

Mr. Podsnap, a character from Charles Dickens' *Our Mutual Friend* (1854), was talking with his friends after dinner when a man came up to them, who makes:

> a highly unpolite remark; no less than a reference to the circumstance that some half-dozen people had lately died in the streets, of starvation. It was clearly ill-timed after dinner. It was not adapted to the cheek of the young person. It was not in good taste." Podsnap says that he did not believe that people were dying in the streets, and put "it behind him." But the man "was afraid we must take it as proved, because there were the Inquests and the Registrar's returns." Podsnap responds: "Then it was their own fault" (Dickens, *Our Mutual Friend*, 1854, Chapter 11).

Unfortunately, this caustic attitude toward the poor has not died out in modern society. Consider this quote from a conservative writer in 2021, describing the impoverished persons he saw on the streets and subways of New York City:

> A growing mass of fat, lazy leeches, slugs, thugs, gangbangers, rule-breakers, whiners, and perpetual ne'er-do-wells. . . . **I refuse to humanize those who cannot be bothered to lift a finger to humanize themselves. The mentally ill need our care. The rest need the whip** (bolded in original) (Zubatov, 2021).

Besides complaining about how many persons of color are in the city, he mocks the concept of structural racism. In his opinion, only the liberal elites who are too rich to encounter any street person would suggest such a ludicrous idea. Mr. Podsnap probably would have approved of his attitude toward the poor—even the whip.

Not surprisingly, the impact of stigma can be shattering on a person. Even as children, we knew that it hurts to be socially excluded and verbally attacked by others. Researchers have developed the concept of rejection sensitivity, "a personality disposition characterized by the tendency to anxiously expect and overreact to rejection" (Breines & Ayduk, 2015, p. 1). Rejection sensitivity can lead to:

- Hostile behaviors toward others;
- Depression instead of happiness;
- Low feelings of self-worth;
- Negative self-talk;
- Self-harm (Breines & Ayduk, 2015).

Besides the impact of stigma, this chapter focuses on the punishing effects of poverty and their relation to the opioid crisis. Unlike the contemporary writer who refuses to humanize the poor if they "cannot be bothered to lift a finger to humanize themselves," social workers do honor the dignity and worth of all persons. Although an individual can make bad decisions regarding money, experts stress the systemic nature of poverty that is both complex and capable of being solved by good policies.

The concept of poverty

What is poverty? The word "poverty" includes many dimensions that extend far beyond the media images of urban devastation. First, financial poverty is only one kind of deprivation. Consider these other variations:

- Time poverty, which can be described as "Working long hours and having no choice" (Bardasi & Wodon, 2010), causes a person to be too busy to get enough rest or recreation. For example, the family responsibilities of parents/caregivers may make it impossible to take a day off to unwind. College students who balance work hours and school commitments may also experience time poverty.
- Cultural poverty, the scarcity of cultural and life-enriching benefits, such as music and art, is a subtle form of deprivation. In this book's context, "cultural poverty" should not be confused with the controversial "culture of poverty" idea (i.e., that some cultures discourage the work

ethic and other means of escaping poverty). Sometimes parents are too busy or otherwise unable to provide cultural opportunities for their children. One summer, I was mentoring a teen who had little access to libraries, museums, or other places for intellectual stimulation. My friend's daughter, in contrast, was able to attend computer camps and visit museums.
- Spiritual poverty, which is defined by a charity website as "hopelessness . . . Oftentimes, people in poverty struggle with feelings of worthlessness and despair. Children are especially vulnerable to these emotions and the message of despair poverty sends" (www.compassion.com).

Discussion question

Select one of the types of nonfinancial poverty listed above and relate it to the opioid crisis. For example, do you see a possible link between time poverty and drug use?

Besides these holistic views of poverty, the U.S. government has established the 2020 Federal Poverty Line (FPL) at $12,880 for individuals and $26,500 for a family of four (www.healthcare.gov/glossary/federal-poverty-level-fpl/). Researchers have disputed the validity of the FPL, also known as absolute poverty, because it is based too much on food expenses to the exclusion of housing and other material needs. Also, "where the poverty line is actually drawn has an arbitrary element to it" and does not measure the inequality in the United States (Rank & Hirschi, 2015).

Relative poverty, in contrast, is measured by comparison to the rest of the population. Persons living in the bottom 20th percentile of income distribution, or having one-half of the median income, would be "poor." Based on this definition, the majority of Americans are going to experience a period of poverty sometime during their adult lives: "61.8 percent of the population will experience a year below the 20th percentile" (Rank & Hirschi, 2015).

Discussion question

Why would policymakers who want to restrict social spending be more likely to stress the FPL instead of relative poverty measurement?

As stated above, most Americans are going to experience a period of poverty sometime during their adult lives (Rank & Hirschi, 2015). A recent historic example of widespread poverty was the Great Recession of 2008 that caused layoffs, foreclosures, and other signs of economic distress. One economist noted that "One in five employees lost their jobs at the beginning of the Great Recession. Many of those people never recovered; they never got real work again" (Cappelli, Barankay, & Lewin, 2018). Poverty became more visible in the suburbs, where white-collar workers with college degrees found themselves in line at the food pantry.

In 2020, the lockdown caused by the COVID-19 pandemic also created a contingent of the "new poor"—people who never thought they would need to apply for benefits or visit a foodbank. Only seven months after the lockdown had started in March 2020, at least eight million Americans fell into poverty (Sykes, 2020). With millions of workers laid off or put on furlough (temporary work stoppage), the economic consequences appeared worse than the 2008 recession. As of 2021, it is too soon to tell the full economic impact of the lockdown and other COVID-19 consequences. It seems likely, though, that the pandemic will make many reconsider poverty as a systemic problem instead of an individual failing.

The power of hierarchy

In 2020, several cities erupted in protests over the death of George Floyd and others killed by police actions. The Black Lives Matter (BLM) movement reverberated with the realization that systemic racism was still alive and well. Police violence was only one indication of how the United States oppressed persons of color through job discrimination, overincarceration, housing segregation, and other harmful practices. Illustration 4.1 shows how the power of the BLM movement inspired young persons.

As Americans grappled with renewed awareness of hierarchal power, a new book (Wilkerson, 2020) added to the debate by arguing that the concept of "caste" applied to U.S. race relations. "Caste" is defined as "an artificial construction, a fixed and embedded ranking of human value that sets the presumed supremacy of one group against the presumed inferiority of other groups based on ancestry and other immutable traits. . . . A caste system uses rigid, often arbitrary boundaries to keep the ranked groupings apart, distinct from one another and in their assigned places" (Wilkerson, 2020, p. 17).

THE PUNISHING EFFECTS OF POVERTY   63

Illustration 4.1 Black Lives Matter (Shutterstock # in picture).
Credit: ©Michal Urbanek/Shutterstock

Wilkerson proposes eight pillars of caste, which include:

▸ Purity versus pollution. The dominant caste is allegedly pure and must avoid contamination from the "polluted" lower castes. In India, the "Untouchables" clean the toilets and perform other menial, undesirable tasks. For decades in the United States, African Americans were the "untouchables" who were forbidden in the same swimming pools or even access to the same drinking fountains as whites. This "polluted" status worsens with the stigma of drug addiction because of the incorrect assumption that most drug users and dealers are African American. For example, former Governor Paul LePage stated in 2016 that "90-plus percent of those pictures in my book, and it's a three-ringed binder, are black and Hispanic people from Waterbury, Connecticut, the Bronx and Brooklyn" (Whittle & Sharp, 2016). In my practice experience, people (even drug users themselves) may regard drug users as unclean not only in the physical but moral sense. Using the terms "clean time" and "testing dirty" indicates the power of language regarding drug use. Telling my clients that I will not use those terms because of their derogatory undertone has sparked many discussions about stigma.

- ▹ Occupational hierarchy. In India, caste determines the employment options for workers. Despite the United States claiming to be the land of opportunity, persons of color are more likely to work in low-paying, low-status jobs, such as janitors. Historically, African Americans belonged in the "mudsill" category—a mudsill is the foundation of a house that "bears the weight of the entire structure above it" (Wilkerson, 2020, p.130). The predominance of race-based job segregation had tragic consequences in 2020 when the COVID pandemic struck. COVID afflicted persons of color much worse because they were more likely to be service workers and not be able to work from home (Needham, 2021).
- ▹ Dehumanization and stigma. Defining outgroups as "an undifferentiated mass of nameless, faceless scapegoats" (Wilkerson, 2020, p. 142), Wilkerson stresses how the caste system deprives persons of their individuality. Slave auctions epitomize this point because the dominant class prodded, poked at, and examined the "merchandise" as if they were inanimate objects. This dehumanization has resulted in a criminal justice system that over-punishes the African American on the assumption that they must all be lawbreakers. For example, the story titled "'Because they can get away with it': Why African Americans are blamed for crimes they didn't commit" describes the increase of whites calling 911 when they see Blacks/AA birdwatching or doing other innocuous activities (Carrega, 2020).

In this race-based caste system that included slave auctions as pictured in Illustration 4.2, poor whites remain in an ambiguous position. They need the caste system to feel better about their lives, especially since "nothing could take away this whiteness that made you and your way of life 'superior'" (Smith, L. cited in Wilkerson, 2020, p. 182). The presidency of Barack Obama, then, shocked many whites because they had lost some of their perceived superiority. The dominant class creates "unsustainable expectations" (Wilkerson, 2020, p. 184) for those poor whites who believed that their birth entitled them to superiority. As President Lyndon Johnson once said, "If you can convince the lowest white man he's better than the best colored man, he won't notice you're picking his pocket. Hell, give him somebody to look down on, and he'll empty his pockets for you" (Moyers, 1988). (Historical note: In 1960, using the term "colored" was considered appropriate.)

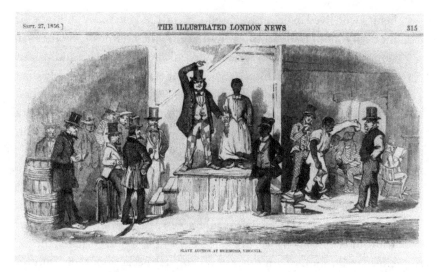

Illustration 4.2   1856 slave auction.

Poor whites are also the focus of Isenberg's *White Trash: The 400-Year Untold History of Class in America* (2016). Instead of focusing on a race-based caste, Isenberg emphasizes class as the basis for the social hierarchy in the United States:

First known as 'waste people,' and later 'white trash,' marginalized Americans were stigmatized for their inability to be productive, to own property, or to produce healthy and upwardly mobile children—the sense of uplift on which the American dream is predicated. . . . At all times, the white trash remind us of one of the American nation's uncomfortable truths: the poor are always with us (Isenberg, 2016, p. xxvii).

Key aspects of the history of "white trash" include:

- Being called "human waste" in the 17th century by the British, who shipped these undesirables to the American colonies. These "lubbers" lived in Lubberland and were too lazy to work. Allegedly, their deformed faces made them look subhuman and they lived in cattle pens without roofs.
- In the 19th century, squatters owned no land but had to live as tenants with no permanent homes. Society regarded squatters as inferior

beings who lived in primitive dwellings and bred too many children. (In modern times, "trailer trash" would refer to their homes.) Another version of white trash was "crackers," allegedly both aggressive and vulgar.

- Although southern whites (e.g., hillbillies) were more likely than northerners to be considered white trash, northerners such as Abraham Lincoln were also called "mudsills" and other insults. His agricultural background and gangly appearance even caused his critics to call him the "original gorilla" (Bowden, 2013).
- In the early 20th century, poor whites were classified as "morons" who were born with low intelligence. Their lack of education, besides medical problems such as hookworm, alarmed eugenicists (those who believed that good breeding would save society from being overrun with "inferior" offspring.) In 1927, for example, a court ordered the forcible sterilization of a mother and daughter because of their "moron" and "feebleminded" rankings (Isenberg, 2016, p. 201).

Nobody would ever argue that the "white trash" population had suffered as much as African Americans during slavery and its cruel aftermath. However, Isenberg's descriptions of how society has treated "white trash" throughout U.S. history compels us to consider the impact of class apart from race. The "white trash" meme shown in Illustration 4.3 illustrates the ongoing contempt for low-income whites.

Discussion questions

- After reading this section, what is your opinion of this crucial question: How much of the social hierarchy in the United States is based on race and how much on economic class alone?
- Using a search engine such as Google Images, look up these terms: "white trash Walmart," "welfare Barbie," "trailer trash," and "white trash outfits." How do these images affect you on a gut level? Do they reinforce or challenge any perceptions you may have had of poor whites? Box 4.1 describes how using art for social justice in Appalachia can challenge such harmful stereotypes.
- Do you agree with Wilkerson's assertion that the United States has a race-based caste system that is rigid or do you think that the United States has a more fluid class system? Support your answer.

THE PUNISHING EFFECTS OF POVERTY   67

Illustration 4.3 "White trash" meme (Shutterstock number in picture).
Credit: © Ron Leishman/Shutterstock

- Explore the Black Lives Matter (www.blacklivesmatter.com) and related websites. How does this movement affect your understanding of Wilkerson's ideas about caste?
- Consider the class differences between powder and crack cocaine. In the 1980s, a silver spoon symbolized the prestige of using powder cocaine because it was relatively expensive. As Robin Williams once said, "cocaine is God's way of telling you that you're making too much money" (cited in azquotes.com). Earlier, society had regarded powder cocaine

users as glamourous, fast-talking, and hard working. When crack cocaine exploded on the drug scene in the late 1980s, though, this cheap product evoked derisive names such as "crackhead" and "crack whore." Of course, racism also played a role in the contrasting depictions of these two versions of the same substance. Do you think that the harsh punishments against crack cocaine resulted only from racism, or did class prejudice play a role?

Box 4.1 Appalachia: Using art for social justice

Appalachia, the rural and mountainous region in the eastern United States, has been the butt of jokes regarding hillbillies who marry their sisters and hide their moonshine stills. In 1873, one writer called it "A Strange Land and Peculiar People" as he described the "otherness" of Appalachians with their alleged facial deformities (Shapiro, 1978, no page).

The Appalachian hillbilly theme emphasizes whiteness despite the region's diverse populations. For decades, several leaders have "all painted the portrait of Appalachia the same way: poor, backward, and white. While the economic despair and major health epidemics are an unsettling reality for the region, a glaring omission has been made from the 'poverty porn' images fed to national audiences for generations: Appalachia's people of color" (Baird, 2014).

Even the recent film *Hillbilly Elegy* (2020) has received negative attention for its traditional emphasis on whites to the exclusion of other Appalachians (Johnson & Byrd, 2020).

One scholar (Campbell, 2011) states that "The myth of whiteness is, of course, not only due to misinformation, invisibility, complacency, or the institutionalization of racist structures. Overt racism is part of political agendas that benefit from the diversion of attention from the problems of African-Americans" (Campbell, 2011, p. 5).

Whatever the causes of the myth of whiteness, it provided the backdrop for recent white supremacist rallies. In 2017, a neo-Nazi rally met in Piketon, Kentucky. Disturbed by this upcoming event, local artist Lacy Hale created a logo with the message "No Hate in my Holler." "This piece just came to me. . . . It just popped in my head—'no hate in my holler.' Don't bring that here. Don't try to bring that fear and lie to us under the guise of helping poor white families. You're bringing hatred and trying to fool people into supporting your cause" (Adams, 2017). The "No Hate in my Holler" slogan then appeared in subsequent protests (Jojack, 2018). Since then, Hale's advocacy through art has included murals, art workshops, and even artwork for masks during the 2020 pandemic (Marietta, 2020).

Besides the visual arts, literature can also promote social justice. Frank X. Walker, who confronted the assumption that all Appalachians were white, started the Affrilachian literary movement for black Appalachians. "Ever since high school, words have continued to serve as my first weapon of choice and my salvation. Many of life's challenges need creative solutions. I believe creativity—in all its many forms—can change the way we think and operate" (Walker, 2006).

Both artists are examples of the potential of creative expression in social movements. Words have power, as evident in Walker's term "Affrilachian" that fights the invisibility of black Applachians. Simple messages such as "No hate in my holler" can resonate throughout several communities and inspire thoughtful activism.

Discussion questions

- If a white supremacist rally were to occur in your area, would you go to a counter-protest or consider other options? Discuss the reasoning behind your answer.
- Research the Affrilachian writers and other persons of color in Appalachia. How would you publicize their achievements to shift the popular misconceptions of Appalachian culture toward a more inclusive version?
- Consider the term "poverty porn" mentioned earlier. This may be related to the concept of "ruin porn" associated with Detroit and other impoverished areas. "On the surface, Detroit can be summed up in one image: an abandoned and gutted home. Detroit is one of the most photographed cities in the world and the general narrative is of ruin, abandonment and decay" (Doucet & Phelp, 2016). What is the appropriate response of social workers toward these portrayals of hopeless poverty in Appalachia and cities such as Detroit? Do these images advance or block the cause of social justice?

The power of capitalism

Appalachia, home of the "white trash" stereotype, became the subject of controversy in 2020 when the film *Hillbilly Elegy* was released. Based on J.D. Vance's 2018 book titled *Hillbilly Elegy: A Memoir of a Family and Culture in Crisis*, the film evoked discussions on the causes of rural poverty. Vance, who was elected as Senator in Ohio in 2022, has told the story about his troubled family. His mother's SUD and his town's poverty apparently proved that Appalachia was a "culture in crisis" because its residents had given up on themselves. One critic is historian Anthony Harkins, who notes that "A common theme across those examples (e.g., Vance's story) is the idea of a dysfunctional community that a person has to rise above in order to be successful" (Devega, 2020). This "culture in crisis" concept thus leads to the question of whether escaping poverty is simply a matter of having enough personal determination and not related to structural barriers, such as lack of good job opportunities. Instead, Harkins wants public attention on the "real Appalachia, with the diversity of the people there—the political activism, the idea of simply being children and a celebration of life, rather than this vision of death and despair" (Devega, 2020).

Another historian, Steven Stoll, explicates the impact of capitalism on this region in his book *Ramp Hollow: The Ordeal of Appalachia* (2017).

> Poor whites also became a despised race defined by their own circular argument. Descriptions of mountaineers emphasize their supposed degeneracy and grotesqueness, which came from their isolation, causing moral depravity, resulting in... degeneracy and grotesqueness. Once a racial type is in place, any worsening of a subject people's condition reinforces the type, providing proof after proof.... Inventing a race of people and depriving them of land not only required the force of law, it required a story. (Stoll, 2017, p. 21)

The story of Appalachians, then, stressed a geographic isolation that Stoll claims was exaggerated to justify the exploitation by lumber and coal corporations. "Isolation ... doesn't really describe location. It describes an unholy remove from civil society, an outlier status. Like race, it doesn't really exist, but the story requires it" (Stoll, 2017, p. 22). These corporations deprived the residents of their common lands which had helped them survive in an agrarian society. By robbing the people of their lands, the capitalist system took away the "ecological base" (Stoll, 2017, p. 74) of their hardscrabble existence. No longer could Appalachians use the common lands for hunting, gathering, and herding.

This dispossession of a devalued group of people does not spontaneously occur, nor is it ever inevitable. Policies are always essential in actions such as the Indian Removal Act of 1830, which created a catastrophe for the Cherokees and other tribes when they were forced to leave their lands. On the Library of Congress website, the caption for a map reads: "A map of that part of Georgia occupied by the Cherokee Indians, taken from an actual survey made during the present year 1831, in pursuance of an act of the general assembly of the state: this interesting tract of country contains (4,364,554) acres, many rich gold mines & many delightful situations & though in some parts mountainous, some of the richest land belonging to the state" (retrieved from https://www.loc.gov/item/2004633028/). During the 1830s, Native Americans faced violence from both the military and civilians. The Trail of Tears, which occurred in 1838, started when the military "forced the Cherokee into stockades at bayonet point while whites looted their homes and belongings. Then, they marched the Indians more than 1,200 miles to Indian Territory. Whooping cough, typhus, dysentery, cholera and starvation were epidemic along the way, and historians estimate that more than 5,000 Cherokee died" (History.com editors, 2020).

When the corporations dispossessed the Appalachians, the results were not as horrific as the Indian Removal Act but still disruptive. Dillon's Rule of 1868, for example, "allowed state legislatures to sanction corporate activities without gaining the consent of anyone whose life might be interrupted"—even if a railroad company wanted to lay tracks in the middle of a city (Stoll, 2017, p. 136). Congressmen also supported the corporations' "scramble for Appalachia" that disregarded the residents' rights (Stoll, 2017, p. 137). As a result of these structural factors, generational poverty became the norm for Appalachians and other dispossessed peoples.

Discussion questions

> Do you think that the phrase "dispossession of a devalued group of people" applies to those with opioid use disorder (OUD)? In what ways are persons with any form of substance use disorder (SUD) devalued

and perhaps dispossessed? Box 4.2 describes the financial costs of SUD, which adds to the problem.

> If capitalism had been one cause of the structural poverty that still exists in Appalachia, it also played a major role in the opioid crisis. As discussed earlier, pharmaceutical companies had promoted Oxycontin and other addictive opioid medications without regard to the patients' well-being. Countries in the European Union, though, had stricter

---

Box 4.2 The costs of SUD on a personal level: A case study

Tess, a woman in her twenties, started using opioids after being prescribed them for bronchitis. "When I ran out, I started looking for them on my own, through dealers. . . . Because I was sick. Jittery. Diarrhea. All of it. I looked up my symptoms and what I'd been taking, and I realized, holy crap, I'm probably addicted" (Macy, 2018, p. 197). She switched to heroin when the pills became too expensive. Working as a waitress, "I worked just to use, and I used just so I could work. There was no in between" (Macy, 2018, p. 199). She was earning $800 a week, besides helping drug dealers to get free drugs—but she still needed more money, more drugs.

After a jail term during which she found out she was pregnant, her family found a treatment center that cost $20,000 (insurance paid all but $6,500). Fortunately, the baby was born without any symptoms of neonatal abstinence syndrome (NAS) due to buprenorphine that made her "feel normal" (Macy, 2018, p. 211). Insurance paid for 80 percent of the medication, but the cash-only doctor charged $700 up front for the visits that cost up to $100 each. Weekly visits would cost $400 a month. If she had used Vivitrol instead of buprenorphine, it would have cost $1,500 a month without insurance.

Because of a relapse that resulted in a hospital stay for Hepatitis C, she did another stint in inpatient rehabilitation that would cost her family an additional $12,000. Additional costs included airfare to the facility, besides replacing her lost driver's license. Her mother had been caring for the infant for months.

Discussion question
Design a wraparound program that would ensure the best quality care for persons like Tess.

regulations on opioid use including prohibitions on advertising. As a result, their rate of OUD is much lower than the U.S. rate (Cleveland Clinic, 2018). Now capitalist entrepreneurs are profiting from the opioid crisis by opening up suboxone clinics and other treatment programs. In this context, should the government be more proactive in restricting the capitalist aspects of the opioid crisis?

Policy analysis: Poverty Bill of Rights (2020)

In 2020, Representatives Barbara Lee (D-CA) and Marcia Fudge (D-OH) sponsored a resolution called the Poverty Bill of Rights. Lee stated in a press release, "We are facing a pandemic and a poverty crisis in this country—both of which disproportionately impact communities of color. This is a national emergency. The COVID-19 pandemic has exposed just how deep inequality runs in this country, with 17 million people unemployed and 23 million renters facing the threat of eviction" (Retrieved from www.lee.house.gov). Fudge's press release also stressed the impact of the pandemic. "During this time of great need, we must uplift low-income Americans and recognize their rights to equal opportunity, a living wage, housing, education, quality health care, and assistance in times of need. Declaring the fundamental economic rights of all Americans is the first step towards building a future where (Americans) do not suffer the effects of poverty" (Retrieved from www.fudge.house.gov).

Below is an abridged version of House Resolution 1048 (full text is available on www.congress.gov).

Expressing the sense of the House of Representatives that the Congress should enact the Poverty Bill of Rights to reaffirm the right of all Americans to live a life free from poverty and its impacts.

- ▸ Whereas according to the Census Bureau, more than 38,000,000 people, including 12,000,000 children, lived in poverty in 2018 based on the official poverty measure;
- ▸ Whereas more than 17,000,000 people lived in deep poverty, defined as living in a household with a total cash income below 50 percent of the poverty threshold;
- ▸ Whereas poverty disproportionately impacts communities of color, with the poverty rate at 20.8 percent for blacks, 17.6 percent for

Hispanics, and 10.1 percent for Asians, versus 8.1 percent for non-Hispanic whites;

▸ Whereas the top one percent of United States households have experienced income growth before taxes and transfer payments nearly seven times faster than the bottom 20 percent of households since 1979;

Resolved, that it is the sense of the House of Representatives that the Congress should enact the Poverty Bill of Rights to reaffirm the right of all Americans to live a life free from poverty and its impacts, including the right to:

(1) equal opportunity, irrespective of race, gender, or socioeconomic status;
(2) working family tax credits, such as the Child Tax Credit and the Earned Income Tax Credit, that are proven to lift families out of poverty, free from onerous eligibility requirements;
(3) a livable wage that is enough to ensure adequate housing, food, clothing, and other basic household needs;
(4) robust paid leave programs so they can care for themselves, their families, and dependents without fear of financial devastation;
(5) emergency financial assistance in times of unemployment;
(6) unionize to negotiate for higher wages, better benefits, and safe working conditions;
(7) financial security for themselves and their families during retirement years;
(8) quality, affordable health care and prescription drugs;
(9) clean air through robust environmental and public health policies;
(10) high-quality, affordable, and reliable childcare;
(11) accessible, affordable, safe housing;
(12) safe, clean, and affordable water and wastewater services;
(13) affordable, reliable energy service;
(14) equitable access to technology and telephone and broadband services;
(15) adequate access to affordable and nutritious foods;
(16) reliable, efficient, and affordable public transportation;
(17) high-quality, equitable PreK–12 public education;
(18) safe public schools that promote racial and socioeconomic diversity;

(19) access to affordable higher education, registered apprenticeships, and other vocational training opportunities;
(20) live with their families and not be separated from each other on the basis of poverty;
(21) safe neighborhoods, where they are protected by law enforcement, not targeted, profiled, harassed, and brutalized;
(22) equal treatment in criminal justice settings, free from discrimination;
(23) equal representation and participation in democracy through unfettered, unabridged access to the ballot box, accessible polling places, and alternatives to traditional in-person voting, such as early voting and voting by mail.

Discussion questions

- Pick the top five items that you consider to be related to the opioid crisis.
- Look up the status of this resolution on the Congressional website (www.congress.gov). In 2020, the House leadership assigned HR1048 to a committee but no further action was recorded in early 2021. Use both "HR1048" and "poverty bill of rights" as search terms.
- The American Rescue Plan, which was passed in March 2021, overlaps with some items in this resolution. Identify at least one and discuss its importance.
- The first part of the resolution includes several "Whereas" statements. Do they make a convincing argument for the need for the Poverty Bill of Rights? Look up the full text to see if you would have included more "Whereas" statements (www.congress.gov).
- After reading the 23 items in this resolution, determine which one is the most critical in the fight against poverty. Why did you pick it?
- Mark the items with these numbers: 1—easy; 2—moderately hard; and 3—impossible. Compare your analysis with your classmates for discussion.
- What would be the strongest argument *against* the Poverty Bill of Rights? Write a paragraph from the conservative/far right perspective.
- Since HR1048 is a resolution and not legislation with practical consequences, there is no need for a cost estimate by the Congressional Budget Office (CBO). If one of the items (e.g., increased access to the

internet for poor families) were to be implemented and the CBO estimate was in the millions, how would you justify the government spending?
- Lee is a social worker and led the Congressional Social Work Caucus in 2021. Discuss the possible influence of social work values on HR1048.
- Lee's website also states that she was a single mother who had used public assistance while going to college. In 2021, she was chair of the Democratic Whip Task Force on Poverty, Income Inequality, and Opportunity. Discuss the concept that "the personal becomes the political" in her career. Has that ever happened to you or someone you know?
- Other issues mentioned by Lee include diaper assistance for needy families and funding for COVID-19 funerals. Are there other poverty-related issues that often get overlooked by policymakers? Box 4.3 provides how the War on Poverty could still be relevant today.
- Several organizations had endorsed HR1048, including the Children's Defense Fund and the Center for Law and Social Policy. Look up those two organizations, then brainstorm about other possible endorsers. Why is it important to gain support from organizations like these?
- In 2021, Representative Lee and Senator Cory Booker reintroduced legislation for the United States Commission on Truth, Racial Healing, and Transformation (TRHT) to "examine the effects of slavery, institutional racism, and discrimination against people of color, and how our history impacts laws and policies today" (Press release on Lee's website www.lee.house.gov). Discuss the link between the historical impact of racism and current poverty issues.
- In 2021, Representative Fudge became the Housing Secretary under President Biden. Research her accomplishments in this new role. Is there any overlap with the Poverty Bill of Rights?

Role of Medicaid in the opioid crisis

Low-income Americans often have no access to private insurance, usually because their jobs do not provide that benefit. Medicaid, the federal program that provides medical care to many (but not all) persons without health benefits, is funded by both the federal and state governments. This means that every state has a different Medicaid program, which can lead to health inequities. For example, Schor and Johnson (2021) note that "Children's

Box 4.3 The War on Poverty: Echoes in 2021

In 1964, President Lyndon Johnson announced a "War on Poverty" campaign that resulted in Medicaid, Medicare, and several other social service programs (Matthews, 2014). Despite the recent assassination of President John Kennedy, a sense of optimism made the idea of ending poverty seem achievable. However, cutbacks on spending appeared in the following decade as politicians opposed the expansion of social spending. When Ronald Reagan was elected president in 1980, his popularity was partly due to his repetitions of the "welfare queen" story of one woman who had defrauded the system (Levin, 2019).

For 40 years, the War on Poverty appeared as quaint and obsolete as candy cigarettes. It seemed to be common wisdom that this war had failed "largely because people rely on the official poverty rate, a horrendously flawed measure, which excludes income received from major anti-poverty programs like food stamps or the EITC (Earned Income Tax Credit)" (Matthews, 2014). However, some experts have argued that the rate of poverty did decrease significantly because "Today's safety net—which includes important programs and improvements both from the Johnson era and thereafter—cuts poverty *nearly in half*" according to the Census Bureau's Supplemental Poverty Measure (Parrott, 2014).

When Congress passed the American Rescue Plan in 2021, it temporarily revived the war on poverty ideal by a huge expansion of the Child Tax Credit provision. For 18 years, Representative Rosa DeLauro advocated for families receiving government grants to raise their children. (As of 2021, this is only a temporary program that Congress would need to renew.) In a press release, she states that "The Child Tax Credit is a lifeline to the middle class, cuts child poverty by 55 percent this year. . . that helps them (families) with the costs of food, childcare, diapers, healthcare, clothing, and taxes. Poor, working, and middle-class families—90 percent of our children will receive the same monthly benefits" (retrieved from delauro.house.gov/media-center/press-releases/delauro-marks-child-tax-credit-week-action).

This expansion of the Child Tax Credit lasted only for 2021, and is unlikely to be expanded again soon (Leahey, 2022). Was it a good idea? Below are some arguments for and against it:

- Almost all European countries have had a similar child allowance for decades. Some programs were universal (i.e., applied to every citizen), and some were needs-based (as in the U.S. model) (Matthews, 2016b);
- Besides European countries, Canada instituted a child allowance in 2006, and workforce participation increased (Sperling, 2021);
- The EITC, another tax credit, has boosted workforce participation among low-income recipients (Sperling, 2021);
- "We must recognize that what keeps many Americans out of the workforce is not the prospect of a child allowance but the barriers of extreme poverty, the costs of child care," and other issues (Sperling, 2021);
- The allowances would encourage "more single parenthood and more no-worker families, both of which could worsen entrenched poverty in the long run" (Winship, 2021, p. 2);
- People would start to rely too much on government allowances (Winship, 2021);
- The expansion is too generous to the middle class, which "could change the way the middle class thinks about the role of government in their lives" (Strain, 2021);
- Voters might expect politicians to provide even more generous benefits (Strain, 2021).

Discussion questions

- How could a policy such as the child tax credit affect persons recovering from SUD?
- In the eight points for and against the child tax credit, four support the program and the other four oppose it. Three of the "pro" arguments are from Gene Sperling, the economist who was appointed by President Biden to implement this program, besides other provisions of the American Rescue Plan. The four "con" arguments are from the American Enterprise Institute, a conservative think tank. Review the eight points, looking for the biases.
- Pick the strongest "pro" argument and write about why you think it is effective. Then pick the strongest "con" argument and do the same.

health greatly depends on where they live. States' policies and actions or inactions yield geographic and sociodemographic inequalities in children's health and health care" (Schor & Johnson, 2021). In 2012, the Supreme Court made it optional for states to expand Medicaid by the Affordable Care Act (ACA, also called "Obamacare") provision. The federal government encouraged states to expand their Medicaid coverage so millions more people could get health care. Eleven states, mostly in the South, have still refused to expand the coverage (Kaiser Family Foundation, 2023). As the opioid crisis has worsened, this limitation of Medicaid coverage has harmed recovery efforts. The article titled "Coverage for opioid addiction treatment varies dramatically across the nation's Medicaid programs" (Bluvas, 2022) states that Medicaid provides services for around 40 percent of persons with OUD.

Even if a patient does have Medicaid coverage, their treatment may not be adequate. "The frailties of Medicaid are numerous. Opioid use disorder typically requires more than a medication, yet only 13 state Medicaid programs cover all four levels of care recommended by the American Society of Addiction Medicine: standard outpatient, intensive outpatient, residential inpatient, and medical inpatient" (Humphreys, 2018).

Any kind of Medicaid coverage can be problematic because of the stigma of poverty. For example, I remember seeing people lobbying at the Ohio Statehouse for expanding Medicaid coverage. They wore tee-shirts that read "I am on Medicaid" to connect a human face to the marginalized population. When I was working for a Medicaid waiver program that allowed seniors to stay at home instead of going to nursing homes, I remember one person calling for help. When they heard the word "Medicaid," though, they hung up because it was such a bad word for them. It seemed that they would rather deprive themselves of services rather than demean themselves of this valuable government program.

Obviously, Medicaid has many problems—but that would be another book topic. The key point is that Medicaid provides funding for thousands of treatment programs that are desperately needed during the opioid crisis. Allowing the stigma of poverty to detract from its potential to fight OUD would be tragic. One legislator who fought the stigma of poverty is featured in Box 4.4.

Discussion questions

> Did your state support or oppose Medicaid expansion? The interactive map on this site could help you find out: www.kff.org/medicaid/issue-brief/status-of-state-medicaid-expansion-decisions-interactive-map/.

› In an article about conservatives reconsidering their anti-expansion stance, one Oklahoma lawmaker stated, "I believe [expansion] improves lives of working individuals and gives them an opportunity to be healthy and ultimately flourish in society. From a conservative aspect of it, I think it makes sense for Oklahoma to have our own tax dollars to come back to our state to help out citizens" (Ollove, 2019). Do you think this is an effective argument? Can you think of a good counterargument to his point?

Box 4.4 Macro and macaroni-and-cheese issues

"I started off fighting for abused children, making sure they were placed in safe homes. Today I am a social worker with power. Every day I (am) working on both the macro issues and the macaroni-and-cheese issues that support the day-to-day needs of families." (cited in Esposito, 2015).

Senator Barbara Mikulski (D-Maryland), who retired in 2016, exemplifies macro social work because she recognized the link between individual clients and the bigger picture. Although child maltreatment occurs on all income levels, poverty is one salient risk factor. In 2015, she co-sponsored REBUILD (Rebuilding Urban Inner Cities is Long Overdue Act) to provide $1.2 billion to fight systemic poverty. "This bill is about rehabilitating neighborhoods, making them healthier and safer, and creating jobs tomorrow for communities that need it most. By supporting small businesses, rebuilding infrastructure, expanding opportunity for our young people and tackling crime, we will lay the foundation for a brighter future" (cited in House Committee on Oversight and Reform, 2015). Although REBUILD did not pass committee, it did foreshadow the major spending bills passed in 2021 that were intended to rebuild the economy.

Discussion questions
› Should a bill such as REBUILD only apply to inner cities or be expanded to other impoverished areas?
› Considering the items in the bill (e.g., rehabilitating neighborhoods and supporting small businesses), do you think that your community could benefit from a smaller version of REBUILD?
› If REBUILD had passed in 2015, do you think it would have had any impact on the opioid crisis? Why or why not?

5
Child welfare and the opioid crisis

Introduction

At the Parents in Recovery program in Pennsylvania, participants learn how to be parents again. The program teaches about how to talk to children about addiction, besides how to deal with the shame and guilt related to past behaviors. One participant stated, "I like that it goes deep into how you feel in recovery. I figured out that I wasn't a bad parent... I was a good mom in a bad addiction."

Pennsylvania Family Support Alliance, 2016

The impact of the opioid crisis on the child welfare system requires consideration of the term "child welfare." Since the word "welfare" simply means one's well-being, the term "child welfare" could include all aspects of raising happy, healthy children: education, food, and even playgrounds. Unfortunately, so many families are in crisis that the term often connotes the need to rescue children from neglect and/or abuse. As a result, the term "child welfare" is sometimes used only in reference to child protective services (CPS).

The United Nations Convention on the Rights of Children (1989) presents several points of reference for the U.S. child welfare system. For instance, Article 9 states: "States Parties shall ensure that a child shall not be separated from his or her parents against their will, except when competent authorities subject to judicial review determine... that such separation is necessary for the best interests of the child" for cases such as abuse or neglect (UNICEF, n.d., www.unicef.org.uk/wp-content/uploads/2017/09/Our-rights_UNCRC.pdf). No matter the issue, the "best interests of the child" is the key term used in this document.

Discussion question

Do you believe that there are universal rights that apply no matter the culture, or do you think that rights should be culture-specific? A traditional group such as the Amish, for example, may end their children's education after age 13. Does this practice violate the children's right to an education? Another example would be a child forced to attend religious instruction despite their objections. Present an argument both for and against the universal rights of children.

Impact of the opioid crisis on the child welfare system

In 2017, Substance Abuse and Mental Health Services Administration (SAMHSA) issued a report that one in eight children "lived with at least one parent who had a past year substance use disorder" (SAMHSA, 2017). Around 8.7 million children, then, were directly affected by opioids, other street drugs, and alcohol.

The opioid crisis is only one cause of child maltreatment, but its impact is obvious. In many hard-hit states, over half of the new CPS cases involve drug abuse and its effects on parenting (Radel, et al., 2018). The detrimental effects may include:

- Financial distress;
- Neglect of both emotional and physical needs of the child;
- Developmental delay due to child maltreatment;
- Abuse caused by the parent's lack of impulse control due to drug use; and
- Incarceration (Child Welfare Information Gateway, 2019).

The relationship between child maltreatment and SUD is even more complicated because "poverty is a stronger predictor of both child welfare involvement and substance use. Since not every county has the same poverty rate, not taking poverty into account may mask the true relationship between child welfare and substance use prevalence" (Radel, et al., 2018, p. 3). One may assume that the rise in overdose deaths would automatically increase the caseloads, but research indicates that this is not always true. Another vital research finding is that opioid-related cases are more problematic than other cases because of factors, such as longer hospital stays for the parent (Radel, et al., 2018).

Illustration 5.1 Child in distress (Shutterstock number in picture).
Credit: © fasphotographic/Shutterstock

One compelling point is the age of the children being removed from homes due to SUD since they are more likely to be five or younger (Neilson, 2019). Also, the rate of infants affected by neonatal abstinence syndrome (NAS), is rising sharply (Agarwal, et al., 2018). These infants often develop medical and developmental problems long after their initial hospital stays.

Racial and ethnic aspects

A controversial aspect of this epidemic is the concern that policymakers are worried about it because only whites seem to be affected by it. (Note: I use the term "white" reluctantly, but I stopped using the term "Caucasian" after finding out that this term was coined by a white supremacist—see Mukhopadhyay, 2016). More than one journalist has noted that recently more and more drug-related CPS cases involve white families who are not living in urban areas (Neilson, 2019). However, persons of color are also affected by SUD issues whether it is opioids or other substances.

Jamelia Hand, an SUD expert who works with Black/AA communities, states that the drug problems have been going on for a long time but that the overdose deaths of those who do not fit the drug addict stereotype have raised awareness. As discussed in Chapter 7, policymakers have targeted Blacks/AA and other minorities with punitive laws. "So even today, we have more black and brown people in jail than white people for minor drug offenses, where people probably need treatment versus jail. And black communities simply weren't offered that option. What's happened as a result of that is black people don't trust systems" (Newman, 2018).

This distrust, of course, would extend to the child welfare workers who would be seen as the enemy. One caseworker asserted that for the mothers, "Not trusting people has helped them to survive. . . . They build up a strong, rough edge and they really have problems letting it down. . . . It might be hidden or dormant, but it comes out when they feel they're being threatened or when they're uncomfortable. It comes back out real, real fast" (Blakey & Hatcher, 2013).

The Latinx population may also feel a distrust of "the system" but for different reasons. In 2019, the FBI reported a sharp increase in hate crimes against Latinx people fueled by the immigration debate (Hassan, 2019). Whether or not a Latinx person was born in the United States, they may feel targeted by racists. The CPS system may not be overtly discriminatory, but one study (Finno-Velasquez, Seay, & He, 2016) indicates a striking service gap. Legal immigrants involved with the CPS system received far fewer SUD services than the U.S.-born Latinx. The researchers speculated that caseworkers may be underreporting the SUD issues of immigrant parents because of language and/or cultural barriers.

In fact, the immigration debate has intersected with child welfare issues in a dramatic fashion since 2017, during the Trump administration. Although

Latinx migrants are not the only foreign-born persons affected, they are at the center of anti-immigration sentiment. The border wall and the "zero tolerance" policies are concrete examples of this trend. Finno-Velasquez and Dettlaff (2018) encourage social workers to advocate against the "punitive" measures of immigration enforcement, especially on the state and local levels. "Finally, the narrative around immigration and immigrants in this country has always ebbed and flowed around dominant U.S. values, morals, and who is considered to be deserving and undeserving. As professional social workers, we must use our voices to contribute to framing the public narrative around immigration enforcement as a humanitarian crisis" (Finno-Velasquez & Detlaff, 2018, p. 737).

This humanitarian crisis involves the child separation policy for migrant families, a policy which has a troubled history. Not only were black slave families often broken apart by their oppressors, but Native Americans have their own historic trauma of child separation policies. From the 1870s to the 1970s, whites kidnapped Native American children or forced the parents to give them up for forced assimilation in boarding schools or with white families. The attempts to "civilize" them meant that the children were not allowed to speak their own language or show any signs of their cultural heritage. One school founder wrote, "In Indian civilization I am a Baptist because I believe in immersing the Indian in our civilization and when we get them under, holding them there until they are thoroughly soaked." (Brown, 2018). By 1974, 25 to 35 percent of all Native children had been removed from their families (United States Congress, 1978).

The Indian Child Welfare Act (ICWA) of 1978 ended this cruel practice. This law promotes the placement of Native children with families from their own tribe over non-Native families. Tribes are now allowed a voice in decisions regarding a Native child's future. The guide for Tribal Governments and Leaders stresses the theme of "Our Children, Our Sovereignty, Our Culture, Our Choice" (ICWA Guide, n.d.).

The ICWA, though, is not without controversy. Like other minority populations, the opioid crisis has hit the Native population with a punishing blow (Jones, 2018). Native Americans are more likely to die from overdose than the national average (13.7 deaths per 100,000 vs. 13.1 per 100,000) (AASTEC Fact Sheet, n.d.). As more and more Native families struggle with addiction, fewer placements become available within a tribe. One child welfare official in Wyoming said, "We try to place them with family members or with other tribal members in the community, but we just don't have enough homes. We are spread so thin that our entire staff works 70 to 80 hours a week, with no end in sight." (Brewer, 2018). The goal of ICWA of keeping Native children in their tribes, then, is facing a difficult challenge due to the high rate of addictions in the Native communities.

Discussion question

Another challenge to ICWA is the criticism that the law is outdated and does not always apply to Native children. One non-Native adoptive parent, for example, writes about how he had to fight this law to keep his sons. "Whereas we had been, according to our social worker, on a fast track to adoption, we were now considered unfit to raise the boys due to nothing other than their eligibility for membership in a tribe they had never heard of, and their Indian mother was not even certain she belonged to" (Moore, 2018). Court cases such as Brackeen v. Bernhardt assert that the ICWA is unconstitutional because it discriminates based on race. (e.g., look up www.narf.org/cases/brackeen-v-bernhardt/). After researching this controversy, state the strongest argument FOR and AGAINST the adoptive parents' opposition to ICWA.

Parents in recovery

> Our general approach to drug use in the United States has long been predicated on removal: asylums, prison, foster care. Readying the foster care system for influx is the obvious short-term strategy. But long-term remedies will only become apparent when we take a compassionate approach to supporting people who use drugs to maintain meaningful and healthy lives. (Dasgupta cited in Neilson, 2019)

How much "clean time" should a parent have before regaining custody of their child(ren)? When should a parent's rights be terminated permanently? These are painful questions for both policymakers and social workers.

Focusing on the treatment of parents instead of punishment has emerged as one trend in child welfare. One study (Traube, et al.,

2015) stresses that the parents' desire to be reunited with their child(ren) is a major motivation for treatment. In this context, interagency collaboration between children's services and drug/alcohol services can be effective. Another study (He, 2015) indicates that interagency collaboration is less functional in areas with a high rate of child poverty. As mentioned earlier, SUD issues and poverty are often interlinked so policymakers should keep this in mind.

The current debate on the rights of parents in recovery is related to the Child Abuse Prevention Treatment Act (CAPTA), which was first passed in 1974 and been amended since then. This federal law gives funding to the states, besides direction on how to best fight child maltreatment (Child Welfare Organization, 2019). Maltreatment includes both abuse and neglect. For instance, an addicted parent may neglect the child's basic needs, such as food. "Although CAPTA was enacted amid concern about physical abuse of children, the vast majority of founded instances of child maltreatment today are due to neglect. . . . Among children determined to be victims of maltreatment, 75 percent experienced neglect, while 18 percent were physically abused and nearly 9 percent were sexually abused" (Casey Foundation, 2019).

Related to CAPTA is the Family First Services Act, which will provide funds for prevention services for families affected by SUD and other issues (Casey Foundation, 2019). As stated earlier, policy is about values. The value of keeping a family intact by providing services instead of separating children from their parents is clearly manifest in this law. Another policy change is the SUPPORT (Substance Use-Disorder Prevention that Promotes Opioid Recovery and Treatment) for Patients and Communities Act of 2018. At the time of writing this chapter, it is too soon to tell if these policies will be effective or even funded properly.

On the practice level, these policies affect the parents in recovery because of the stress on case plans. Parents who have lost custody of their child(ren) must comply with these case plans to prove that they are able to provide a safe home for their children. As a counselor, I have met numerous clients who came in for an assessment and other services because it was mandated by a case plan. In other cases, a client may ask for counseling even it is not mandated because it would "look good" to their caseworker. Box 5.1 explicates the elements of a case plan. Box 5.1 explicates the elements of a case plan.

Box 5.1 What is a case plan?

Clients in recovery may sometimes refer to a case plan when discussing their attempts to regain custody rights. In most states, the child protective services (CPS) system has an established protocol for helping families in crisis.

The goal of case plans is to ensure the safety, permanency, and well-being of children. According to the U.S. Department of Health and Human Services website, "Permanency is defined as a legal, permanent family living arrangement and may involve the child's reunification with his or her family, guardianship, adoption, or another planned permanent living arrangement." Before the stress on permanency, children were lost for years in a limbo of foster care and/or temporary stays with their families.

Components of the case plan include:

- Assessment, including both the threats to the child's safety and the family's strengths;
- Outcomes for:
  - the child, such as behavior control;
  - the parent/caregiver such as abstaining from drugs;
  - the family, such as better communication;
  - the environment, such as less social isolation;
- Goals, which must be SMART (specific, measurable, achievable, realistic, and time-limited);
- Tasks which include a timeframe (e.g., a parent must go to counseling).

Federal law requires that when a child is removed from a home, the parent(s) and worker must develop a case plan within 60 days. Both federal and state laws affect the rules regarding a child's reunification with the parent(s). (U.S. Department of Health and Human Services, n.d.).

Permanency planning

Since the 1970s, child welfare experts expressed concern about foster children in limbo—not being adopted but also not reunified with their parents. In 1997, the Adoption and Safe Families Act stressed that the child deserves a permanent home within a timely manner. (Health and Human Services, n.d.). In most cases, twelve months is the time limit for a permanency plan (Beckerman, 2017). This time limit means that parents may lose their custody rights forever so the child can be eligible for adoption.

Many parents may be incarcerated due to drug-related offenses, so the time limit imposed by permanency planning may hinder the effort to regaining custody. Beckerman (2017) states that caseworkers may find it difficult to determine whether an incarcerated mother is complying with a case plan. Worse yet, the requirement of permanency planning to maintain close relations between mother and child can be impossible in a jail/prison setting.

Whether or not the parent is incarcerated, one critical element of permanency planning is the number of visits between parents and child(ren). Higher levels of visitations correlate with higher rates of parent/child reunifications. Less than 30 percent of parents, though, have had monthly visitations. Each child welfare agency has a different set of rules regarding visitations, rules that might create barriers for the parents. Other barriers include the parent's chaotic situation, transportation, and overwhelmed caseworkers. Recovery coaches can help the parents overcome these barriers (Choi, 2019).

Discussion questions

- After reading this section, what policy recommendations would you propose to improve the likelihood that a parent stay sober and reunite with their child(ren)?
- The value of keeping a family intact is one implicit value of child welfare policies. What other values do you see in these policies—and do they really address what is in the best interest of the child?

Grandparents and other kinship providers

At a rally for grandparents called GrandRally: Building a Community of Hope, one former foster youth spoke out. "'Since my mom's rights were terminated my only hope and dream was to live with my grandmother with my brother and sisters.... She saved us from many years of turmoil, trauma, and the many dynamic issues youth face from the foster care system.' This rescue is what every foster youth deserves" (Children's Defense Fund, 2017). Although grandparents and other relatives have provided care to foster children for decades, not until recently have policymakers paid attention to this issue. Up to thirty percent of children in foster care are cared by relatives (Greef, 2018A). Kinship foster care can be advantageous for both the relatives (who know that the children are safe with them instead of being in a stranger's home) and the children (who are living with somebody with whom they already have a bond). States one child, "Grandma took us away from all of the drama and made us feel wanted." (cited in Generations United, 2017).

However, grandparents often face financial struggles that include the lack of health care and the inadequacy of Social Security payments. Generations United, an advocacy group for kinship providers, estimates that these relatives save the government four billion dollars a year. Child welfare agencies may or may not be flexible regarding licensing requirements, which means that these relatives may not be paid at all for caring for these children. One suggestion is to use the National Family Caregiver Support Program to help these families.

The emotional toll of raising traumatized children can also be hard. "I thought because my grandkids were babies . . . they were not going to have any problems. Boy was I wrong! They had problems with separation anxiety; it was so painful to see them go through this." (grandmother cited in Generations United, 2017). Kinship providers may need counseling, support groups, and classes. West Virginia, for example, provides the Healthy Grandfamilies program to help both the grandparents and children cope with the new living situation. Says the founder, "We have grandchildren who for the first years of their lives lived on soda pop, potato chips and candy" (CBSNews, 2018). Basic nutrition is one class topic.

Another dilemma for the relatives is how to interact with the biological parents who may be going in and out of recovery. One grandmother said that she wished she had known from the beginning that the arrangement was going to be permanent. "You do live in a bit of a fantasy world. You see 'Oh, they got clean for a while or stayed (sic) out of jail for a while' and then bam, they're back to doing whatever" (Matthewson, 2016). The question of when a relative should file for adoption is a difficult one—one which is affected by permanency planning policies.

When a biological parent dies of an overdose, the problem is not about custody but about grandparents grieving their loss while raising the child(ren).

Said one grandmother, "You get good at hiding it, the pain. You learn to cry at night by yourself instead of in front of the children. You have to be there for them" (Leonard, 2018a). Grief support, then, is another possible intervention for these care providers.

Discussion questions

- Greeff (2018a) notes that women are more likely to be kinship foster parents, so they are more likely to be exploited by the state if they do not get enough support. The traditional view of women as nurturers who do not need a financial reward could have an impact on policymakers' decisions. How would you remind policymakers that kinship providers need support even if they are acting out of family love and duty?
- If there is a family dispute over the best way to raise a child, who gets to decide what is in the child's best interest? When should the state intervene, and when should it stay out? For example, an aunt may want to move the child to another city away from the other relatives (Greeff, 2018b).
- One assumption about kinship providers, of course, is that they are not abusing drugs or alcohol themselves. However, SUD can affect extended families and not just the parent (Serres, 2018). What are the policy implications of this reality—for instance, should kinship providers be required to take drug tests?

Box 5.2 discusses the schools' responses to the opioid crisis, while Box 5.3 describes the process of aging out of the foster care system.

Box 5.2 Schools' responses to the opioid crisis

In some communities, teachers find themselves on the front line when dealing with their students' trauma. "Teachers console children whose parents have died, gone to jail, or disappeared as foster care rates increase, often resulting from drug abuse. Sleep-deprived youngsters come to school hungry and dirty, describing drug busts in their homes. Sometimes, the abusers are the students themselves. Overloaded school counselors struggle to assist hundreds of kids and parents" (Hefling, 2018). As parents with SUD become less involved in their children's lives and grandparents become caregivers, counselors and teachers must cope with this major shift (Klein, 2018).

What is it like to be a student in a classroom who is "experiencing the chaos of addiction, including the fear that their parents might not survive an overdose"? One school counselor notes: "The unknown of whether a parent will live is a certain kind of trauma. . . . if you are a child who has experienced trauma, school itself can have a lot of demands" (Gotbaum, 2018). School-based counseling and psychiatric services, then, have become a major component for children affected by their parents' addictions.

In 2018, Congress authorized $50 million for five years for school districts and other entities to help students access mental health care. However, one expert warns that federal money is not enough because "This investment will really be a drop in the bucket. What I hope is that states don't turn their back. . . just because Congress has passed this bill" (Klein, 2018).

Another challenge for schools during the opioid crisis is providing treatment services for teens in recovery. One intervention is recovery high schools (also called sober high schools), which specifically educate this population. These schools started in 1979, but only recently have they become more prevalent (Botzet, et al., 2014). According to researchers (Gonzalez, et al., 2012), two major triggers for teens in recovery are school stress (e.g., failing classes) and socialization pressures, such as peer pressure.

Discussion questions

> ➤ Do you agree that funding and other forms of support must come not only from the federal government, but also the local government? Present an argument for and against this assertion.
> ➤ Recovery high schools sound like a good idea, but do they really work? Why is proving the efficacy of programs such as these a policy issue? Consider how you would measure the success rates of these schools (see Botzet, et al., 2014).

Box 5.3 Aging out of the foster care system

According to the National Council for Adoption (Soliz, 2017), 22,000 foster youth "age out" of the system at age 18. What happens to them? The answer varies because it depends on where the youth lives. Geography is destiny—a youth could have well-funded support to help with the transition or almost no services at all.

As a former "host parent" who had helped a youth age out of the foster care system from the Franklin County (Ohio) Children's Services, I saw firsthand the quality of services offered to her. During her senior year, she received senior pictures, a yearbook, and the chance to take a college admissions test. The agency paid me $800 a month for living expenses, with the caseworker coming monthly with the check to pay us a brief visit. The young lady attended a weekend retreat with other youths to learn about independent living skills. During the summer between high school and college, she worked at the Therapeutic Arts Program that was designed to help with emotional healing. She was president of the Youth Advisory Board, which enabled youth who were aging out to speak about their experiences and make recommendations. Several years later, she now reflects that the services were somewhat helpful, but she also had other sources of support for her college plans. Other college-bound youth are not as fortunate if they lack support. Not surprisingly, foster youth are half as likely as the national average to go to college, and less than 10 percent of foster youth achieve a bachelor's degree as compared to the national average of 32.5 percent (National Working Group on Foster Care and Education, 2018).

For those who do not go to college, the youth were assisted with the rental deposit and first month's rent for their transition. They also received donated furniture and other necessities. Another option besides independent living is transitional living (staffed group homes provided for those not ready to live on their own).

On the national level, aging out can be catastrophic for the youth. Advocacy groups, such as Shared Justice, note that "The statistics are devastating.... One in five of these youth will become homeless after turning 18. Only half will obtain employment by 24. Over 70 percent of female foster youth will become pregnant by 21, and one in four former foster youth will experience PTSD" (Shared Justice, 2017). Without proper support services, thousands of youths are left stranded. The opioid crisis is going to make this problem even worse unless social workers and others change policies—and save lives.

Discussion questions
> Mentoring is one micro-level intervention for these youth. What policies in your local area need macro-level interventions? Research the transition services offered by your local children's services agency and make some recommendations.
> Stigma is another barrier faced by foster youth. One disturbing example appears in the TV series *Unbelievable*, which tells the true story of a former foster youth who reported a rape. Not only did she face skeptical police officers, but she was convicted of filing a false report. This woman's lack of credibility stemmed from the fact that she had been in foster care. What advocacy efforts would you suggest for fighting this stigma?

Fathers' rights and responsibilities

This section will explore the basic policy aspects of fatherhood when the parents split up. Since substance abuse is often correlated with relationship stress (Hendy, et al., 2018), considering the father's rights and responsibilities is vital for social workers.

Who's the daddy?

According to Althauser (2019), "marriage creates a presumption of paternity." If the couple is unmarried at the baby's birth, they can sign an affidavit to acknowledge paternity. Although the affidavit is used by the child support system, it does not ensure visitation rights.

As a result, a male client in a recovery group may feel frustrated that he is paying to support a child that he is not allowed to visit. The term "baby mama drama" indicates the resentment of fathers toward these mothers, a term that I have heard used by males of different ethnic groups.

Many states have a child support enforcement system that pays for paternity testing. If the biological fathers are forced to pay child support, then the unmarried mothers do not have to rely so much on SNAP (food stamps) and other government programs. Child support became a controversial topic in the 1980s with "deadbeat dads" being blamed for poverty and other social ills.

Deadbeat dads

The demonization of fathers who did not pay for child support started in the 1980s with Ronald Reagan's proclamation on child support enforcement. The rhetoric shifted from the broader concept of "neglectful parent" to "deadbeat dad" in the 1990s when Bill Clinton signed the "welfare reform" bill (PRWORA, see Chapter 3). Battle (2018) notes that he "shifts the moral focus of the consequences of nonpayment from a gender-neutral conceptualization of parents to fathers specifically and 'deadbeat dads' in particular become the subject of punitive enforcement policies" including severe financial penalties and even jail time (Battle, 2018, p. 253). This focus has a racial overtone, since it is related to the "welfare queen" stereotype of an African American single mother.

Why don't nonresident fathers get more involved in their children's lives? One qualitative study (Arditti, et al., 2019) asked that question of mothers and children, resulting in a complex set of reasons. "Environmental press indicators included structural complexity in fathers, mothers, and children's lives (e.g., repartnering, whether children resided or remembered residing with fathers, moving, children in multiple households), challenging life circumstances (e.g., incarceration, illness, unemployment" (Arditti, et al., 2019, p. 73).

Breaking down this list of indicators would deepen the understanding of "deadbeat dads." The ripple effects of poverty can affect these indicators. For instance, transportation barriers can include lack of gas money and/or bus fare. Other possible factors could be:

- Did the mother get another partner?
- Did the children reside with their father? If so, do they remember it?
- Did the mother move to another city or another state?
- Are there other households involved?
- Was the father incarcerated?
- Did health issues prevent the father from regular visits or paying child support?

> Did unemployment affect the father's ability to pay child support?

Discussion question

If your client believes that he has been treated unfairly as a father trying to visit his children, what resources would you recommend?

Adverse childhood experiences

In 1998, a pioneering study of 9,508 adults (Felitti, Anda, Nordenberg, & Williamson, 1998) shocked many with its conclusion that adverse childhood experiences (ACE) were much more common than believed—over half of the subjects reported at least one. "One of the most striking findings of the ACE study is that within the cohort, all generations with one or more early-life adversities were at greater risk for substance abuse, mental illness, and perpetuating violence compared to those reporting no ACEs. Thus, ACEs science provides empirical support on the importance of breaking the intergenerational cycle of these early-life exposures" (Dube, 2020, p. 3).

Different versions of the ACE test have emerged over the past 20 years. One typical question is: "Before your 18th birthday, did a parent or other adult in the household often or very often ... swear at you, insult you, put you down, or humiliate you? Or act in a way that made you afraid that you might be physically hurt?" (a full version of the ACE test is available in Starecheski, 2015). Depending on the test, at least two questions about substance misuse are included.

In the original study, the adults were middle-class. Since then, the assumption that the stressors of poverty would increase the likelihood of more ACEs has been validated by many studies (e.g., Hughes & Tucker, 2018). Other ACE test versions have included bullying and community violence (Ports, et al., 2020).

Likewise, multiple studies have confirmed the link between SUD and ACEs. The first part of one article, "The traps started in my childhood" illustrates the undeniable impact of ACEs on persons with SUDs (Boppe & Boyer, 2021). Although the positive relationship between the two is evident, the mechanisms of how SUD and ACEs interact require more study (Leza, et al., 2021).

Illustration 5.2 Overcoming adversity.
Credit: © YuryImaging/Shutterstock

OUD and ACEs also have a strong connection. In one study of mothers with OUD, 95 percent reported at least one ACE, and 65 percent reported four or more ACEs (Gannon, et al., 2021). However, one promising study suggests that resilience can mediate the harm done by ACEs for persons with OUD (Wang, et al., 2021).

One form of mediation appears in the CDC prevention strategies for ACEs. Below are these strategies:

- Strengthen economic supports to families;
- Promote social norms that protect against violence and adversity;
- Ensure a strong start for children;
- Teach skills;
- Connect youth to caring adults and activities;
- Intervene to lessen immediate and long-term harms (www.cdc.gov/violenceprevention/aces/prevention.html).

Discussion questions

- As Illustration 5.2 suggests, children can overcome adversity. Pick one of the CDC strategies to prevent ACEs. Suggest three ways to implement it.
- If you had to write your own ACE test, what items would you include? For example, would the COVID-19 lockdown be considered an ACE?
- Research one of these advocacy groups regarding kinship providers: Children's Defense Fund, American Association of Retired Persons (AARP), Casey Family Program, and National Kinship Alliance for Children. Pick a policy suggestion. Determine the level—local, state, or federal? For example, state laws may limit the amount of financial support for kinship providers. Look up which state legislators to contact about your concern. Remember, registered voters are taken more seriously by legislators!
- Fighting the stigma of children affected by SUD (e.g., foster children or those being raised by relatives) is critical for their success. Create a public awareness campaign to make people realize how valuable these children are, then use social media to amplify this message.

6
Women and OUD

Introduction

In a hospital room, a Black/AA woman with OUD was resting after delivering a stillborn child. Speaking to a group of residents, a doctor commented on this patient within earshot. He said that had the infant survived, they would probably have had neonatal abstinence syndrome (NAS, which is the withdrawal symptoms of a drug-exposed infant) and go into foster care. "This, sadly, is a typical case. These women are in such a bad way. It feels like there is very little we can do. They should be given an IUD along with their methadone. It's terrible to say, but it might be a blessing that the baby didn't survive" (Knight, et al., 2019).

Against medical advice, the bereaved mother left the hospital with a roll of toilet paper to use for her bleeding. She then lost her access to methadone because she had lost the baby. Having relapsed and living on the streets, she became pregnant again and delivered another stillborn child. Before the delivery, she consented to a tubal ligation—permanent sterilization. One ethical question echoes in this case study: was it informed consent, or was there any coercion or pressure used on her? (Knight, et al., 2019).

This woman's story delineates some of the challenges faced by women with OUD. This chapter's first section, the criminalization of pregnancy, discusses how the "crack baby" myth of 30 years ago still affects policymakers today. Without reproductive justice (defined here in the social context, such as access to healthcare), women such as the one in the above case study will probably continue to suffer. Also, OUD exacerbates the harm to marginalized women who need treatment instead of incarceration.

The second section, human trafficking, explicates how this issue has been inextricably linked with SUD for decades. The opioid crisis has only worsened the situation. Although males and nonbinary persons are also trafficked, females (both children and adults) are the primary victims (United Nations Office on Drug and Crime, 2009). After a brief overview of

Illustration 6.1 Pregnant woman behind bars (Shutterstock number in picture).
Credit: © TatyanaKar/Shutterstock

human trafficking, the section will focus on the intersection of it with both substance use disorder (SUD) and opioid use disorder (OUD).

Lastly, the issue of women in prison is related to the discussion of the War on Drugs in Chapter 7. As the rate of incarceration of women climbs, it is critical to examine its relationship to the opioid crisis. As Illustration 6.1 shows, pregnant women behind bars is a compelling issue.

The criminalization of pregnancy

Women who use opioids are at risk for unintended pregnancy for several reasons, including lack of access to birth control. For example, one study of 50 women in medication assisted treatment (MAT) found that 84 percent of them had had unintended pregnancies (Smith, Morse, & Busby, 2019). An unintended pregnancy for any woman can be devastating if there is not enough medical or social support. For women with SUD, the impact can be even more severe because they may be charged with a crime even if a miscarriage or stillbirth cannot be conclusively attributed to their substance use.

In the late 1980s, the media and politicians spoke about a "crack baby" epidemic caused by pregnant women using crack. "Women, particularly minority women of lower socioeconomic status, who used cocaine while pregnant were perceived as immoral and irresponsible" (Coles, 1993, p. 290). So-called experts claimed that crack babies were more likely to be born early, besides being "born addicted and quivering, to experience a host of neurological, digestive, respiratory, and cardiac problems, and to be headed toward a childhood of learning difficulties, hyperactivity, and ultimately, delinquency and jail" (Ortiz & Briggs, 2003, p. 44). This was related to the idea that a child born in poverty in the United States was somehow damaged at birth, as opposed to the "resilient" orphans adopted from Rumania and other desirable locations (Ortiz & Briggs, 2003).

However, research has shown that the "crack baby" problem did not even exist. By 2001, the Journal of the American Medical Association had published a systematic review of research on children's growth an development after prenatal cocaine exposure—definitive proof that the "crack baby" issue was only a myth (Frank, Augustyn, Knight, Pell, & Zuckerman, 2001). Also in 2001, the Journal of the American Medical Association printed a commentary that asked, "Why then all the hullabaloo about crack babies? Why then the prosecution of 200 women who used cocaine while pregnant? Why was a program established to pay $200 to crack-using women to become sterilized?" (Chavkin, 2001, p. 1626). Unfortunately, society still demonizes pregnant women who abuse drugs despite the medical evidence that treatment—not punishment—works best for both mother and child.

During the opioid crisis, the concern about fetal health has focused on NAS/NOWS (neonatal abstinence syndrome, which applies to many substances; neonatal opioid withdrawal syndrome, which applies to opioids). When fetuses are exposed to opioids, the results may include:

> Lower birthweight;
> Respiratory complications;
> Long hospitalizations for the newborns;
> Huge costs to state Medicaid programs, since they are usually the payer (NIDA, 2019).

Newborns may also experience symptoms, such as "excessive high-pitched crying, abnormal fussiness, trouble sleeping, a type of skin discoloration known as 'mottling,' difficulties in feeding, tremors and diarrhea." One volunteer "cuddler" noted that "it's very difficult because they're in a lot of pain. Sometimes they're just very fussy. They can just be really rigid, and they just need holding" (Gluck, 2019).

Another consideration regarding NAS/NOWS is the potential long-term effects of opioid use during pregnancies. An Australian study, for instance, associated NAS with poor school performance (Oei, et al., 2017). Another study, based in Tennessee, concluded that infants who had NAS later developed educational disabilities (Fill, et al., 2018). However, one meta-analysis of 27 studies on former "crack babies" (now adolescents) reminds us of how dire predictions of brain damage and behavioral difficulties can be overstated. Family background and community violence can account for the lower test scores of these adolescents—not prenatal exposure to cocaine (Associated Press, 2013).

Despite the mixed research about the effects of prenatal substance use, many state legislatures have responded to it as a criminal problem instead of a public health concern. For example, Tennessee passed a law that criminalized substance use by pregnant women in 2014. This resulted in women avoiding prenatal care or leaving the state for medical care. Although the intention was to push pregnant women into treatment, advocates believed that this approach could backfire and lead to more drug use. "It's no surprise that people under stress, scrutinized by the state, with the threat of their baby being taken away—that they would experience stress that could lead them to use again" (Ganeva, 2015). Two years later, this law was not renewed (Levinson-King, 2021).

A pregnant woman who uses street drugs can even be charged with murder, as evident in the 2020 case of a California woman who had used methamphetamine and delivered a stillborn fetus (Associated Press, 2020). In 2021, though, these charges were dismissed. As one legal expert wrote, a murder conviction could "subject all women who suffer a pregnancy loss to the threat of criminal investigation and possible prosecution for murder" (Paybarah, 2021).

In another case, a Native American woman was convicted of manslaughter after having a miscarriage at four months and admitting to drug use (Levinson-King, 2021). According to the Mayo Clinic, more than 20 percent of pregnancies end in miscarriage for a variety of reasons (www.mayoclinic.org/diseases-conditions/pregnancy-loss-miscarriage/symptoms-causes/syc-20354298). Pregnancy Justice, formerly known as National Advocates for Pregnant Women, states that being poor and a person of color makes it far more likely to be arrested for being pregnant while using substances. The organization also documented over 1,200 cases of women who were arrested and/or prosecuted for being pregnant from 2006 to 2020. "Pregnancy criminalization disproportionately targets poor people; nearly 85% of cases involved criminal charges against a pregnant person who was deemed legally 'indigent,' meaning that they faced considerable financial hardship" (Pregnancy Justice, 2022, p. 2).

The personhood movement, which has stressed the rights of the fetus as a person over the mother's rights, has resulted in 23 states considering substance use during pregnancy to be child abuse. "At the root of these cases is the idea that women, once they become a mother, should put their foetus first no matter what" stated a British legal scholar, who adds "The fact that the state has failed to give them the help and support during their pregnancy and prior to their pregnancy is the fault of the state" (cited in Levinson-King, 2021).

Besides criminalizing pregnancy, many states are restricting access to abortion that could have been an option for pregnant women. One striking example is the 2021 Texas law as described in this article, titled "Gov. Greg Abbott signs into law one of nation's strictest abortion measures, banning procedure as early as six weeks into a pregnancy" (Najmabadi, 2021).

Not surprisingly, public health advocates stress the need for improved SUD services. Barriers to these services include provider shortages (especially for Medicaid patients), lack of transportation and/or childcare, stigma, and fear of legal consequences (Saunders, et al., 2018). In Appalachia, many MAT providers were cash-only and did not accept any insurance—especially Medicaid (Patrick, et al., 2018). Even in cities, long wait times due to provider shortages have stymied the efforts of pregnant women seeking services (Bedrick, et al., 2020).

Possible solutions to the barriers to service include:

- Coordination of treatment that includes wraparound services, such as nutrition;
- Trauma-informed, family-centered care;
- Telemedicine;
- Provider awareness and training;
- Modifying billing practices so insurers are more likely to pay;
- Decreasing the stigma (Kroelinger, et al., 2019).

Thus, the context of this policy dilemma is related to reproductive justice. As mentioned earlier, this concept stresses more than reproductive rights such as keeping abortion legal. Sister Song, originally called the Women of African Descent for Reproductive Justice, began as an advocacy organization in 1994 to promote sexual health for marginalized women. "The right to have kids (or not), to survive, and thrive is universal, and one of the basic building blocks of liberation. When we fight for reproductive justice—we show up for people who are harmed the most" (www.sistersong.net/visioningnewfuturesforrj).

Advocating for the right to have children, for example, is critical for women of color because of the legacy of forced sterilizations.

Through the criminalization of pregnancy, the legal system is oppressing vulnerable women who need treatment instead of punishment. The intersection of being a woman of color, having a stigmatized condition, such as SUD, and/or poverty is related to this injustice.

Discussion questions

- Pick one of the possible solutions to the barriers to service. Design a three-part plan to implement that solution.
- Do you think that the stigmatization of pregnant women who use drugs is related more to race, class, or gender prejudice? Explain your answer.
- Research the website of Sister Song (www.sistersong.net). Do you consider this organization to be effective in communicating its message? How would you amplify their message?
- Which social work value best applies to this issue?
- If you were a social worker working with a pregnant client who uses drugs, what would be your ethical concerns? How would you address them? Box 6.1 addresses compassion fatigue.
- One study (Tyler, et al., 2018) notes that over two billion dollars were spent on infants with NAS between 2004 to 2014. Since states provide one-half of Medicaid funding, what would be the impact on the state budgets of hard-hit states such as West Virginia? If you were the governor of a hard-hit state, what policy solutions would you suggest? What should the federal government do about this ongoing problem?

Box 6.1 Compassion fatigue

Although NAS and NOWS are both treatable (NCSACW, n.d.), it can be upsetting to watch the infants cope with the symptoms. Nurses at the neonatal intensive care unit (NICU) departments, for example, try to comfort the infants who cry incessantly and show other signs of distress. One nurse stated "I want to take a recorder and just record their crying (and force the mothers to listen). 'Listen, we have to deal with this weaning process that you put them through. And you just get to come at the end of this and say, "Okay, I'm ready to get my baby"'" (Recto, et al., 2020). This frustration, besides the resentment toward the mothers whose drug use caused the infants' distress, can lead to compassion fatigue.

Related to burnout, compassion fatigue is defined here as the reduction of empathy in service providers, such as nurses and social workers. One expert said it could happen to "any professionals who use their emotions, their heart. . . . It's like a dark cloud that hangs over your head, goes wherever you go and invades your thoughts" (Clay, 2020). During the COVID-19 pandemic, of course, compassion fatigue became a policy issue because of the high rate of resignations among medical staff. One article title expresses it well: "'I've seen more death than ever': ICU nurse tells news crew she is QUITTING due to 'compassion fatigue' because of the number of sick and dying who failed to get their shots" (Thaler, 2021). The concept of self-inflicted harm—"they did it to themselves"—also applies to persons with SUD.

The opioid crisis has presented even more challenges for those trying to avoid compassion fatigue. Winstanley (2020) states that overdose-related compassion fatigue (OCF) has affected many communities that have witnessed too many overdoses. Unfortunately, OCF can even lead to hostility toward opioid users in hard-hit areas, such as West Virginia. One woman who was revived from an overdose stated, "it was attempted suicide and I used the heroin to do it.[. . .] Woke up, the paramedics were around me and I heard a cop—he didn't know I could hear him—but he said, 'You should have just let the junky bitch die'" (Ondocsin, et al., 2020). The policy implications of such hostility include the closure of a needle and syringe program in Charleston, WV in 2018, which was caused by a backlash against the harm reduction approach. Reluctance to use Narcan to revive overdose victims also appeared as a disturbing trend (Ondocsin, et al., 2020).

> Discussion exercise
> Develop an action plan to combat compassion fatigue regarding the opioid crisis in your community. Consider the following points in your plan:
>
> - Education for both service providers and the general public can be useful, but it is not as effective as personal contact with a stigmatized person. Researchers stress the importance of in-person contact as having much more impact than a virtual meeting or recorded video (Recto, et al., 2020).
> - Avoid eliciting pity for persons with SUD, since regarding them as helpless and incompetent will not help with their recovery efforts (Recto, et al., 2020).
> - For nurses involved in maternal substance abuse, the ACTS script has assisted staff to address stigmatizing comments from their coworkers. The components of ACTS are: Acknowledge the comment instead of criticizing it; Create circumstance for reflection; Teach; and Support. The social work field could use this concept. Apply ACTS to this scenario of a social work colleague who says this about a client who just gave birth to an infant with NAS: "How can she do that to her baby? She is a terrible mother. She doesn't even deserve her baby—what kind of life will that child have?" (adapted from Marcellus & Poag, 2016).

Human trafficking

In a rest stop in rural Ohio last weekend, I was in a bathroom stall when I saw the "STOP" sign as I closed the door. The outreach poster asked if "you or someone you knew" was being forced to sell sex or work against their will. Below this message, slips of paper had the hotline number for trafficking victims. A few of the slips had been torn off. I had to wonder, did somebody in trouble stand in this same stall and need this hotline number?

This outreach effort reminded me of the Save Our Adolescents from Prostitution (SOAP) project founded by Theresa Flores, a trafficking survivor. At one SOAP event that I had attended, she spoke about the experience of going into a motel bathroom to wash herself after sex with a "john." She realized later that soap wrappers with hotline information could save a trafficked person who has limited contact with others. After we volunteers wrapped the soaps, others delivered them to local motels and hotels along with anti-trafficking education to staff. In *The slave across the street: A human trafficking survivor's spiritual journey of healing*, Flores states that "It is my greatest hope that as our society continues to unravel the dynamics of power and its abuses, more people will understand that mine is the story of the sexual exploitation of a child. The victim is a child. A child who feels and believes there are no options" (Flores, 2019).

Human trafficking is a complex topic that involves the sex trade and forced labor (e.g., working in agriculture, restaurants, and nail salons). Although media attention usually focuses on sex trafficking and international crime rings, most trafficking involves small-scale, localized operations. For example, one couple recruited a Nigerian woman to work as a domestic. Once she was in the home, they took her documents and forced her to work for 16 hours a day every day for eight years (case studies found in www.humanrightsfirst.org/resource/who-are-human-traffickers).

One major component of this problem is sex trafficking, "in which the commercial sex act is induced by force, fraud or coercion, or in which the person induced to perform such an act has not attained 18 years of age" (www.acf.hhs.gov/otip/fact-sheet/resource/fshumantrafficking). Although pimps and other exploiters have been prostituting vulnerable persons for centuries, new awareness of this practice has troubled many. Others see prostitution as a victimless crime with this dichotomy: men are the buyers, women are the sellers. However, Davidson (2005) states that this framework is troubling because it assumes that women have equal power in the transaction. The historical—and current—reality is that adult males are in an advantageous position. In many cases, females (and other trafficked persons) are noncitizens who cannot enter a business contract with adult male citizens as equals.

The sex trade also exemplifies racism because so many prostitutes are women of color and from a disadvantaged class. In Canada, feminists have spoken out about the disproportionate number of prostitutes who are indigenous. "Race, class, and sex intersect in the worst ways to subjugate Native women—and in the act of prostitution it's *the* most racist, *the* most sexist.... And the man holds all of the economic power in that," stated one advocate (Murphy, 2014). The colonial legacy of treating indigenous women as not fully human amplifies the perception that they can be discarded. If girls are growing up in poverty and enduring abuse, they are more likely to believe that their "bodies aren't actually ours but that they are to please men" (Murphy, 2014). As Illustration 6.2 indicates, public awareness is essential in the fight to end human trafficking.

In the United States, women of color are more likely to become involved in sex trafficking than white women. According to the Department of Justice website (www.bjs.ojp.doj.gov), "Confirmed sex trafficking victims were more likely to be white (26%) or black (40%)," although whites comprise 75 percent and Blacks/AA comprise 13 percent of the of the U.S. population (2010 census—census.gov). Also troubling is the reported increase of Latino residential brothels that feature female immigrants who entered the United States for either a boyfriend (who turned out to be a pimp)

Illustration 6.2 Anti-trafficking poster (Shutterstock # in picture).
Credit: © dramaj/Shutterstock

or for job opportunities. The Polaris Project, an advocacy organization against human trafficking, states that brothels run by Latinos and other ethnic groups are spreading throughout the United States (www.polaris project.org).

Despite these disproportionate numbers, an article in *Ebony Magazine* discusses the media's focus on only white victims of sex trafficking.

> Black females are 40% of confirmed sex trafficking victims in the United States but under-represented in news coverage on missing children and over-represented among women and girls arrested for prostitution. Perhaps as a function of the deafening silence on their presence "in the market," African American girls remain vulnerable to (sex trafficking). TeamEBONY, 2014.

This media silence about Black/AA victims may be related to the Jezebel stereotype that legitimized sexual violence against Black/AA women for centuries. MISSEY is one organization that is intervening on behalf of women of color being trapped into prostitution. The Thrive program, for example, provides job training and other career services for the young women to build their lives (www.misssey.org).

Discussion questions

- Using the term "little black ho" on a search engine, research the portrayal of black prostitutes on the internet. Write a paragraph about your reaction.
- In your opinion, is there any connection between the "video ho" meme and the high rate of black trafficking victims? Can you think of other examples of hypersexualized women of color who will do anything for money?
- Do you agree that women of color have been underrepresented in the media's coverage of human trafficking stories? Research ten stories on the mainstream media websites about human trafficking and share your results with the class. Box 6.2 provides a larger context for the human trafficking issue.

Box 6.2 Fighting forced labor on a global scale

Globally, around 25 million persons are victims of forced labor—a number that includes cotton pickers in Uzbekistan, farm workers in North Carolina, and domestic servants in the Middle East. One-fourth of the victims are children. The International Labor Organization (ILO) uses the term "forced labor" to include sex trafficking, which involves 4.8 million persons. Sixty-three percent of all those in forced labor are women and girls. Coercion methods include violence, threats against the worker and/or their families, withholding wages, and even forcing the workers to use drugs or alcohol (ILO, 2018).

Through the ILO Forced Labour Protocol of 2014, the ILO is on the forefront of fighting forced labor. Working with other international organizations, such as United Nations Children's Fund (UNICEF), the ILO proposes these four strategies:

- Prevention;
- Protection for the victims;
- Remedies to enable victims to find justice and compensation;
- Enforcement of laws (ILO, 2018).

Forced labor is often entangled with the supply chain of economics. For example, chocolate companies who allegedly used child labor on the Ivory Coast cocoa farms faced a lawsuit from eight former workers in 2021. They "describe being recruited in Mali through trickery and deception, before being trafficked across the border. . . . There, they were forced to work—often for several years or more—with no pay, no travel documents and no clear idea of where they were or how to get back to their families" (Balch, 2021). One child was only 11 when he was trafficked to the Ivory Coast.

Discussion questions
- One aspect of prevention is Fair Recruitment, which ensures that workers are not deceived or coerced when being recruited. The Ivory Coast workers are one striking example of forced labor using deception for recruitment. Also, East European women were sometimes recruited to be a waitress in the United States but then forced to work in a brothel by the traffickers. How would you set up Fair

> Recruitment practices in an overseas city to ensure that potential workers are protected? How would you monitor the recruiters?

> Another aspect of prevention is to increase awareness of the problem. Not only the public but also the corporations who may be involved in the supply chain need to be informed. Design a poster or write a public service announcement (PSA) to increase awareness of labor and/or sex trafficking, using information from this chapter and other sources.

Intersection of SUD and human trafficking

The quote below exemplifies the intersection of SUD and human trafficking, especially the prevalence of trauma and mental health issues. "I started doing drugs, specifically cocaine down at the local go-go bar, and eventually I tried heroin. I was a mess, wrecked my life, wasted it on drugs because I'd been raped and I didn't think I mattered to anyone" (Lederer & Wetzel, 2014).

Another survivor, Rachelle Limbeck, describes her ordeal in the poem "He sold my soul" including this excerpt:

Counting dollars in your head, one at a time, My pimp might buy me a line.
I need some drugs to take this memory away–hopefully, it'll kill me today (Limbeck, n.d.).

One woman also experienced SUD after she was tricked into working at a strip club, which included having sex in the club when she was not earning enough money. "I lost myself.... I was abusing alcohol and drugs and I'd just numb myself" (Dell, 2019). Even after she left the club and her traffickers, she still worked in the sex trade for years. "I went in a downward spiral, I was depressed, addicted to cocaine and I drank way too much" (Dell, 2019), until she found emotional healing through forgiveness.

How many trafficked persons use or abuse drugs/alcohol in the United States? Not only is it difficult to obtain hard data on human trafficking, but the additional stigma and criminal status of street drugs does not help. One example of research is from a service provider in Maine, which states that 66 percent of their clients reported having an SUD before being trafficked and only 4.5 percent developing a SUD during their ordeal (Smith, et al., 2016). Although this information is valuable, it is impossible to make any generalizations from this snapshot.

Calls to trafficking hotlines can provide more data about the link between SUD and human trafficking. The Polaris Project, an anti-trafficking organization, collected data from hotline calls to three centers from 2015 to 2017. All numbers are based on the callers' self-reports and are impossible to verify.

- Potential victims who "had drug use induced or exploited as a means of control in their trafficking situation"—2,238, which is 15 percent of the callers. The hotline workers did not ask about drug use, so this information was volunteered by the callers.
- Potential victims who already had a SUD before being trafficked—926. Twenty-six of them were recruited into trafficking "directly from drug rehabilitation centers."
- Potential victims who were minors involved in drug use—678 (Polaris Project, 2017).

In another study of 102 survivors, Lederer and Wetzel (2014) found that 84 percent of them had used substances. Although alcohol was the most used substance, heroin was used by 22.3 percent. Out of these survivors, 27.9 percent reported being forced to use substances by their traffickers. Dual diagnoses were a salient feature in this study, as almost 90 percent reported depression and over half reported symptoms of PTSD. Most disturbing of all, 41.5 percent had attempted suicide.

Besides this data, the global perspective of the intersection between drug trafficking and human trafficking is enlightening. The United States is not alone in fighting organized crime networks. Shelley (2012) states that diverse drugs are used for diverse reasons, including commercial sexual exploitation and forced labor, such as agriculture and begging. "There is a compelling logic for the criminals of the drug trade to diversify into this lucrative, highly profitable and low risk crime. When caught, the penalties are less. . . . Moreover, drugs and women can be moved along the same routes and sometimes simultaneously providing an economy of scale" (Shelley, 2012, p. 242).

The international picture of drugs and human trafficking

Internation drug and human trafficking usually includes the following aspects:

- Stimulants used to increase production by agricultural workers;
- Hallucinogens used to provoke the violence of child soldiers;
- Former sex workers who are returned home to their villages but are still addicted to both the drugs and the fast lifestyle of the cities;
- Widespread corruption among the police and other government functions (Shelley, 2012).

Discussion questions

- Why should we consider the international perspective of the intersection of drugs and human trafficking?
- If you were writing a grant proposal to research the extent of SUD among persons who were trafficked, what research methods would you suggest? Justify the importance of this topic to potential funders. Box 6.3 describes the importance of critical thinking when addressing the trafficking issue.

Intersection of the opioid crisis and human trafficking

"The physical craving the body develops for opioids is profound and unrelenting. Add extreme brainwashing, psychological manipulation, and physical trauma and you end up with someone who is trapped in a cycle. The power of addiction combined with the coercion of a trafficker can be a lethal combination" (emergency room doctor cited in Roberson, 2017).

As mentioned in the previous section, it is difficult to find conclusive data on how many trafficked persons have an SUD. Finding data on opioid use is even harder. One researcher claims that nearly 25 percent of one group of survivors had used heroin (Stoklosa, Stoklosa, & MacGibbon, 2017) and that one medical professional stated that over half of the trafficking victims she saw in the emergency room were "hooked on heroin" (Stoklosa, 2016).

Box 6.3 When conspiracy theories cause harm

In 2016, a man listened to broadcasts such as Alex Jones' Infowars and started to believe that Hillary Clinton and other evil politicians were conducting child sacrifice inside a pizza parlor's basement. This basement did not even exist. He went inside the restaurant and shot up the place with an AR-15 and other weapons. Fortunately, nobody was killed during this "Pizzagate" incident (Doubek, 2017).

Unfortunately, "Pizzagate" was not the end of these allegations when QAnon and other sources started promoting the same type of conspiracy theories. Even Tom Hanks, the popular actor who played Mr. Rogers, has been the target of their accusations. The belief is that "There is a secret, global cabal of Satan-worshiping pedophiles who control everything— including politicians, the media, and Hollywood—and who engage in child sex trafficking and ritual sacrifice to harvest adenochrome from children, and Trump is here to save us all from their evil" (Reneau, 2020b).

Allegedly, adenochrome is the chemical created by fear. After the child victims are terrorized by evildoers, their blood is drained so that celebrities, such as Oprah and Pope Francis can drink it. Related to this nonsense is the claim that Bill Gates created the COVID-19 outbreak so he could take over the world—or implant microchips in the vaccines, according to another theory (Friedberg, 2020).

Why is this blood harvesting craziness even mentioned in a social work textbook? Unfortunately, misinformation has sometimes overshadowed the real problem of human trafficking. Polaris Project, the anti-trafficking organization, had to issue a factsheet about "#Savethechildren" and other misleading sources. "The information being spread online by people who are involved in or believe in the QAnon conspiracy is distracting from the very real, very important work of fighting sex trafficking. . . . (They) have an agenda that has little or nothing to do with reducing human trafficking and whose real aim is creating an atmosphere of fear (and) division" (www.polarisproject.org).

Confusion among well-meaning but misinformed persons is not the only problem, though. People are calling the police and/or the trafficking hotlines countless times with QAnon-related claims, which interferes with the work of law enforcement and legitimate anti-trafficking organizations. One child advocate noted that "Unfounded conspiracy theories minimize, distract and draw valuable resources away from the tireless work being done by child protection advocates on the ground" (Reneau, 2020a). This advocate was afraid to give their name to the reporter because they were afraid of hate mail or even threats from conspiracy believers.

In 2022, former President Trump showed signs of supporting QAnon on his Truth Social platform. Pressed on QAnon theories that Trump allegedly is saving the nation from a satanic cult of child sex traffickers, he claimed ignorance but asked, "Is that supposed to be a bad thing? If I can help save the world from problems, I'm willing to do it" (Klepper & Swenson, 2022).

Discussion question

Social workers are required to use critical thinking, especially regarding policy. One contention by the QAnon believers is that annually, 800,000 children in the United States are victims of sex trafficking. Research the accuracy of this number by using reputable sources (e.g., www.fawco.org). Why is it critical to avoid exaggerating the extent of a social problem in policymaking?

In a compelling article about how pimps use drugs to control their victims, Roberson (2017) describes the legal consequences of a trafficker who would induce a person's SUD or worsen their SUD as methods of recruitment and exploitation. Andrew Fields, who was sentenced to more than 30 years, had offered drugs and/or even force-fed his victims crushed pills, such as Oxycontin. When the police raided his home, they found almost 9,000 prescription pills and a notebook that recorded the drug debts of the victims who would always owe him money (Roberson, 2017). Fear of withdrawal sickness was another tactic used by Fields, who would watch a victim start going through the excruciating symptoms. He "would compel her to serve another prostitution client by saying, 'I'll give you a pill. I'm not going to give you another until you get up and go to work. And you know you need another'" (Department of Justice, 2014).

Children are especially vulnerable when the opioid crisis and human trafficking intersect. The risk factors for SUD and being trafficked often overlap, especially with poverty and adverse childhood experiences (ACEs), such as abuse and neglect (Roberson, 2017). "Maybe you're listening to my story and you're thinking, 'how foolish is this girl!' But I wasn't foolish. I was vulnerable, I was naïve, and I was a perfect target. I didn't have a sense of belonging. I didn't feel wanted or valued for anything other than my body" (Diamond, 2020). This statement reminds us that stigmatizing a trafficking victim/survivor (or those who voluntarily work in the sex trade) violates the social work ethos of respecting the individual's dignity and self-worth. This stigma is related to jokes about "hos" and other hostile language. Also, we should be vigilant about protecting those who might become the "perfect target" for a trafficker. Children, teens, and young adults all deserve to feel valued for themselves and not for the commodity value of their bodies.

Amaya (2015) was another girl who left a troubled home only to be trafficked on the streets of New York, which caused her "deep shame." She was only 12 when she started working the streets for 10 years. "I became heavily addicted to heroin. And heroin saved my life. It numbed me to the existence that I was surviving. I don't want to say I was living because I was merely surviving all those years, over a decade" (Amaya, 2015). Opioid use also had a positive effect on this survivor: "Now I look back, not promoting substance abuse or opioid use, but I feel strongly that for me, if it was not for the opioid use, then I would probably be in a mental institution today. And I like truly, truly believe that" because it helped her to dissociate from her traumas (ACF, 2018).

Despite the ambiguity toward opioid use expressed by these women, the damage caused by the opioid crisis continues to affect children. As more parents become impaired by SUD, their children are at higher risk for being trafficked not only by strangers but by the families themselves. According to the Administration for Children and Families (ACF), 63 percent of child sex trafficking victims were trafficked by a family member—and almost half involved a parent or guardian (ACF, 2018). To view child sex trafficking as mostly done by kidnappers working for criminal networks, then, is to ignore the perils faced by children in their own homes.

Lastly, Amaya (2015) is but one of the advocates who has spoken out on behalf of survivors who had been children but still had criminal records. Years after leaving the streets, she experienced difficulties trying to expunge her record in New York state despite having been a trafficked child. Although child rape is a crime in all states, most state laws did not realize that there is no such thing as a "child prostitute" and thus prosecuted trafficking victims under 18 as if they were criminals. Safe harbor laws are one way to undo this injustice by protecting the victims. Through "child protection proceedings, they give sexually exploited children access to specialized services. Safe harbor laws also promote the use of safe houses rather than juvenile detention for child survivors of sex trafficking" (National Council of Jewish Women, 2016).

Discussion questions

- Research your state's position on safe harbor laws. Does your state have one? How strong is it? Shared Hope International, an anti-trafficking organization, issued a "report card" on states and safe harbor laws in 2019 (available on sharedhope.org) that might be useful.
- Victim identification is critical in the fight against sex trafficking, especially for police officers. In one research study, Novak (2016) analyzes the training materials for Texas law enforcement and notes the absence of three groups of possible victims: males, Native Americans, and LGBT+ persons. Research Native Americans or LGBT+ persons and their unique risks for trafficking.
- Despite popular perceptions, females are not the only ones who are trafficked. According to the anti-trafficking website Love146 (https://love146.org), "As of 2019, in Love146's programs in the United States and the Philippines for victims of child sex trafficking, we've seen 13.5% are boys and 1.6% non-binary youth. Some research suggests this number of boys affected could be as high as 30–50%." Propose policies to increase awareness of victims who are male or nonbinary and to develop programs for those groups.
- Besides gender, race plays a critical role in human trafficking because children of color are more likely to be trafficked. One trafficked male noted that "race can add an additional layer of oppression. This is especially true when noting that white peers were sometimes sold for more money simply because of their race. My dark-skinned friends and I were sold for less" (Young, Johnson, Bidorini, & Williamson, 2019). Propose a way to integrate anti-racist initiatives, such as Black Lives Matter, with anti-trafficking efforts.
- One barrier to victim identification is that she may be arrested for using heroin instead of being recognized as somebody who needs to escape her trafficker (Roberson, 2017). Suggest a policy to ensure that law enforcement and prosecutors become aware of this dilemma. Box 6.4 provides a case study of a woman who esca

> **Box 6.4 Case study**
>
> Survivors of trafficking have gone through wrenching experiences that often involve SUD. For example, Eleana was not yet 13 when she met her "boyfriend" who later became her pimp. Having lived in both foster care and with her crack-smoking mother, she was street smart. She knew how to cook "dope" (make crack out of "soft" cocaine), which she sold to her mother and her mother's friends in her Minneapolis neighborhood. During the "grooming" phase, her "boyfriend" gave her expensive presents—including good-quality weed. She became a sex worker and called herself Destiny. Sometimes she got high with her johns so she could earn more money. Because she was in love with him, she never hesitated to give him her earnings because she thought they were a couple. Then one night he locked her in a gas station restroom and whipped her with a coat hanger. He forced the bleeding girl into the trunk. She was confused by this violence, which she knew was not needed because she loved him. Later she found out that this was part of the "breaking/turning out" phase used to overpower a victim's sense of self. Now she was "terrified of him" (Lukes, 2020a, p. 113).
>
> Then law enforcement, including the FBI, arrested her pimp and the criminal gang that had harmed so many people. After her pimp was sentenced to 85 years in prison, she was free from his control. She went home to her mother and tried to figure out her life. She was 15.
>
> For four years, she engaged in polydrug use as she continued in the sex trade by herself. Getting high made her feel free. In her second memoir titled *Don't Call Me Destiny; That's Not My Name: A Sex-Trafficking Story of Survival*, she describes her SUD after her pimp went to prison.
>
>> The scary part of using cocaine and smokin' crack is that I loved the way it made me feel, and too much was never enough. With me, that was how the cycle began, going on calls, which led me to use, then using led me to go on more calls to support the expensive habit of using. I could not have one without the other, and I couldn't abandon either without something better to look forward too (sic) (Lukes, 2020b, p. 54).
>
> ### Discussion question
> "Rescuing" a trafficking victim is more complex than arresting the traffickers. The impact of trauma and SUD can have long-lasting effects. If you were the advocate for women like Eleana, what program ideas would you recommend to your state legislator?

Women in prison

In the United States, the impact of the opioid crisis becomes glaringly obvious in the mass incarceration of women. According to advocacy group The Sentencing Project, the rate of incarcerated women has escalated almost 10 times since 1980, from 13,258 to 113,605 in 2012. "The number of women in prison, a third of whom are incarcerated for drug offenses, is increasing at nearly double the rate for men. These women often have significant histories of physical and sexual abuse, high rates of HIV infection, and substance abuse" (www.sentencingproject.org). Women of color are more likely to live in jail or prison, according to these striking numbers: all women have a one in 56 chance of being incarcerated; white women, 1 in 111, Black/AA women, 1 in 18, and Latinas 1 in 45. With the racial disparity being even worse for males, the mass incarceration in the United States has had a profound impact on the disproportionately affected.

As a result of this high rate of incarceration, family ties—especially the mother/child relationships—are damaged. Rathbone (2006) describes her research setting at MCI-Framingham (in Massachusetts):

> The housing units were crowded, dark, and noisy, and the aimless vacuum of the daily life there often made you want to curl into yourself on your thin little bunk up close to the ceiling and cry. But it was nothing, *nothing*, like Denise thought it would be. There were the locks, of course—including, most impressively, the one to her own cell—to which she would never hold a key. And there were the guards and the continually blaring intercoms, which controlled the smallest minutiae of her everyday life. There were full, bend-over-and-cough strip searches both before and after a visit, and random urine checks, and cell searches (called raids), which left her prison-approved personal items (mostly letters and drawings from her son, Patrick) scattered all over the floor. She'd heard there were punishment cells too. Dismal, solitary cages with nothing but a concrete bed and a seatless toilet, to which women sometimes disappeared for months.
>
> Despite all this, Framingham seemed more like a high school than a prison. Some of the guards were rougher than teachers would ever be, of course. Dressed in quasi-military uniforms and calf-length black leather boots, a few also flaunted their power, making irrational demands simply because they could. For the most part, though, Denise found it easy to keep

out of the way. No, it was the inmates, not the guards, who reminded her of her days at Wecausett High—as did the unfamiliar experience of being with so many women ... the overwhelming majority were mothers, as well, their walls decorated not, as she'd imagine, with images of muscle-bound men but with photos of their kids and sheets of construction paper scrawled over with crayon—valentines and birthday and Christmas cards saved year after year (Rathbone, 2006, pp. 4–5).

This mother/child separation violates one key tenet of reproductive justice, the right to raise a family with dignity. In the article titled "Reproductive justice disrupted: Mass incarceration as a driver of reproductive oppression," the authors assert that "the disproportionate hyperincarceration of Black individuals and other historically marginalized groups violates the principles of reproductive justice" (Hayes, Sufrin, & Perritt, 2020). According to the Women and Prison website (womenandprison.org), at least 65 percent of incarcerated women have a child under 18. Fifty-three percent of the 1.5 million people held in United States prisons by 2007 were the parents of one or more minor children. This percentage translates into more than 1.7 million minor children with an incarcerated parent, children who are disproportionately Black/AA and Latinx.

Previous research has shown a close yet complex connection between parental incarceration and adverse outcomes for children, including an:

- Increased likelihood of engaging in antisocial or delinquent behavior, including drug use;
- Increased likelihood of school failure;
- Increased likelihood of unemployment;
- Increased likelihood of developing mental health problems (Women and Prison website, www.womenandprison.org).

Besides being the custodial parent, many incarcerated women had also contributed to the community as a caregiver to an elderly parent or a disabled friend. Incarceration affects not only the immediate family, but also the wider social network.

Another aspect of prison life for women is loneliness. According to Owen (2005), women prisoners are less likely to be socialized as criminals or gang members. As a result, they have fewer social ties in prison. Lack of privacy is another stressor although most women's prisons allow for bathroom stalls.

> Women in prison rarely escape the male gaze.... While privacy is already eroded by crowded conditions, shared housing units, and the need for surveillance, the presence of male staff further undermines one's ability to attend to personal hygiene and grooming without the scrutiny of men. (Owen, 2005, p.272)

Why are so many women in prison? As explained in Chapter 7, the War on Drugs has been one major cause of the rise "with its emphasis on street-level sweeps of those engaged in the drug trade and harsh mandatory sentencing.... Despite their roles as relatively minor players in the drug trade, women—disproportionate numbers of them African American and Latina—have been 'caught in the net'" ("Women and the drug war" article on drugwarfacts.com). Mandatory sentencing policies, intended to capture the drug lords, have caused women with minimal involvement in the drug trade to be harshly punished.

Prostitution may also lead to the higher rate of incarceration, although these sex workers probably need treatment for childhood trauma instead of a jail term (Belknap, 2014). Another risk factor is being a previous victim of violence (e.g., getting beat up by a gang or a husband).

Another aspect of women in prison is their urgent need for substance abuse treatment (Women's Prison Association website: www.wpaonline.org). In fact, jails/prisons may be the only place where women can access any health services—a fact that is explicated in Sufrin's ethnographic work on "jailcare" (Sufrin, 2017).

> Jail, and the carceral system more broadly, have become an integral part of our society's social and medical safety net.... The whittling away of public services for impoverished people, coupled with the exponential escalation in the number of jails and prisons serving as sites for the care of the indigent, define this American tragedy. The poorest of the poor in America have come to expect that they will go to jail. While there, they know that they will not only be subjected to a regimented, disciplinary environment, but that they will also receive certain services. For the worst off in America, jail is the new safety net. (Sufrin, 2017, p. 5).

Incarcerated women, then, may benefit from the treatment they could find only behind bars. Jailcare, an unintended consequence of the War on Drugs, deserves further attention from social workers and policy makers.

Although stigmatization of this population still occurs, public awareness is shifting. For example, a blog by a woman who visited a facility in Marysville, Ohio, to sing in a choir performance states: "As the program starts, I look at these women, our audience. I am struck by their *ordinariness*. They look like the women I see downtown, in the grocery, in my neighborhood. Many are chomping gum—the prison is a non-smoking facility. They could be my daughters and my grandmothers" (The women in the mirror: A first-hand account of MUSE's visit to an area women's prison, https://www.citybeat.com/arts/the-women-in-the-mirror-12175163).

Discussion questions

- You work at an agency located in a neighborhood that is economically depressed. When you start seeing more and more female ex-felons on your caseload, you realize that some people at the agency (both client and staff) express resentment at how many resources "those women" are getting. How do you generate more social acceptance for the stigmatized women at your agency?
- Sufrin also writes that "I use the term carceral-therapeutic state to describe our contemporary set of carceral institutions—ostensibly for punishment, confinement and containment of criminals—that is increasingly dominated by therapeutic ideologies and processes. Among a diverse and varied drug treatment industry, how have carceral institutions become the largest mental health and addiction service providers for the poor?" (Sufrin, 2017, p. 9). Discuss the policy implications of the "carceral-therapeutic state" model that provides substance abuse treatment to incarcerated persons.

7
Special populations

Introduction

The special populations covered in this chapter are: Blacks/AA, Hispanic/Latinx, Native Americans, older adults, veterans and active military personnel, and transgender persons. Unfortunately, it is beyond the scope of this book to cover other populations such as Asian Americans and sexual minority persons (e.g., gay or bisexual). It is my hope that this chapter inspires the reader to explore these other groups.

Although each of these populations has unique gifts, they also face unique problems such as racism, xenophobia, ageism, and transphobia. For them, the fight to avoid being erased by society is critical to their overcoming the opioid crisis. The "Invisible Man" motif (the title of Ralph Ellison's 1952 book that describes life as a Black/AA man) resonates in this chapter. None of these folks deserve to be invisible or unheard. As the opioid crisis affects them, listening to their concerns is fundamental to the well-being of all Americans.

Blacks/AA

To write about the opioid crisis in the Black/AA population without first acknowledging their historic and current traumas would be unthinkable. Historic trauma, of course, remains unresolved as we grapple with the troubling legacy of slavery and other abuses. The 1619 Project has shared the story of the early Africans who arrived in Virginia in 1619 to be indentured servants. Not until 1661 did slavery (i.e., lifetime ownership of another human) become legal—a pivotal point in U.S. history that was determined by lawmakers, not inevitable fate. The 1619 Project reminds us that we must recognize the significance of not only slavery and its aftermath for the past 400 years, but the proud heritage of African Americans (www.1619project.org).

Current traumas also affect Blacks/AA, as proven by the need for the Black Lives Matter (BLM) movement that has protested police violence and other injustices. These protests have generated widespread support in my city as indicated by the numerous BLM signs at homes and businesses. On many downtown walls, talented artists have painted the faces of those killed by police violence along with messages of peace. As of late 2020, at least 23 million Americans have participated in BLM protests. One optimistic writer notes that

> There has never been an anti-racist majority in American history; there may be one today in the racially and socioeconomically diverse coalition of voters radicalized by the abrupt transition from the hope of the Obama era to the cruelty of the Trump age (Serwer, 2020).

Whether or not the BLM and related movements will shift the United States toward a more just society, the opioid crisis presents a test for Black/AA communities. Unfortunately, the crack cocaine problem that started in the 1980s appeared as a "black" problem, while the opioid crisis seemed like a "white" problem. This popular perception is wrong. One op-ed writer states, in an article titled "The opioid crisis isn't white," that the media covers opioid misuse more sympathetically than for other drugs, such as crack: "It's notable how this kind of coverage emphasizes the humanity of opioid users. Phrases like 'introduced to,' 'caused by' and 'fell into' are increasingly used to describe pathways to addiction" (Shihipar, 2019).

Like other experts, Substance Abuse and Mental Health Services Administration (SAMHSA) agrees that the opioid crisis is not "white." Although the rate of opioid use among Blacks/AA is the same as the national rate (four percent), the rate of opioid deaths rose 40 percent for Blacks/AA from 2015 to 2016. This rate is almost double the rate of increase for whites (SAMHSA, 2020a).

One reason why people believe that Blacks/AA are not as affected by the opioid crisis as whites is because doctors prescribe fewer opioids to Blacks/AA. This disregard for the pain of Blacks/AA patients, who are 29 percent less likely to be prescribed appropriate medication, is an ethical question for the medical profession because under-prescribing can be as harmful as over-prescribing (SAMHSA, 2020A). The providers' beliefs (e.g., believing that black skin is tougher than white skin or that blacks are mostly drug seekers) can be dangerous when some patients turn to their families or the streets for pain relief, thus taking opioids without medical supervision

(Stevens-Watkins, 2020). Unfortunately, the topic of Blacks/AA and opioid prescription misuse is not well researched. In analyzing the differences between rural and urban Blacks/AA regarding this topic, Rigg and Nicholson (2019) stress that this population is not a "monolith" as several variations occur, such as education level and religiosity.

Instead of opioid medications being the cause of so many overdose deaths of Blacks/AA, fentanyl is blamed for this rise because other drugs such as cocaine have been contaminated with this synthetic (and deadly) opioid. (A full discussion of fentanyl is in Chapter 8.) SAMHSA also notes that "Opioids are not the only substances of concern and are likely not being misused in isolation. An understanding that intergenerational and polysubstance use are common among some impoverished communities, and that disentangling the behaviors of a person's social network, including their family, are challenging yet critically necessary" (SAMHSA, 2020a).

Intergenerational drug use, then, has emerged as a risk factor for OUD since many Black/AA families have a decades-long history of drug use. Besides intergenerational drug use, polysubstance use can endanger a person's recovery. One study of methadone clients concludes they are more likely to have positive drug screens and drop out of the program if they had family members who were drug users and/or using cocaine (Lister, Greenwald, & Ledgerwood, 2017).

OUD, of course, can lead to overdose deaths. SAMHSA explicates the risk factors for overdose deaths—including incarceration because a newly released prisoner may not realize that their body's tolerance level had diminished. The War on Drugs has also resulted in the reluctance to call 911 if somebody is overdosing. Besides avoiding any emergency personnel and police involvement, many Black/AA persons also distrust outreach programs, such as needle exchanges (SAMHSA, 2020). One drug counselor said,

> black people don't trust systems. Criminalizing drug use has truly left a hole in black families and the community as it relates to the criminal justice system. There is a huge divide, and we haven't done much to sort of repair that distrust. Medical systems are no different (Newman, 2018).

Likewise, distrust of medication assisted treatment (MAT) has been problematic for Blacks/AA. The racial divide appears in the type of MAT, with persons of color more likely to use methadone (which requires daily clinic visits) rather than buprenorphine (which requires weekly or less frequent doctor visits). Many did not deem methadone programs as safe because "some African Americans believe white community outsiders were 'experimenting' on them and that these programs served to locate and potentially isolate opioid-dependent African Americans in their own communities" (Stevens-Watkins, 2020). This suspicion of methadone clinics is not unfounded since researchers have found that the clinics have regularly under-dosed their Blacks/AA patients. Another issue is that

> Treatment is complicated for Medicaid patients due to the inconsistent funding or time-restrictions that are imposed by Medicaid insurance. This is detrimental to the patient as it can impede their success for treatment due to the higher chance of relapse with sub-optimal dosing of methadone (Santoro & Santoro, 2018).

Besides methadone, buprenorphine (e.g., suboxone) is another MAT option. The barriers to using buprenorphine include lack of private insurance or cash, lack of prescribers in their neighborhoods, and childcare (Stevens-Watkins, 2020). Interestingly, racial/ethnic segregation plays a role in the availability of buprenorphine for both Blacks/AA and Hispanic/Latinos. If a white resident was less likely to interact with either group, the more likely that this form of MAT would be available in their area.

These findings describe a racialized treatment landscape for OUD in the United States, where the racial/ethnic composition of a community may significantly determine whether residents will be able to access methadone rather than buprenorphine and vice versa when seeking treatment (Goedel, 2020).

Discussion questions

- Goedel (2020) writes of the "racialized treatment landscape for OUD." Despite decades of government efforts, racial/ethnic segregation still exists. How segregated is your community? Write a policy suggestion to reduce segregation.
- Many in the Black/AA population continue to distrust the medical system and other options for recovery. How would you design an outreach effort that would engender trust? For example, how would you recruit pastors or other community members?

SPECIAL POPULATIONS 127

> Om (2018) writes that "Largely because of media portrayals of crack as violence-inducing, the number of Americans who believed drug abuse was America's most pressing concern rose from 3 to 64% from 1986 to 1989; however, a meta-analysis of 55 articles . . . on the opioid crisis revealed that only 9% called for criminal justice approaches." Was the portrayal of crack as violence-inducing an accurate one? Researchers in the 1990s and later (e.g., Baumer, 1994) did find crack to be related to a rise in urban crime rates. One study even associates the doubling of the murder rate of young black males to the introduction of crack into the cities (Evans, Garthwaite, & Moore, 2018).
  o The drug trade can be a violent one, but the opioid crisis is not associated with a rise in violence as was the crack crisis (Szalavitz & Rigg, 2017). Do you think that race/ethnicity or other factors can explain this difference?
  o Cocaine (both powder and crack) is a stimulant, so this substance is more associated with violent behavior (Vaughn, et al., 2010) than depressants, such as opioids. Do you think that this could be a factor

Illustration 7.1 Stock photo of "Addict" (Shutterstock number in picture).
Credit: © Lipik Stock Media/Shutterstock

128   THE OPIOID CRISIS

in the different views of the "crack addicts" vs. the "innocent" users of opioids—or is race/ethnicity the only explanation for this difference?
- Study Illustration 7.1 of a Black/AA "addict" and consider its implicit messages. If you were running a public awareness campaign about the opioid crisis in the Black/AA community, would you use this type of picture? Why or why not? If not, what type of picture would you use and what messages would you want to convey?

Case study: Washington, DC

As cited earlier, the rate of Blacks/AA dying of opioid overdoses is increasing at an alarming rate. In Washington, DC, the rate of these deaths for Blacks/AA was 74.6 per 100,000 in 2017—the second highest in the nation (SAMHSA, 2020a). Eighty percent of the overdose deaths in DC, a city hit as hard as any Appalachian area, were Black/AA, although only 65 percent of the city's population is Black/AA (www.census.gov). "In this new explosion of deaths, the nation's capital is ground zero" (Jamison, 2018b).

Unlike the stereotypical opioid user whose SUD started with Oxycontins or other pills, many of the Black/AA opioid users in DC had been using heroin for decades. These users "had developed a semblance of functional addiction, getting by with menial jobs on factory floors and construction sites. Until they began dying" (Jamison, 2018a). With fentanyl contaminating their heroin, drug use had become more lethal. Even after two near-fatal overdoses, one user described the fentanyl feeling like "'taking a hundred coats off,' whose pleasure—while much diminished since the early days of their addiction—was still powerful enough to obscure the uglier details of their lives" (Jamison, 2018a).

With the arrival of fentanyl in the city's drug supply, policy debates have emerged. Frustration has appeared in some debates because of the formidable grip of SUD. One city health official stated, "You can't beat the addiction for them. You have to be there to meet them and help them. But at the end of the day, they have to find a way to come off this drug before it kills them" (Nirrapil, 2020). Policies that have been proposed and/or implemented include:

- Allowing fentanyl test strips to be used, a form of harm reduction;
- Decriminalizing drug paraphernalia;

- Increasing the number of city employees carrying Narcan (resuscitation drug);
- Revising the "Good Samaritan laws" that allow drug users to avoid arrest if they call 911 (for a full explanation of these laws, see Chapter 10);
- Promoting access to buprenorphine for Medicaid patients and those covered by private insurance;
- Ensuring that jail inmates receive drug treatment (Narrapil, 2020).

Despite these initiatives, the city government has received criticism for the low rate of Narcan distribution. Another concern is that too few persons with SUD have been referred to services despite federal funding efforts (Jamison, 2018b).

Discussion questions

- Design a public health campaign with the theme of "Beyond Narcan: Roads to Recovery" to stress that follow-up is essential for overdose survivors. In your community, are there any services that you could include in this campaign?
- In 2021, the U.S. Congress debated on the possible statehood of the District of Columbia. If DC were to gain statehood, and thus achieve more political power, how could this affect its opioid crisis? For instance, do you think that local officials would be able to gain more resources?

Hispanic/Latinx

"We Hispanics are the ones who are dying," stated one Hispanic/Latino man in recovery. He had lost several family members to overdose deaths and said he felt lucky that a Spanish-language facility had a bed available. Now "I see a good future for me. Many of the counselors here went through this program and that gives me hope that it can be done" (Carrasco, 2021).

According to SAMHSA, the rate of opioid misuse among Hispanic/Latinos was similar to the total U.S. rate at four percent in 2018. Over half of the opioid-related overdose deaths involved synthetic opioids, a trend that resembles the total U.S. rate (SAMHSA, 2020).

This report was based on pre-COVID-19 data, and no national update was available at this time. However, an update from Maryland provides a glimpse of how the pandemic affected this population. For the first nine months of 2020, opioid-related overdose deaths among Hispanic/Latinos rose 27.3 percent, much higher than among non-Hispanic whites (16 percent) and non-Hispanic blacks (13 percent). The pandemic had affected the transport of heroin, so fentanyl was more available—and deadlier (Carrasco, 2021).

One possible reason for the disproportionate rise in these overdose deaths could be the stress caused by workplace exposure to COVID-19. The higher prevalence of Hispanic/Latinos in manual and service jobs made it impossible for these workers to work from home. One expert stated that "Particularly for front-line and essential workers, among whom Hispanics are overrepresented, COVID-19 is an occupational disease that spreads at work. Hispanics were on the front lines and they bore a disproportionate cost" (Caldwell, 2021). These workers were not only risking themselves, but the health and lives of their families and friends.

Aside from the grim realities of the pandemic, the disproportionate rate of Hispanic/Latinos in manual labor has resulted in more use of opioid pain medications and later OUD. The research on whether Hispanic/Latinos are prescribed fewer opioids than whites is unclear. Even if Hispanic/Latinos are prescribed opioids, they may not be able to get them at their pharmacies. Because so many in this population may be suffering from chronic pain that is undertreated, SAMHSA recommends that we "need to consider how pain intersects with opioid use and misuse" (SAMHSA, 2020, no page).

Besides workplace injuries as one cause of the rate of overdose deaths, many Hispanic/Latinos are reluctant to call for emergency services when needed. One drug counselor said that on the streets, "It's not cool to be calling 911. . . I could get shot, and I won't call 911" because "it's a machismo thing. . . . To the men in the (recovery) house, the word 'help,' sounds like degrading . . . (it) is like you're getting exiled from your community" (Bebinger, 2018).

Another reason for the reluctance to call 911 is the fear of deportation, a fear felt even by the Hispanic/Latinos who are documented. As a result, the first responders to an overdose emergency are often family members or others in the community (SAMHSA, 2020).

Discussion questions

- If you were the public health official for a Hispanic/Latino neighborhood, would you focus your efforts on providing naloxone (Narcan) to the unofficial first responders in the community? Or would you instead focus on improving relations between the community and official first responders (e.g., ambulance crews)? What are the pros and cons of either option?
- Despite popular misconceptions, 80 percent of U.S. Hispanic/Latinos are U.S. citizens (Ortiz, 2020). Anti-immigrant attitudes, strengthened by racist antagonism toward persons of color, have built a barrier between Hispanic/Latinos and treatment services. If you worked in a city government and wanted to decrease these negative attitudes, what program(s) would you suggest?

Although families remain an essential component in the Hispanic/Latino communities, this is not always beneficial to persons with SUD when drug use occurs within the family. In some multigenerational households, opioids and other substances may be used together by grandparents, parents, and older children (SAMHSA, 2020). Also, overcrowding can be a stressor (Ortiz, 2020). These factors can stymie the recovery for somebody who wants to stay close to their family but still abstain from drug use (Bebbinger, 2018).

Another barrier to recovery is the language barrier for those with limited English proficiency. One reporter noted that some Hispanic/Latinos "describe sitting through group counseling sessions, part of virtually every treatment program, and not being able to follow much, if any, of the conversation. They recall waiting for a translator to arrive for their individual appointment with a doctor or counselor and missing the session" (Bebbinger, 2018).

Besides language barriers, research shows that discrimination plays a role in the rates of SUD among Hispanic/Latinos. However, subgroups (e.g., gender and country of birth) within the population merit further research because not all subgroups were affected (Otiniano Verissimo, et al., 2014). Another study states that using culturally appropriate techniques are essential but they "cannot be a one-size fit all approach and require more tailored approaches that can only come from subregion and subgroup patterns" (Valdez, Cepeda, Frankeberger, & Nowotny, 2022).

Two other risk factors are the immigration experiences for first-generation Hispanic/Latinos and the level of acculturation for second and subsequent generations. Obviously, the traumas related to the migration process (either as a documented or undocumented person) can have consequences for years. The level of acculturation also plays a role in SUD because traditional families are a protective factor against SUD while being more "Americanized" raises the risk of SUD (Ortiz, 2020).

To address these risk factors, SAMHSA and other experts advise emphasizing the role of community building. One outreach worker stated "Understanding how Latinos view mental health and addiction is critical to implementing a culturally and linguistically responsive approach to prevention efforts. Latinos are heterogenous representing a wide variety of national origins and cultures, but a common theme will always remain, and that's the importance of building trust and relationships with our community" (WSYX/WTTE, 2020).

One example of building trust is evident in the use of Mexican traditional medicine. Sorrell (2020) presents the case study of Oswaldo, who was referred for services by one of the abuelas (lay health advisor) at his church. The abuela assisted with the assessment and then the family meeting in which they discussed treatment options. The family decided that MAT was the best option. Later, the abuela or her colleagues participated in the induction process in which he started the medications and provided herbs to alleviate his anxiety. Mexican traditional medicine, then, provided him with cultural competent care that was also holistic.

Discussion questions

- The intersection of stigmatized conditions affects Hispanic/Latinos who are actively using or in recovery: SUD, ethnicity, and possibly class status and/or language proficiency. Think about how stigmas are fluid and can diminish over time. For example, same-sex couples were once severely stigmatized and now they have weddings with plenty of well-wishers. Pick one of the stigmas associated with Hispanic/Latinos and suggest ways to diminish the stigma.
- The impact of the deportation of a family member or friend is one risk factor for the misuse of prescription opioids among U.S. citizens (Pinedo, 2020). Research the current policy on deportation and discuss how it might impact the rate of SUD in the Hispanic/Latino community.
- Hispanic/Latinx face many barriers to treatment, including the stigma associated with drug use and mental health. One doctor suggests that

mental health counselors be available when people come in for their physicals (Carrasco, 2021). Do you consider this idea to be feasible? If so, how would you justify the costs?

Native Americans

It is impossible to generalize about the Native American population (also known as AI/AN—American Indian and Alaskan Native) because of its diversity with its 570 tribes and the urban/rural differences. However, a disturbing trend has emerged among the AI/AN population—a rate of overdose deaths as high as whites from 1999 to 2016. Also disturbing are the data from two urban areas from this period, which indicate a disproportionate number of AI/AN overdose deaths:

- Minneapolis with a rate of 42.4 per 100,000 AI/AN persons but only 5.7 for non-Hispanic whites; and
- Seattle with a rate of 31.2 per 100,000 AI/AN persons but only 13.6 for non-Hispanic whites (Tipps, Buzzard, & McDougall, 2018).

These rates vary considerably from state to state. Both North Dakota and South Dakota, for example, show a low rate of overdose deaths. Researchers speculate that the Native Americans had less access to prescription opioids when the drugs were being over prescribed, and that the drug traffickers may not find it profitable to travel such long distances for such a small population. Also, methamphetamine is widely used in the Dakotas because it can be made at home (Tipps, Buzzard, & McDougall, 2018).

The context of the opioid crisis among the AI/AN population includes centuries of historic trauma that include genocide and dehumanization. These tragedies were neither spontaneous nor inevitable, since policymakers created the laws that still affect the AI/AN populations today. For example, the 1956 Indian Relocation Act attempted more assimilation by encouraging Native Americans on reservations to move to cities. The Bureau of Indian Affairs paid for the moves while their flyers promised "good jobs," "happy homes," and "the chance of a lifetime" (Hunt, et al., 2020, p. 761). Unfortunately, good jobs were scarce in the cities, and social support was even scarcer for the newly urbanized AI/AN. "Without home and community as protection, relocated Indians were left both detached and disenchanted in their new environments," especially because the "policy of dispersal" broke apart several communities (Hunt, et al., 2020, p. 762). In 1950, only eight percent of the AI/AN population lived in urban areas, but that number rose eightfold by 2000 to 64 percent. When they returned to the reservation for visits, they "found they did not 'fit in' with those who stayed behind" (National Archives, 2016).

Although the Indian Relocation Act was not the only cause for the urbanization of AI/AN, its impact deserves further study as an underlying cause of the opioid crisis in this population. In one qualitative study, a psychologist stated that " 'I think the fact that some Natives have grown up in the city, but they don't know about their traditional cultural practices. Some of them know they're Native, but they don't even know their Tribe . . . if you have a loss . . . of connection to your tribe or your culture, that's definitely a risk' " (Zeledon, et al., 2020, no page).

Besides the rapid urbanization of AI/AN, another unique aspect of this population is the complicated relationship between tribal and non-tribal governments. Some tribes have their own court system, so they can administer justice in a more culturally appropriate way. For example, the Tribal Healing to Wellness Courts resemble state drug courts with their emphasis on treatment instead of incarceration. However, reconnecting to culture and addressing historic traumas are unique components of the Healing to Wellness programs. The Medicine Wheel Teaching (see Illustration 7.2), which emphasizes a holistic view of the person/community such as physical and emotional, is often used. "Because situations taking place in human life are believed to be interdependent, interrelated, and joined, addiction is viewed as an inevitable life 'conflict' which is actually not an enemy but a necessary friend that is needed, for it provides clarity" (Mukosi, 2020, p. 46).

Despite the intuitive appeal of the healing to wellness courts, their efficacy is not fully established. "The scant research that is available does suggest that participation in the courts decreases recidivism, primarily for adult clients; however, because of a lack of extensive and rigorous evaluation we cannot be sure whether these courts are superior to other options such as criminal courts" (Aseline & Antunes, 2021, p. 202). The authors also note that the courts themselves do not share adequate information about their operations. Besides not being evidence-based, these courts face the following policy issues:

Illustration 7.2 Medicine wheel (Shutterstock number in picture).
Credit: © Argo Studio/Shutterstock

- Dependence on federal and other outside funding, which can be unpredictable;
- Dependence on local treatment services, which are often underfunded and thus understaffed;
- The complicated jurisdictions between tribal lands and non-tribal areas—should a case be tried in a county or tribal court? (Aseline & Antunes, 2021).

The Tribal Healing to Wellness courts may require more research on their efficacy, but the key message of this program and other interventions is the importance of reinforcing cultural pride. As one client said after completing a recovery program, "I'm proud to be a Native now. I'm proud for who I am. I know my identity. I don't care if anybody calls me a dirty Indian, lazy Indian.... Well, so what? I'm still a human being... today I'm very proud for who I am" (Gone, 2013, p. 693).

Discussion questions

- For the Center for Disease Control and Prevention (CDC), one difficulty in obtaining accurate data about overdose deaths in the AI/AN population has been that rates "may be substantially affected by differential racial misclassification on death certificates as well as potential under- or overcounting of AI/AN in Census Bureau data" (Tipps, Buzzard, & McDougall, 2018, p. 424). Numbers are significant for policy decisions, so this difficulty could affect funding. For example, what would you say to a policymaker who would simply dismiss the problem because it is so hard to measure?
- Stereotypes based on Pocahontas and other images can stymie the efforts of social workers who may know little about AI/AN culture. Pick one tribe (if possible, one located in your state) and write down three ways to increase your cultural awareness of this population. Why would it be wrong to make any generalizations from only one tribe?
- Increasing awareness of OUD among the AI/AN population is essential, but one unintended consequence could be the reinforcement of the "drunk Indian" stereotype. How would you avoid that trap if you were trying to reach out and had to write a public service announcement (PSA)?
- The term "evidence-based" applies to the question of the efficacy of the healing to wellness courts. Without enough evidence, funding by government agencies and support from the public could weaken. Design an evaluation plan that would provide evidence about the courts' success rates. What would be the barriers to your evaluation plan?
- Look up the Indian Health Service (www.ihs.gov) and use the search term "opioid." What do you think about their responses to the opioid crisis?

Older adults

Many social workers have a favorite population, and mine is older adults. Having grown up with little contact with my grandparents, I keenly appreciate my experiences with folks who are older and wiser than me. Social work students would sometimes comment that working with this population would be depressing. An oral history assignment usually made the students realize the richness and joys found in connecting with older adults.

On my mantel is a photo of my aunt Sister Celine, who lived past 100. Once during late October, she had asked me what I was planning to be for Halloween. I had scoffed at that question, stating that I was too old to dress up. She had said that nobody is too old for Halloween. In the photo, she is dressed as a witch as she waves at the camera. And she was right—nobody is too old for Halloween. As Illustration 7.3 indicates, successful aging is possible.

Successful aging

My aunt exemplified the ideal of successful aging because she thrived instead of just surviving the physical decline and multiple challenges associated with living 10 decades. Successful aging means defying the beliefs that all old people are cranky and just sit around waiting to die. Ageism (i.e., negative attitudes toward older persons) focuses on the problems of aging instead

Illustration 7.3 Successful aging (Shutterstock number in picture).
Credit: © Rawpixel.com/Shutterstock

of valuing older adults for their ongoing contributions. In its most extreme form, ageism assumes that older adults are expendable. During the early days of the COVID-19 pandemic, some commentators even suggested that older adults be sacrificed for the sake of avoiding the economic damage caused by lockdowns. As one young woman said, "Coronavirus only kills old people, and they are going to die anyway" (Neutill, 2020).

Ageism also influences the issues of OUD and older adults, as evidenced by the sparse research on this topic (Daoust, et al., 2018). Based on my personal and professional experiences, I am concerned that medical providers and others may overlook the symptoms of OUD (e.g., mental fogginess) as just "old age" or misdiagnose OUD as dementia or other age-related conditions. This concern extends to possible unrecognized mental health conditions, such as depression. I will be forever grateful to the doctor who treated another aunt of mine (and yes, another Catholic sister!) when she had been "zoning out" and becoming lethargic while in her 80s. After she went on antidepressants, she became her old self and lived several more fulfilling years.

In this context of ageism possibly affecting the medical care of older adults, pain management emerges as a pressing issue regarding OUD. Few would dispute that chronic pain is common among older adults, with one study stating that 57 percent of persons 65+ had pain that lasted at least a year (cited in Levi-Minzi, et al., 2013). For all persons with chronic pain, there is a "lack of consensus among prescribers across the United States on the proper use of opioid pain medications" with 20 percent of patients with chronic pain being prescribed opioids (Sterling, 2018).

One question about this population is simple but perplexing: how old must you be to be considered an older adult/senior/elderly person? Different studies present numbers that range from 50 to 65. In general, any opioid use by older adults can result in overdosing caused by the body's accumulation of the substance (Sterling, 2018). Falls are another serious risk, especially when bones become more fragile with age. Not surprisingly, older adults may experience cognitive deficits and psychomotor impairments due to opioids (Joshi, Shah, & Kirane, 2019). One woman in recovery stated, "I had a spinal fusion and so I had been taking opiates for a period of time. You know, the older we get the more aches and pains we get.... We injure ourselves, we have surgeries. So, for people in recovery it's a slippery slope" (Davidson, 2018).

Unfortunately, doctors must balance the risk of undertreatment of pain with the risk of OUD because untreated/undertreated pain can trigger opioid misuse. In one study, over 80 percent of older adults misusing opioid medications and/or buying street drugs reported that pain was the cause. One respondent said, "Sometimes the pills wear off and the pain come back and I take some more... The prescription that they gave me, the amount that they tell me to take, just don't do nothin. So I take more than what they tell me to take" (Levi-Minzi, et al., 2013, p. 1726). Also, medical providers sometimes fail to screen for pain while their patients are often fatalistic about the pain, believing that it is an inevitable part of aging.

Besides chronic pain as a factor in the OUD crisis among older adults, the possibility of decades-long use of substances by baby boomers (i.e., those born from 1946–1964) is important. One study states that "their drug use initiation and experience appears to span over the entire age spectrum" (Chhatre, et al., 2017). Those with a long history of drug use are called "early onset" users as opposed to those whose drug use started when they were already older adults (Carew & Comiskey, 2018).

"Early onset" users are more likely to have polysubstance use which may include opioids, alcohol, and marijuana. According to another study, the older adults who were entering treatment from 2000 to 2012 reported these drugs of choice:

- Heroin at a 26 percent increase;
- Non-prescription methadone at a 200 percent increase;
- Other opioids at a 221 percent increase (Chhatre, et al., 2017).

More older adults are seeking treatment for OUD with an approximate 50 percent increase from 2004 to 2015 (Huhn, et al., 2018). Although the MAT medications have not been tested for this specific population, researchers still recommend MAT and other general treatment options (LaGrotta, 2020). However, older adults may not feel comfortable with their younger counterparts in treatment groups because of their rough language and the pressure to be surrogate parents for the younger members (Brown, 2018).

Another recommendation is that providers integrate gerontology into treatment programs for older adults.

We are witnessing now the magnitude of the intersection of aging and substance use. For health care systems to adequately care for the complexity of aging, chronic medical conditions, and substance use among its aging populations, a framework that draws from both geriatric-based principles and from harm reduction is required (Han, 2018).

The impact of the opioid crisis on the older adult population is not only about their OUD but also the consequences of relatives (usually their adult children) having an OUD. Chapter 4 discusses how grandparents have had to raise another generation. Financial exploitation and abuse are also concerns when elderly parents have children who need money for their habits. In my practice experience, I have comforted clients who had lost thousands of dollars and—worst of all—their trust in their own family. This sense of betrayal can cut deep.

Policymakers have become aware of this problem. Stories like these help them understand the connection between the opioid crisis and older adults: "Mrs. B's recently unemployed granddaughter moved into Mrs. B's house at her invitation. Over time, the granddaughter began stealing Mrs. B's social security checks and other income, using the money to buy opiates. She also began blocking visitation attempts by Mrs. B's other relatives and friends" (Teaster, Lindberg, & Gallo, 2020). Another consideration is the increase of drug-related cases, which is estimated to be at a 25 to 35 percent increase. The front-line workers in this small study also stressed that they needed more resources and data to help them (Teaster, Lindberg, & Gallo, 2020).

Financial abuse is not the only result of the opioid crisis. Front line staff "also indicated that when desperate perpetrators had gone through the money, the drugs, or both, older adults were psychologically and physically abused. Their abusers isolated the older adults in their own homes so that they could not reach out to others to help them" (Singletary, 2019).

Elder justice is the policy response not only to elder abuse/neglect, but also the improvement of this population's well-being. Under this definition, programs such as Social Security and Medicare are part of elder justice (Nerenberg, 2019). The Elder Justice Act of 2010, though, only focuses on adult protective services and not this broader vision. Although the Act was comprehensive enough, the programs have received very little funding (Teaster, Lindberg, & Gallo, 2020).

Discussion questions

- One source (Joshi, Shah, & Kirane, 2019) estimated that 5.7 million older adults would have an SUD in 2020. However, the National Institute on Drug Abuse reports that only one million older adults had an SUD in 2018 (www.drugabuse.gov/publications/substance-use-in-older-adu

lts-drugfacts). If you were writing a grant to obtain funds for a treatment program that focuses on older adults, how would you present this data? Would you cite only the higher number or mention this big discrepancy? Discuss the ethics of this situation.
- The Office of Inspector General for Health and Human Services reported that in 2017, 90,000 Medicare beneficiaries were at risk for opioid misuse or overdose. One man "received 62 opioid prescriptions during the year, which is more than one prescription per week. All of the prescriptions were for fentanyl or oxycodone. The beneficiary had an average daily MED of 3,130 mg . . . almost 35 times the level that CDC recommends avoiding. All but one of these opioids were prescribed by one family medicine physician" (https://oig.hhs.gov/oei/reports/oei-02-17-00250.pdf). If you were the Inspector General, how would you ensure that the Medicare system flags down these cases of overprescribing?
- One study (Chhatre, et al., 2017) notes that providers must be able to properly diagnose SUD in older adults, so more geriatric education for the providers is urgently needed. Write a two-sentence "mini-proposal" to request funding for this education.
- Look up the National Council on Aging factsheet on elder abuse. Using this factsheet, apply the information from this section. Design an advocacy tool to increase funding for the Elder Justice Act.

Veterans and active military personnel

In 2006, Corporal Jimmy Cleveland Kinsey II was a soldier in Iraq when a roadside bomb shattered his leg. The doctors had to amputate the leg. For four years, he struggled with the pain and the opioid misuse that resulted. His widow writes, "I first noticed something was wrong when he would fall asleep sitting up while smoking a cigarette, the ashes growing so long they'd ash themselves. Once, he fell asleep with his face down in a bowl of Cheerios. In 2008, he overdosed for the first time" (Fugett, 2020). During the four years between his injury and death by overdose in 2010, he was unable to obtain appropriate services from the Veterans Administration (VA) because the opioid crisis was not yet recognized.

Now it is widely recognized that veterans are twice as likely as civilians to die from an opioid overdose (Goldberg, 2017). the Veterans' Health

Administration and the Department of Defense offer several programs to fight the opioid crisis. The Opioid Safety Initiative, for example, has reduced the number of opioid prescriptions in favor of other pain management interventions (Lin, et al., 2017). At first the author was going to only focus on veterans, but the research results indicate an undeniable overlap between active military personnel and veterans of the wars in Iraq and Afghanistan.

Almost 2.8 million service members have served in Iraq and Afghanistan since 2001. "We have an opioid epidemic in the military population. That is well known. And nearly three million deployed since 9/11, so what is the impact of this combat?" (Cesur quoted in Kime, 2019). During their deployments, they were exposed to these risk factors:

- Easy availability of opium in Afghanistan, which produces 80 percent of the world's supply;
- War injuries, especially due to improvised explosive devices (IEDs, also called road bombs) which account for one-third of the OUD cases;
- Combat trauma (Cesur, Sabia, & Bradford, 2019).

The authors of the research study titled "Did the War on Terror ignite an opioid epidemic?" (Cesur, Sabia, & Bradford, 2019) also note that the VA has not properly monitored the patients' prescriptions as do the states with their prescription drug monitoring programs. As a result, patients can "doctor shop" and/or obtain multiple prescriptions without a database tracking what they are taking. For instance, a patient could obtain benzodiazepines from one doctor and opioids from another—a highly lethal combination because both medications suppress one's breathing.

Physical pain is another issue for those in uniform (Illustration 7.4), since one veteran stated that "In the veteran population, we have a lot of people with neck and back injuries. Just about anyone who carried around a backpack of 100 pounds [or] 120 pounds ended up with arthritis or some other pain—and there's a big push for opioids." Drugs were "everywhere he landed," a problem that was exacerbated when he was offered any pain medication he wanted in Iraq after being injured (Military Officers Association of America, no author, 2017).

Besides the easy availability of opioids for active military personnel, they were also exposed to the risk of post traumatic stress disorder (PTSD). PTSD, called "battle fatigue" and "shell shock" in previous wars (Friedman, no date),

SPECIAL POPULATIONS   143

Illustration 7.4 Veterans and military personnel (Shutterstock number in picture).
Credit: © Bumble Dee/Shutterstock

is described by one veteran: "When you have PTSD, the world feels unsafe. You may have upsetting memories, feel on edge, or have trouble sleeping. You may also try to avoid things that remind you of your trauma—even things you used to enjoy" (video quote retrieved from www.ptsd.va.gov/understand/what/ptsd_basics.asp).

For Iraq/Afghanistan service members, the rate of PTSD is one in five (Cesur, Sabia, & Bradford, 2019). Likewise, Vietnam veterans have experienced PTSD. One veteran shares a glimpse of combat trauma in this quote:

> The most important event was just seeing real war. We walked endlessly and waited for someone to shoot us. . . . Earlier in the day, 20–30 women came running out of the village and our soldiers were shooting and I yelled stop shooting, they are women and children but they kept shooting. . . . These are the people we were told that we were there to protect against Communist monsters . . . I was flabbergasted at other soldiers' bad behavior but rarely said anything. . . . It was nine months of hell for me (Hart & Stough-Hunter, 2017, p. 27).

This quote also indicates a moral injury, which is caused by action(s) that violate one's personal morality, or by not acting such as the soldier who rarely said anything when he saw his comrades' "bad behavior." This condition is not the same as PTSD, although they may overlap. "While PTSD is more fear-based, moral injury is shame-based" (Hart & Stough-Hunter, 2017, p. 6). One study notes that moral injury poses a higher risk for suicide than PTSD for both veterans and active military members (Ames, et al., 2019).

Another veteran dealing with a moral injury returned to Vietnam in 1994 to visit a village where hundreds of civilians were killed.

> I went back to this village where our battalion killed 272 people—old men, women and children. It's where I got my first Purple Heart from a Bouncing Betty (an explosive device). There is a memorial in that village for the people we killed and I spent one day on my hands and knees and placed three burning incense sticks at each grave, one of which was a mass grave for 23 children. I made it a point to tell the people from that village that I was one of the guys who did this and there was absolutely no hostility toward me. So now when I think about that place I have different pictures in my brain besides the people we killed and my buddies who bled with me. I have pictures of people who are happy there now, who are my friends, and who have forgiven me (Hart & Stough-Hunter, 2017, p. 85).

Moral injury can also be associated with the feeling of being betrayed by the U.S. government by soldiers who view the war they fought in as immoral. The Vietnam Veterans Against War started in 1967 when six veterans participated in a peace demonstration (website: www.vvaw.org). When President George W. Bush announced the upcoming invasion of Iraq in 2003, worldwide protests erupted in almost 800 cities (Bennis, 2013). Even the ongoing occupation of Afghanistan, which had been invaded in 2001 in response to its support of Osama bin Laden, has caused controversy. According to one veteran, the U.S. government got away with dishonesty about the war in Afghanistan "because of public apathy, because of the 'low cost' of the war—an acceptable number of casualties, a relatively low footprint. We learned how to fight a war that nobody cared about" (Terkel & Ahmed, 2021).

A veteran, then, may experience chronic pain, PTSD, and/or moral injury. Another risk factor for OUD is traumatic brain injury (TBI), often caused by the reverberations from roadside bombs. A veteran with a history of TBI is at more risk (1.55 times) to die from suicide than other veterans (Brenner,

Ignacio, & Blow, 2011). This suicide risk is related to the 80 percent probability of psychiatric diagnoses, including SUD, in this population (Carlson, et al., 2010). Veterans with TBI are highly likely to have chronic pain, which is an additional risk factor for opioid misuse. However, they are also more likely to be prescribed opioids despite these risks (Seal, et al., 2018).

As veterans face OUD and other challenges, homelessness and/or housing instability may ensue. One cross-sectional study of over five million veterans (Manhapra, Stefanovics, & Rosenheck, 2021) states that homeless veterans were 12 times more likely to have an OUD than other veterans. In another study, the researchers suggest that veterans seeking MAT should be screened for housing issues and be referred to housing assistance if needed (Bachhuber, et al., 2015).

Discussion questions

- Calling moral injury an "invisible wound," Yan (2016) urges better screening and services for this condition because of its overlap with PTSD and other issues. Design a poster or write a paragraph calling attention to moral injuries affecting the health of the veterans.
- Review the VA's strategic plan to end homelessness for veterans (available on www.va.gov/HOMELESS/docs/VHA-Strategic-Plan-External-Final_508.pdf). What are three key points that you would emphasize in a presentation to local agencies?

OUD and transgender/nonbinary persons

Before discussing OUD in this population, certain terms require definition. According to the Human Rights Campaign:

- Transgender is "an umbrella term for people whose gender identity and/or expression is different from cultural expectations based on the sex they were assigned at birth";
- Cisgender "describe(s) people whose gender identity aligns with the sex assigned to them at birth";

> Nonbinary "describe(s) a person who does not identify exclusively as a man or a woman." This term may include genderqueer, genderfluid, and others who do not fit in the male/female binary (Human Rights Campaign, 2020, p. 8).

For many transgender/nonbinary persons, their personal lives became political footballs in 2021, when at least 250 anti-trans bills were proposed in most states. These bills include prohibition of trans youth playing on sports teams that are "consistent with their gender identity" (Schneiberg, 2021) and receiving gender-affirming health care such as puberty blockers and hormone treatment. Both children and teens testified in state hearings to explain why these bills would be harmful. Also, the "bathroom bill" issue arose again in 2021 when Tennessee also passed bills restricting access to public bathrooms for transgender persons (Kreusi & Mattise, 2021).

In reaction to the wave of anti-trans bills, President Biden spoke out clearly in his first speech to Congress. "To all transgender Americans watching at home, especially the young people. You're so brave. I want you to know your president has your back" (Biden cited in Sopelsa & Yurcaba, 2021).

However, one trans activist stated:

> It's very hard to be us. This is not easy. If you are a cis(gender) person... probably you can hop in your car, go to Target, go buy something, and come back without having to think about 20 different ways that you're going to keep yourself safe.... We have the weight of having to be unwanted in a world.... Most human beings would rather have us not exist and want us dead, not here, not existing ("Why trans people react the way they do" video on Facebook page of activist Jeffrey Marsh).

In this political climate of overt hostility to transgender/nonbinary persons, it is not surprising that OUD is at a higher rate in this population than for cisgender persons. An analysis of the U.S. Transgender Survey of over 26,000 persons reveals that nonbinary persons faced a higher risk for prescription drug misuse than binary persons "possibly due to less societal affirmation." Also, minority-stress correlated with prescription drug misuse, so this study "highlights the importance of interventions to reduce discrimination" against transgender/nonbinary persons (Kidd, et al., 2021).

Unfortunately, research on this population and SUD (much less OUD) is scarce. One meta-analysis (Glynn & van den Berg, 2017) also notes that:

- Research on interventions is "alarmingly scarce";
- Several treatment programs claimed to have culturally sensitive services but do not (only eight out of 911 programs actually had specific services);
- Treatment providers should either create services specifically for transgender/nonbinary persons or incorporate cultural sensitivity into the general services.

Discussion questions

- On the federal level, the policy response to the states' anti-trans legislation is the Equality Act (HR 5) that passed the House in 2021. Look up the status of the bill—did it become law? Discuss the fate of this bill.
- On YouTube, look up the testimonies of young trans activists, such as Kai Shappley about the anti-trans bills. How would you rate their effectiveness in persuading legislators? Suggest ways to build on their testimonies.
- One parent of a six-year-old trans child encourages cisgender adults to speak out. "I want to watch her grow without simultaneously watching the brightness of her incrementally dulled. What she needs, now, is for adults to get loud. She and the other trans children . . . need adults to do the heavy lifting because they are only kids" (Declan, 2021). Write down three ways to advocate for trans rights for both children and adults.

8
The role of criminal justice in the opioid crisis

Introduction

As a community activist on the South Side of Chicago, John Eason participated in the "Operation Holy Ground" effort to reduce drug trafficking. Several churches and community members in this predominantly African American area marched through the streets and prayed outside of the drug houses. The police came along to arrest many alleged dealers.

Afterward, some of the marchers met in a church basement and expressed their second thoughts about the arrests. One person said, "I know we're standing up for our neighborhood, but we are having our black children arrested here in the city for what? *White folks downstate to get jobs*!" Another stated, "*You either get a job or you become a job*" while somebody noted that "Black folks don't grow drugs or import them into our neighborhood, so why are we imprisoned the most for selling drugs?" (Eason, 2017, p. ix).

This story illustrates the problematic role of the criminal justice system in the opioid crisis. Nobody wants to live next door to a crack house. Small business owners in drug-saturated areas do not want customers to avoid their stores because of the obviously impaired persons loitering outside. The sight of used needles littering a sidewalk is troubling. Most cities have a notorious area where drug use and criminal activity prevail. The "west side" of Columbus, Ohio is one of those spots, a neighborhood I would frequent when I mentored the foster youth living there. One adolescent girl could not even walk the short distance to her school on her own because of the street harassment and drug offers she would have faced. Johns often drove in that neighborhood looking to pay for sex, knowing that female drug users were vulnerable and needed money.

The author's bias regarding the criminal justice system reflects the marchers' ambivalence, since the system may be necessary for a stable society but is also deeply flawed. In my practice experience, I have met clients who started their recovery journeys while incarcerated. Some clients received excellent services, including in-depth counseling and meaningful psychoeducation about topics such as coping skills. Others, unfortunately, received little or no assistance for their SUD or mental health issues while behind bars. This inconsistency appears based on which county or city they served time in—not the level of need.

The criminal justice system continues to be a critical component of the opioid crisis. One client told me that he was on a meth binge, which he could not stop until he got arrested. Forced to get "clean" while in jail, he was able to reset his life. Another client cried with relief when telling me that her son, an active user who was living on the streets, had been arrested again so there was new hope he could link up with recovery services. In some cases, then, incarceration might be the last resort for those with advanced SUD.

This chapter strives to expose the reader to the complex intersection of the criminal justice system with the opioid crisis, especially the impacts of mass incarceration. These issues are too complex and multifaceted for any easy answers, so further research and discussion are essential as we strive to incorporate more "justice" into the criminal justice system. Box 8.1 presents a case study of a justice-involved individual who needs relapse prevention and other services.

Box 8.1 Case study

Maria, 32, had started using opioids in her teens. Her parents had sent her to treatment three times as they struggled to help her. She was on probation for several offenses, mostly drug possession and shoplifting. While out of jail, she lived at home and was actively using to the point of crisis. Her father believed that only being arrested again would stop her downward cycle. He reported her drug use to the probation officer and she was arrested. Then she was released again, returning home to live with her parents with three months of "clean" time. She comes to your agency one week after her release.

Micro level:

▷ Relapse prevention is obviously the highest priority for Maria. What interventions would you suggest so Maria can maintain her sobriety?
▷ How would you help her to get a job, the first step toward independence?

> If Maria is angry at her father for contacting the probation officer, what interventions would you suggest for the family to resolve the tension?

Mezzo level: After Maria leaves the building, you hear a coworker complain about "junkies just out of jail" and other derogatory language. If you were the supervisor, how would you ensure agency-wide changes to ensure that persons with SUD are treated with dignity and respect?

Macro level: Maria is fortunate to have a supportive family, but many persons with SUD are estranged from their friends and family because of their past behaviors (e.g., stealing from them to buy drugs). These persons will need more intensive services to get back on their feet.

> What ideas do you suggest for persons just released from jail or prison who are new in their recovery?

The era of mass incarceration

The concept of mass incarceration in the United States is certainly hard to dispute, since prisons/jails have experienced an explosive growth since 1980. Although the United States has only 5 percent of the world's population, it has 25 percent of the world's total of incarcerated persons—a statistic often attributed to "misguided drug laws and draconian sentencing requirements" (Howard University, n.d.). Incarcerated persons may be serving long sentences in prison, or they may cycle in and out of jail (called jail churn). In 2020, five million persons went through jail churn and faced a higher risk of contracting COVID-19 in those cramped facilities (The Justice Collaborative, 2020).

A review of these numbers confirm that mass incarceration does exist:

The American criminal justice system holds almost 2.3 million people in 1,833 state prisons, 110 federal prisons, 1,772 juvenile correctional facilities, 3,134 local jails, 218 immigration detention facilities, and 80 Indian Country jails as well as in military prisons, civil commitment centers, state psychiatric hospitals, and prisons in the U.S. territories (Sawyer & Wagner, 2020).

The high number of facilities shows the fragmentation and complexity of the system, besides the impossibility of generalizing about any average experience.

The causes of mass incarceration are interlinked and controversial. Below is a partial list of possible causes:

- Moral panic, the term that describes a population overreacting to a social problem that is exaggerated by the mass media (Cohen, 1972). This results in the public's overwhelming fear of crime despite the decreased crime rate of almost 50 percent since the 1990s (Farrell, Tilley, & Tseloni, 2014);
- The "tough on crime" stance taken by politicians who want to win votes. One example is California's Proposition 184, called the "Three Strikes and You're Out Law." Enacted in 1994, it mandated life sentences for the third conviction. "It was intended to 'keep murderers, rapists, and child molesters behind bars, where they belong,'" but around half of the prisoners were serving time for nonviolent offenses. In fact, some "clients have been given life sentences for offenses including stealing one dollar in loose change from a parked car, possessing less than a gram of narcotics, and attempting to break into a soup kitchen" (Stanford Law School Three Strikes Project, no date). In 2012, voters approved a reform bill to release prisoners convicted for nonviolent and minor offenses.
- The War on Drugs, which will be discussed below;
- Structural unemployment, leading to more property crimes (Gilmore, 2007);
- Racial cleansing, an attempt to incarcerate as many persons of color as possible, as evidenced by the disproportionate number in jail or prison (Gilmore, 2007);
- The rise of private prisons, which creates the profit motive for stricter laws and more prisoners (ACLU, no date);
- The employment opportunities for rural Americans where most prisons are located, especially for prison guards. This has raised concerns that the United States has shifted from being dominated by a military-industrial complex to a prison-industrial complex (Gilmore, 2007).

Whatever the causes of mass incarceration, the disproportionate impact on persons of color is well documented. Blacks/AA represent 13.4 percent of the U.S. population but comprise 38.1 percent of the incarcerated population (www.census.gov/ and www.bop.gov/about/statistics/race). Michelle Alexander, author of *The New Jim Crow: Mass Incarceration in the*

Age of Colorblindness (2012), writes that "We have not ended racial caste in America; we have merely redesigned it" (Alexander, 2012, p. 20). "Jim Crow" is the term used for the Southern racial segregation laws in force after the Civil War until 1968. Black codes, for example, forced Blacks/AA to work for lower pay and even in labor camps (no author, 2021). She also writes that "The system of mass incarceration is based on the prison label, not prison time.... Mass incarceration, like Jim Crow, helps to define the meaning and significance of race in America. Indeed, the stigma of criminality functions in much the same way that the stigma of race once did. It justifies a legal, social, and economic boundary between 'us' and 'them'" (Alexander, 2012, pp. 40, 43–44).

In this context, it is indeed disturbing that Blacks/AA are the most likely group in the United States to be incarcerated—six times more likely than whites. Latinx are also overrepresented in the prison population because they are three times more likely than whites to be incarcerated (www.fwd.us/news/coronavirus-disparity/). The War on Drugs, as discussed below, is one explanation for the striking racial/ethnic disparities.

Discussion question

The author cited the "fwd.us" organization as one source for the above section. Look up this organization and determine if this was a credible source. Their report used the Sentencing Project as a source. Look up the "About us" tab for this organization and determine its credibility. What is your criteria for your determinations?

Other gaping inequalities also appear in the criminal "justice" system, including class and geography. For example, a civil rights group wrote the report "Too Poor to Pay: How Arkansas's Offender-Funded Justice System Drives Poverty & Mass Incarceration" about how the new version of debtors' prison was trapping low-income persons "too many of them African American or minority, in a cycle of escalating debt and unnecessary incarceration" (Braden, et al., 2019). Even for minor offenses, these persons were charged exorbitant fines and fees. In contrast, Colorado passed a law to ban the practice of jailing persons too poor to pay their fines (ACLU Colorado, no date). It is well advised, then, to be arrested in Colorado rather than Arkansas if you are too poor to pay the fines.

Bail is also an issue, with the median cost being $10,000 in 2016. This bail amount represents eight months of wages for the average defendant (Rabuy & Kopf, 2016). As noted above, race and class intersect on this issue because "Bail practices are frequently discriminatory, with black and Latino men assessed higher bail amounts than white men for similar crimes by 35 and 19 percent on average, respectively" (Onyekwere, 2021). Another aspect of discrimination is that defendants who are unable to post bail are four times more likely to be sentenced time in prison than their counterparts. Being held for an uncertain amount of time can cause so much emotional distress that some defendants commit suicide (Onyekwere, 2021).

Besides debtors' prison, geographic disparities are also evident in the ever-changing marijuana laws that vary from state to state. Five states ban all marijuana use, while 26 permit only medical use. The other states now allow both medical and recreational marijuana uses (2021 status from DISA Global Solutions at disa.com). Meanwhile, Oregon recently decriminalized street drugs, so people are ticketed but not arrested for possession of small amounts (Johnson, 2021).

Discussion questions

"Imprisonment is no longer a symptom of deviance; its sheer extent challenges us to think about incarceration as an increasingly normal event in the lives of young disadvantaged men" (Western, Pattillo, & Weiman, 2004, p. 3). These words were written in 2004, when 1.5 million Americans were incarcerated with the rate of 724 per 100,000 (Department of Justice, 2005). In 2020, 2.3 million Americans were incarcerated with the rate of 698 per 100,000 (Sawyer & Wager, 2020).

- The term "young disadvantaged men" implies what types of disadvantages?
- In your opinion, is it more accurate to stress the total numbers (1.5 million vs. 2.3 million) or the rates (724 vs. 698)? Why is this important for the sake of intellectual honesty?

The War on Drugs

The War on Drugs, defined here as the policy to primarily use law enforcement instead of treatment options to curb drug use, has a centuries-old history in the United States The first federal law was the Smoking Opium Exclusion Act in 1909—even then, opioids were used widely. Subsequent laws have criminalized the use and trade of certain substances. The most notorious one, of course, was the 1919 Prohibition Act that forbade the nonmedical use of alcohol (History.com editors, 2019). Obviously, liquor is now legal for adults, and the reader may even be doing jello shots while reading this chapter.

Others, though, would consider 1971 to be the starting date of the War on Drugs when President Richard Nixon stated that "America's public enemy number one in the United States is drug abuse. In order to fight and defeat this enemy, it is necessary to wage a new, all-out offensive" (cited in Scherlen, 2012). At the time, protests about civil rights and the Vietnam War were occurring, and he thought he needed a creative way to handle the protesters. According to former Nixon domestic policy chief John Ehrlichman, "We knew we couldn't make it illegal to be either against the war or black, but by getting the public to associate the hippies with marijuana and blacks with heroin. And then criminalizing both heavily, we could disrupt those communities. . . and vilify them night after night on the evening news" (LoBianco, 2016).

For decades presidents, such as Ronald Reagan (e.g., "just say no" to drugs) and Bill Clinton (e.g., Plan Colombia), had marshalled enormous resources to reduce drug use in the United States (Scherlen, 2012). However, attempts to cut off the supply on both international and domestic levels have failed. Fifty years after Nixon's speech, a 2021 University of Pennsylvania study concluded that the United States had spent one trillion dollars on this effort.

Commentators from both left and right have stated that the War on Drugs has failed because drug use has only risen. "Law enforcement was given an unprecedented level of authority with measures like mandatory sentencing and no-knock warrants, recently reevaluated after the death of Breonna Taylor, who was shot and killed by police in a botched drug raid" (Lee, 2021).

"'What good is it doing for us?'" asked Aaron Hinton, a community activist profiled in an article questioning the worth of the War on Drugs. As a Black/AA male, he had seen many in his cohort be sent to prison. "'They're spending so much money on these prisons to keep kids locked up,'" Hinton said, shaking his head. "'They don't even spend a fraction of that money sending them to college or some kind of school'" (cited in Mann, 2021). Having seen substance use disorder (SUD) firsthand, including his mother's overdose death from opioids, he believed that the "tough on crime" approach made it much harder for persons like his mother to get help (Mann, 2021).

Besides the massive waste of one trillion dollars, the War on Drugs has played a role in the racial disparity issue in the U.S. criminal justice system. The most outrageous example was the disproportionate 1:100 ratio of penalties for powder cocaine vs. crack. A person (usually Black/AA) arrested with one gram of crack cocaine would be sentenced for the same five years as a person (usually white) with 100 grams of powder cocaine. Whites were the majority of crack cocaine users, but "the overwhelming number of arrests nonetheless came from black communities who were disproportionately impacted by the facially neutral, yet illogically harsh, crack penalties" (Taifa, 2021).

The War on Drugs also has an international dimension, especially since the United States has been involved in Colombia and other countries. The above-mentioned Plan Colombia, for example, was a joint effort that started in 1999 between the United States and Colombian governments to combat narcotrafficking. It appears to have failed. Government planes sprayed fields of coca plants with herbicide, and the farmers found ways to avoid the spraying. Traffickers used different routes to avoid law enforcement. Nearby countries, such as Bolivia, developed their own coca production while the drug cartels' activities spread north into Mexico. Colombia's militarized police heightened tensions within the country, which flared into civil war in 2021. These unintended consequences did not address the major cause of coca production: the high demand for cocaine. "Plan Colombia did little to focus on demand-side strategies to reduce cocaine production. Instead, it relied on supply-side strategies, such as crop eradication and drug interdiction operations" (Lee, 2020).

Another international dimension is that other countries also have their own version of their War on Drugs. UNAIDS, the United Nations organization that fights HIV/AIDS, has presented a blunt message about the impact of the War on Drugs on those most affected:

> "People who use drugs have been the biggest casualties of the global war on drugs. Vilified and criminalized for decades, they have been pushed to the margins of society...(with) Billions of dollars spent, a considerable amount of blood spilt and the imprisonment of millions" not making a dent in the drug trade or number of users (UNAIDS cited in Khindaria, 2019).

From a public health perspective, the War on Drugs has resulted in more HIV infections because punishment instead of treatment was stressed worldwide.

Box 8.2 Is the War on Drugs the major cause of mass incarceration?

If it is hard to dispute that mass incarceration exists, it is harder to determine whether the War on Drugs is the major cause of this problem. Pfaff (2017) argues in *Locked In: The True Causes of Mass Incarceration and How to Achieve Real Reform* that other causes are to blame. Before reviewing his position, a critical reader should first analyze the source.

- Who is the author? Pfaff is a law professor at Fordham University, which indicates solid credentials.
- Who is the publisher? Basic Books, a well-established publisher. When considering any book as a potential source, it is wise to look for two red flags. First, a self-published book has probably escaped any peer reviews or other ways to establish credibility. It may or may not be a reliable source. Secondly, some publishers are openly biased with the understanding that readers are aware of it. Regnery Publishing, for example, specializes in conservative books. IG Publisher has periodically published an anthology called "Proud to be a Liberal." Researchers should not reject books from such biased publishers, but acknowledge the bias if appropriate.
- Who has praised Pfaff's work? Conservative periodicals such as *National Review* and the *Economist* have commended his work, besides liberals such as Chris Hayes (MSNBC show host). The book's back cover includes blurbs (positive reviews) from three criminal justice experts.

Now that Pfaff's credibility has been determined, keeping an open mind to his argument is essential. In an interview before the book's publication, he states that the five-fold increase in the prison population since 1980 should be explained by dividing the time period into two periods. Until 1991, a sharp rise in crime created a need for more jails and prisons. Since 1991, though, the crime rate has dropped considerably but more persons were behind bars. He notes that "the probability that a district attorney files a felony charge against an arrestee goes from about 1 in 3, to 2 in 3. So over the course of the 1990s and 2000s, district attorneys just got much more aggressive in how they filed charges" (Neyfakh, 2015).

His book also posits that the "standard story" of the War on Drugs ignores the fact that only a small percentage of state prisoners (the bulk of the incarcerated population) were convicted of drug charges. Instead, violent crimes were the major reason for incarceration. The "standard story" also stresses the length of sentences, another factor which he disputes. Although long sentences are often handed out, "most people serve short stints in prison, on the order of one to three years, and there's not a lot of evidence that the amount of time spent in prison has changed that much" (Pfaff, 2017, p. 6). Also, he counters the "prison industrial complex" concept, which blames the rise of private prisons that profit from more convictions, by emphasizing the public sector's heavy lobbying efforts to keep prisons in their counties.

The standard story, though, does include a topic that he is concerned about—racial discrimination in the criminal justice system. Because of racial segregation, "urban prosecutors (who) are elected at the county level, where political power is concentrated in the wealthier, whiter suburbs" become aggressive and charge an excessive number of felonies (Pfaff, 2017, p. 7).

Discussion questions

> An in-depth analysis of a book's trustworthiness would also include a review of its cited sources. For instance, somebody once gave me a book containing antisemitic accusations of a global conspiracy. The citations showed a poor quality of scholarship, besides enlightenment about the author's mindset. Find a politically controversial book (e.g., Ann Coulter's *Demonic: How the Liberal Mob is Endangering America* or Terry Eagleton's *Why Marx was Right*) and review the citations. What did you learn from this exercise?

> What is the difference between a drug charge and a drug-related charge? For instance, a person may be arrested for burglary due to their SUD but not be charged with drug possession. Pfaff uses the criteria of "drug charges" that may not include other persons with SUD who are incarcerated. Research the rate of *drug-related* convictions on websites such as Prison Policy Initiative (www.prisonpolicy.org). Does this information affect your opinion of Pfaff's argument about the War on Drugs?

Illustration 8.1 The intersection of drug use and criminal law (Shutterstock number is in picture).
Credit: © ERIK Miheyeu/Shutterstock

Discussion question

How has the War on Drugs affected your opinion of a country involved in the drug trade, such as Mexico or Colombia? How much of it is based on fact and how much on media images, such as the drug traffickers featured in the *Breaking Bad* show? Box 8.2 examines the question of whether the War on Drugs is really the cause of mass incarceration.

Drug use and treatment in prisons/jails

Despite being locked up, incarcerated persons can still access substances that are smuggled into the facility. Anecdotal accounts can provide insights, although generalizing from them is not advised. For example, one medical professional who has worked in Ohio prisons for 15 years told me that "if the guys don't want to quit, they don't quit." She said that the treatment programs, including MAT (in this case, Vivitrol), and twelve-step meetings were effective. However, "people just do the programs just to get out early." During the COVID-19 lockdown, outsiders threw packages into the prison so the inmates could still access drugs. She said that most inmates had no drug of choice, since "they do whatever is available." Marijuana, fentanyl, heroin, and suboxone were common. K-2, a form of rat poison, was causing seizures, paranoid episodes, and delusions. She told me about a man who thought he was Superman, so he jumped off a ledge and broke his leg.

Heart problems and abscesses were also some of the drug-related health conditions. Although drug use was mostly a security problem, the medical staff bore most of the burden. Besides being understaffed, the prison had some "dirty staff" who were involved in drug trafficking. She said that she had seen no improvements in the drug problem during the 15 years on the job: "It's there. It's not going anywhere." (Anonymous, 2021).

Besides this professional's experiences with drug use in prison, reports such as "Overjailed and undertreated: How the failure to provide treatment for substance use in prisons and jails fuels the overdose epidemic" (ACLU, 2021) provide a compelling look at the issue. About one-fourth of the prison/jail population has an opioid use disorder (OUD). The report advocates for widespread use of MAT in prisons/jails as "basic healthcare for individuals with OUD . . . MAT reduces the risk of death from any cause by 85 percent, and the risk of death from an overdose by 75 percent in the weeks following release" (ACLU, 2021, p. 4.). As there are three types of MAT (methadone, buprenorphine/suboxone, and naltrexone only/Vivitrol), facilities should make all three types available instead of just one. Forcing a person to go through withdrawal before being administered Vivitrol, for instance, could lead to health complications and even death if the person has a co-morbid condition. Also, suicides and overdoses are more likely to occur if the persons receive inadequate treatment.

Discussion question

In your opinion, what would be the strongest argument AGAINST providing MAT to persons in prisons/jails?

Social costs of mass incarceration

Whether or not the War on Drugs continues to dominate the criminal justice system, its effects will last for a long time. Sampson (2011) proposes the concept of the "incarceration ledger" to examine the costs and benefits of mass incarceration. For decades, criminologists had focused on the benefits of incarceration such as public safety (i.e., the streets should be safer) and deterrence (i.e., potential criminals will decide to obey the law to avoid jail or prison). However, Sampson challenges the researcher to also look at the costs of incarceration that affect families and the wider community.

Related to this concept is "coercive mobilization," which posits that the community is destabilized when several of its members cycle in and out of prison (Frost & Gross, 2012). A city neighborhood, for example, may have to cope with a fraying social network when so many members are missing and so many families are directly affected by mass incarceration. Does locking up so many people really decrease the local crime rate? According to a study of Tallahassee that utilized geocoded data, the answer was mixed. Although the crime rate went down if there were moderate rates of coercive mobilization (i.e., incarceration), the crime rate actually increased if there was a higher rate of coercive mobilization (Frost & Gross, 2012).

In this context, social workers may question whether the social costs of incarceration are worth "getting tough on crime." For example, the health consequences on the female partners and family can be devastating. In an aptly titled article "Things fall apart: Health consequences of mass imprisonment for African American women," Lee and Wildeman (2013) discuss how policymakers should take note of this problem because "an African American female may be the daughter of an incarcerated father, partner of an incarcerated man. . . . We need to better understand what implications experiences with incarceration have at each point in the life course, as well as how cumulative experiences may be particularly detrimental to health and wellbeing" (Lee & Wildeman, 2013, p. 48). These women are at higher risk for obesity, diabetes, and hypertension because of the stress caused by:

- Financial problems as described below;
- Family strain when mothers must become single parents or kinship providers must take in children;
- Social isolation caused by the stigma of being related to an incarcerated man, which may lead to less emotional and financial support;

> Intermittent and often unpredictable arrivals and departures related to prison cycling. A wife or girlfriend of an incarcerated man may be uncertain about starting a new relationship while in this limbo.

However, the authors note that if the partner had been abusive, then the incarceration can be a positive life event for the woman. In most cases, though, the socio-economic status (SES) of these women is diminished at a time when they may be isolated from their communities due to stigma.

As noted above, one major stressor of having a family member behind bars is the often-overwhelming financial cost. A 2015 report titled "Who pays? The true cost of incarceration on families" includes this quote by the wife of an inmate: "I feel like I've been locked up along with my husband for the past 30 years. I work hard to support him and to keep my family from falling within the same cycles of abuse and poverty. But . . . the burden of tens of thousands of dollars in court fees and fines keep our family down" (Ella Baker Center for Human Rights, 2015, no page).

The financial burden of having a family member in jail or prison may include the possible loss of the man's paycheck, besides the subsequent job discrimination later on (Center for Human Rights, 2015). The costs of keeping in touch with him can be expensive. For instance, some 15-minute calls may cost up to $30—or even $60—because the phone system is a monopoly with little federal oversight (Lecher, 2015). Phone and transportation costs have resulted in 34 percent of those surveyed stating that they had gone into debt just to keep in touch with their family member. Court-related costs are an average of $13,607—which is almost the annual income of a minimum-wage worker ($15,000) (Center for Human Rights, 2015).

Discussion questions

> Over 80 percent of the affected family members paying for the costs are women (Center for Human Rights, 2015). Would you consider this to be a feminist issue (i.e., a stress on female empowerment)?
> The Center for Human Rights suggests policy changes to reform the criminal justice system (e.g., reduce mass incarceration and improve re-entry services). Consider proposing a program aimed to address the families' needs. Besides the families themselves, who would benefit from the program? Who would oppose it and why?

Impact of mass incarceration on justice-involved persons

One man describes his prison experience and its aftermath: "It's not the physical danger. It's the mental drain, the spiritual drain, and psychological drain that it puts on a person. The prison was designed to debilitate. To dehumanize you. You're no longer an individual. You're a number, and you are a part of a bunch of other numbers. I spent twenty-seven years just battling the effects of trying to be made nominal. I hate being marginalized. I want to be important" (Miller, 2021, p. 206).

Almost 20 million Americans have a felony record, with 45,000 federal and state laws regulating their lives long after their release. These restrictions, which vary by state, affect:

- Employment;
- Housing;
- Right to vote and hold public office;
- Rights as a parent and even the right to adopt a child;
- Availability of student loans;
- Eligibility for benefits, such as food stamps (SNAP);
- Ability to leave the country or even the state (Miller, 2021).

The story of Yvette exemplifies the ongoing punishments of a felony record years after release. After a sports injury forced her to take off from her steady job, she applied for public assistance. When asked if she had ever been arrested, she said "yes" even though it was over 10 years ago. People then found out that she was an "ex-con. That word got back to her boss. Yvette explained that she was a different person, that the old her was dead and buried. She told him she made a mistake but had been clean for over a decade. She was active in church and needed the job to care for her family. Besides, she was good at her job" (Miller, 2021, p. 156). Nevertheless, she lost her job.

Besides small-scale discrimination such as the one experienced by Yvette, large-scale discrimination can be destructive for persons involved in the criminal justice system. In 1996, the Housing Opportunity Extension Act allowed public housing authorities to evict tenants or reject applicants based on their criminal records. The Act also allowed the rejection of applications with SUD as a possible danger (Weiss, no date). Fortunately, reformers have succeeded in amending this policy. The Housing Authority of New Orleans, for example, has instituted a screening criteria for applicants with records so some may be allowed to live in public housing (Reckdahl, 2016).

Housing instability and even homelessness can result from the 1996 "one strike" regulation regarding persons involved in the criminal justice system. One woman stated, "I lost my apartment. . . . I went to jail for selling drugs, which I wasn't selling at the time. They were for my use. I had some bags on me and I got busted . . . (but) I was not doing nothing in my apartment. I know better. I got kids" (Dickson-Gomez, et al., 2008, no page). Despite having served her time years ago, she still has trouble finding housing and has to live with a man in a destructive relationship. For nonsubsidized housing (i.e., the free market), the major barrier for these persons is the prevalent use of criminal background checks by apartment managers. Box 8.3 describes the impact of digital punishment, in which the internet provides false or misleading information.

Box 8.3 Digital punishment

Imagine getting arrested outside a night club where a fight broke out, but you are released without any charges. All over the internet, your mugshot is displayed, and your reputation is ruined. "It is rather devastating. It is public shaming. Embarrassment is an understatement" (Lageson, 2020, p. 3).Or imagine that a decades-old conviction gets entangled with another man's record, resulting in you being falsely associated with multiple offenses. This results in landlords denying you housing and other forms of discrimination.

> It's too much, it's too frustrating. You ain't done nothing for thirty-something years and then all of a sudden you want to get an apartment and you can't. You're just stuck at where you are at. That's just terrible. It's a bad feeling. It's like I've been on a standstill. But I still keep going because I gotta set an example for my kids and grandkids. That's what I do; I set an example. I had no choice, man. (Lageson, 2020, p. 3)

Many people would like to believe that online felony records are not only accurate but used for appropriate purposes. The book *Digital Punishment: Privacy, Stigma, and the Harms of Data-Driven Criminal Justice* (Lageson, 2020), though, provides startling evidence to the contrary. Background checks can be fragmented, mistake-ridden, and often misused. Because private corporations are making huge profits from obtaining data from the cash-strapped law enforcement agencies, these companies have little incentive to reduce the impact of the digital punishment.

Social justice also plays a role in this issue. "Widespread internet stigma based on criminal justice system contact disparately impacts non-white and poor people, especially those without training in technological systems and those who don't have the resources to make a claim to their personal privacy or their digital identity, increasing the harms" (Lageson, 2020, p. 9). Social workers should be aware that their clients may have to fight the online shaming that could damage their careers and other harms.

Discussion questions
> If a client needs help to expunge or correct their record, what local resources would be available? Research free legal clinics and other options.
> What policy ideas do you suggest to fight digital punishment?

Discussion questions

> *Halfway Home: Race, Punishment, and the Afterlife of Mass Incarceration* (Miller, 2021) advocates for ex-prisoners who face struggles trying to re-enter society. The book includes not only factual exposition but the author's personal stories about being the son and brother of convicted felons. He has served as a chaplain in Cook County Jail and worked with several ex-prisoners. Thus, this book shows the "personal is the political" idea that his direct involvement deserves as much discussion as the "big picture" facts. Do you agree with this approach? Why or why not?
> If you were to write the screening criteria for public housing applicants with a record, how would you determine who could be accepted? For instance, what should be the lookback period for how long ago the conviction occurred—five years? Should arrests without convictions be counted against an applicant?
> For the screening criteria, what rules would you set for an applicant with a history of SUD or who is a current user? For example, you may consider the type of drug (e.g., marijuana vs. fentanyl), the period of

sobriety (e.g., one year or five years), and proof that they are working on their recovery (e.g., attendance slips from a 12-step meeting).

Fixing a broken system

"Our country's criminal justice system is broken—and it has been broken for decades. You cannot deny justice to any American without it affecting all Americans" (Senator Cory Booker, cited in Grassley press release, 2018). The First Step Act, which was passed in 2018, confronted the problems caused by mass incarceration. The Act included these provisions:

- Sentencing reform for "low-risk inmates" to have shorter federal prison sentences (Grassley, 2018). Also, a "safety valve" now allows a judge to issue a sentence that is shorter than the mandatory minimum (Grawert, 2020).
- Prison reform for better conditions in federal prisons, such as no longer using restraints on pregnant women. A renewed focus on rehabilitation instead of punishment is another legislative goal (Grawert, 2020).
- Prevention of "career and violent criminals" to earn time credits if they are seen as high risk (Grassley, 2018).

One year after its implementation, the federal prison population has decreased by at least five thousand. Unfortunately, the COVID-19 pandemic slowed the progress of prison reform for obvious reasons. The Bureau of Prisons (BOP) asserts "Rolling out this system as intended will be a challenge, however, in part because BOP programs are already understaffed and underfunded. Around 25 percent of people spending more than a year in federal prison have completed *zero* programs. A recent BOP budget document described a lengthy waiting list for basic literacy programs" (Grawert, 2020).

The First Step Act exemplifies the need for diligent vigilance regarding a bill's real-life implementation. Indeed, passing a bill is only the first step for any reform (pun intended). Advocates must ensure that agencies involved (e.g., Bureau of Prisons) are provided enough funding and guidance to fulfill the goals.

Three years later, Senator Grassley and his co-sponsors introduced the First Step Implementation Act of 2021 to the Senate. The expansion of this bill would include:

- "Allowing courts to apply the FSA (First Step Act) sentencing reform provisions to reduce sentences imposed prior to the enactment of the FSA;
- Broadening the safety valve provision to allow courts to sentence below a mandatory minimum for nonviolent controlled substance offenses...;
- Allowing courts to reduce sentences imposed on juvenile offenders who have served more than 20 years;
- Providing for the sealing or expungement of records of nonviolent juvenile offenses; and,
- Requiring the Attorney General to establish procedures ensuring that only accurate criminal records are shared for employment-related purposes" (Grassley, 2023).

Box 8.4 describes the reform efforts to correct the injustice of racial disparities in the criminal justice system.

Discussion questions

- Pick one of the provisions in the 2021 Act and write a paragraph that argues for or against it.
- The 2021 Act was endorsed by the American Conservative Union, which likely increased the chances of support among conservative lawmakers. On its website (conservativejustice.org) is a list of the 12 Principles of Justice, including "the harm done by the sentence should never be greater than the harm caused by the crime." Based on these principles, do you think that the American Conservative Union would be a good ally for criminal justice reform despite their stance on voting restrictions and other controversies?

Second look laws

When should a person who has been incarcerated for several years receive a "second look" at their sentences? The Model Penal Code suggests a judicial review after 15 years, while some experts recommend 10 years (Ghandnoosh, 2021).

On the federal level, senators introduced the Second Look Act of 2019 (S2146), but the Judiciary Committee did not act on it. Below is the bill summary from the U.S. Congress website (www.congress.gov/bill/116th-congress/senate-bill/2146?r=6&s=1):

> This bill allows a defendant who has served at least 10 years in prison to petition a federal court for a sentence reduction.
>
> Specifically, a court may reduce the prison term for a defendant if (1) the imposed prison term was more than 10 years; (2) the defendant has served at least 10 years in custody; and (3) the court finds that the defendant is not a danger to public safety, is ready for reentry, and the interests of justice warrant a sentence modification. The bill outlines the factors a court may consider in reducing a prison term.
>
> Further, the bill creates a rebuttable presumption of release for a defendant who is 50 years of age or older on the date of the petition.

Although this bill did not proceed past committee, the issue of older prisoners prompted legislative action when hundreds of them died from COVID-19. Living in a communal setting, such as prison, became life-threatening during the pandemic. Senator Grassley and other senators sponsored S312 in 2021, the COVID-19 Safer Detention Act. In his press release, Grassley noted that "Elderly offenders, the fastest-growing portion of the prison population, have much lower rates of recidivism and are much more expensive to incarcerate due to their health care needs" (Grassley, 2023).

If the second look approach to criminal justice reform had stalled on the federal level in 2021, it has thrived on the state level. Reformers argue that many of the long-term prisoners have been "oversentenced" and deserve a second look at their sentences.

The arguments for second look laws include:

- Expenses of incarceration "without delivering any real public safety return";
- If a prisoner has transformed himself and 'aged out' of the phase in which people are most likely to commit crimes;
- These prisoners are more likely to be older and more vulnerable to health problems, especially during the COVID-19 pandemic;
- Changing social attitudes that had once endorsed severe punishments for drug use such as marijuana (OSU Moritz College of Law, 2020).

Box 8.4 Good news about the racial disparity in sentencing

In the federal court system, the racial disparity for drug crimes has decreased from 47 months (almost four years) in 2009 to nothing in 2018. Blacks/AA and whites are serving sentences that are equal. For other crimes, the racial disparity is less than six months. "This remarkable but unheralded progress reflects 15 years of reforms by the courts, Congress and, most important, the Justice Department" (Lane, 2021).

This progress resulted from the efforts such as the 2010 Fair Sentencing Act to decrease the sentencing gap between crack cocaine and powder cocaine from 100:1 ration to 18:1. Also, "shifts in the prosecutorial use of mandatory minimums played a critical role in decreasing black–white sentencing inequality (Light, 2021). In 2013, the Attorney General told federal prosecutors to stop seeking the maximum sentence for nonviolent offenders.

However, more work awaits the advocates for true criminal justice. This good news only applies in the federal courts—only one-eighth of the incarcerated persons in the United States. State laws dominate the criminal justice system. The ratio of African American persons involved in the entire criminal justice system compared to whites is 5.1 to 1, which had decreased from 8.3 to 1 in 2000 but is still shocking (Lane, 2021).

Mandatory minimum laws also affect the racial disparity. In 2021, Senators Mike Lee and Dick Durbin introduced the Smarter Sentencing Act to allow federal judges to review individual cases of nonviolent drug offenses. Durbin stated, "Mandatory minimum penalties have played a large role in the explosion of the U.S. prison population, often leading to sentences that are unfair, fiscally irresponsible, and a threat to public safety." And Lee stated, "Our current federal sentencing laws are out of date and often counterproductive" (Judiciary Committee, 2021). This is a bipartisan bill, which increases its chances for success.

Action steps
- Look up the current status of the Smarter Sentencing Act. Did it pass the Senate or did it die in committee? Did it become law?
- Look up the supporters of the Smarter Sentencing Act and explore the organizations' websites. Do you consider these supporters to be sufficient or would you suggest other possible supporters?

> Contact your senators and representative about the racial disparity issue. Encourage people to advocate on behalf of fair sentencing.
> Research your state's laws regarding mandatory minimums. Have they resulted in racial disparity or other injustices? A good way to start is to contact your state representative and senator's offices and ask for constituent services. Explain that you are a student who needs research assistance on policy. If the staff cannot help you, they might be able to suggest a resource.

The Sentencing Project is one major player in this reform effort. The research study titled "A Second Look at Injustice" (Ghandnoosh, 2021) states that over 200,000 persons were serving life sentences with nearly half of them African American. Over 25 states have introduced second look laws to provide judicial review of long sentences. California, for example, enacted a law that demonstrates the importance of bipartisan cooperation—especially with the prosecutors' support.

Discussion questions

> Write the strongest argument you can think of against the second look laws. What would be an appropriate response to this opposition?
> If thousands of older prisoners were released without proper preparation for their re-entry into the community, what could be the result? Consider what you would do if you were the mayor of a small city with limited resources and you were just informed that 100 older prisoners will be released next week. Write a plan regarding their housing, clothing, food, and other needs. Also think about how you would ensure that they will get the proper medical care (e.g., help them apply for Medicaid).
> Does your state have a second look law? If so, research on how that has affected your community. If not, do you think that advocating for one is a good idea?

Discussion question

Policy is about numbers—who counts and who doesn't. Census data and other sources of information are critical in decisions about social services and other policy matters. However, incarcerated persons are often overlooked in data collection. In the book *Invisible Men: Mass Incarceration and the Myth of Black Progress*, Pettit (2012) argues that "the exclusion of inmates from most federally administered data collection efforts renders them effectively invisible to policymakers and social scientists. Even after leaving prison and jail, ex-inmates commonly fall outside the purview of policymakers and the microscopes of social scientists" (Pettit, 2012, p. 28). Write a policy proposal that ensures that persons involved in the criminal justice system are fairly counted and no longer invisible. What would be your strongest argument?

9
Ongoing challenges

Introduction

The opioid crisis is like a multilayered, constantly mutating creature with tentacles in most aspects of society. Its rapidly changing nature has required us to keep up with many challenges. The impact of COVID-19, which started in the United States in 2020, is especially troublesome for society. At yesterday's staff meeting, for example, we discussed how the worker shortage was affecting social services. Not only did thousands of workers die from COVID-19, but millions more are suffering from long COVID and cannot work full-time. One estimate is that 30 million working-age Americans have long COVID.

This chapter will explicate the ongoing challenges of the impact of COVID-19, co-use of methamphetamine, fentanyl, and the stigma of substance use disorder (SUD). Please note that the information on fentanyl and other synthetic opioids will need updates, since chemists are inventing new synthetics on a regular basis. For instance, "Frankenstein opioids" (nitrazene) have recently appeared in the United States. An Ohio official warned, "Frankenstein opioids are even more lethal than the drugs already responsible for so many overdose deaths" (Guzman, 2022).

The impact of COVID-19

Working as a drug counselor during the worst of the COVID-19 pandemic, I witnessed the challenges for both clients and staff. Triggers for relapse included the stimulus payments (i.e., easily accessible money being a strong temptation), besides the economic distress and relentless boredom caused by the lockdown. In my view, the worst aspect of COVID-19 for persons with SUD was the social isolation. The inability to see their family or friends increased the risk factors of depression and anxiety. Online AA/NA meetings were available, but anyone who has used Zoom and other meeting sites would understand why some clients grew tired of that format.

As a staff member, I occasionally had to use televisits instead of in-person visits. This format sometimes made it difficult to connect on an interpersonal level with the client. For example, one time a client was holding his phone parallel to his mouth so the camera focused on his nose hairs. (Yes, I am still going to therapy for that incident.)

Since I was working at a suboxone clinic where clients had to come in for their "drops" (urine drug screens), I was able to do most of the counseling in-person. The mask mandate was controversial for some clients, thus starting the session off with a negative tone. Although I strongly support mask wearing in the middle of a pandemic, I felt that it inhibited my effectiveness as a counselor. Clients could only see the top half of my face, and I would have to say, "I'm smiling but you can't see it." Worse, I had trouble reading my clients' facial expressions so I probably missed many nonverbal cues. Another time, a client was wearing a baseball cap that hid the top half of her face while she wore a SpongeBob mask. I had the eerie impression that I was talking to SpongeBob himself. (That incident produced a few nightmares, of course.)

Upon reflection, my experience of counseling persons in recovery during a pandemic has reinforced my pride in them, as they were tested by adverse circumstances. Parents had to balance their children's at-home schooling with their jobs. Those who were laid off or furloughed had to deal with financial stress. Many of my clients, though, coped with these hardships and stayed strong.

Besides these stressors, the disruption of most social service agencies was a hardship for clients and staff during the pandemic. Once during a child welfare emergency at the clinic, I called the hotline number for children's services, but it only accepted voicemail messages. Fortunately, the sheriff's department was able to contact children's services and they were able to intervene for the child's safety.

In this context, it is not surprising that the number of overdose deaths rose from April 2020 to April 2021—over 100,000, which represents a 28.5 percent increase from the year before (www.cdc.gov/nchs/pressroom/nchs_press_releases/2021/20211117.htm). The American Society of Addiction Medicine (ASAM) held a webinar in June of 2020 (i.e., three months after the lockdowns started) to discuss the anticipated impact on SUD treatment. One concern was the interruption of medicine assisted treatment (MAT), which resulted in clients facing the risk of overdose without these medications (Olsen, 2020).

When help was most needed, this disruption of most social services had a severe impact on the homeless (unsheltered) population. All communal living places, whether homeless shelters or prisons or nursing homes, had become a public health hazard because of the contagious nature of COVID-19. Many communities set up alternative care sites (ACS) to reduce the numbers in the homeless shelters. However, the shelter or ACS staff sometimes did not understand about withdrawal or harm reduction, so basic SUD services were not provided (Salisbury-Afshar, 2020).

Discussion questions

> If you were a drug counselor who worked near a new alternative care site, how would you approach the director to offer your services? If you were the local public health official, how would you ensure that SUD services were linked with the agencies that served the homeless?
> One consideration for this population is their limited access to phones and/or internet, which makes televisits impossible. (Salisbury-Afshar, 2020). Brainstorm some ideas on providing the necessary equipment for televisits, keeping in mind that the client needs to be in a private place for the visits.

Another vulnerable population was the newly released prisoners who were re-entering society, especially the estimated 80 percent with SUD (Waller, 2020). Even under the best of circumstances, re-entry can present difficulties in obtaining services, jobs, and housing. The pandemic worsened these difficulties, as these persons had trouble continuing their MAT medications and finding a job during an economic crisis. Another stressor was that they had faced a higher risk for COVID-19 exposure during their prison terms. COVID-19 also caused some states to institute a rapid release program for low-risk prisoners to decrease the prison population, which made social services for re-entry even harder to coordinate.

Discussion question

What ideas would you suggest for a re-entry program that would help the newly released prisoners with SUD to maintain their sobriety or start treatment?

Lastly, many persons with SUD had health conditions that put them at higher risk for COVID-19 complications. Dr. Nora Volkow of National Institute of Drug Abuse (NIDA) stated in 2020 that "We know very little right now about COVID-19 and even less about its intersection with substance use disorders. But we can make educated guesses based on past experience that people with compromised health . . . could find themselves at increased risk of COVID-19 and its more serious complications—for multiple physiological and social/environmental reasons" (cited in Weimar, 2020). These risk factors include the respiratory effects of opioids, methods of using drugs (e.g., inhalation and injection), and their living situations (e.g., unstable housing) (Jarvis, 2020).

Other medical considerations of the intersection between COVID-19 and SUD include:

- Person's fear of going to the ER because COVID-19 is so contagious;
- Symptoms of opioid use resembling symptoms of COVID-19;
- Increased likelihood of a person overdosing alone due to social isolation, so nobody would be around to administer naloxone or call 911; and
- Medical staff being so busy with COVID-19 patients that they may not be able to provide adequate care for patients with SUD (Weimar, 2020).

During the COVID-19 public health emergency, the need for mental health/SUD services increased dramatically with 52 percent of community mental health agencies reporting a rise in demand. However, 26 percent of them had to lay off employees, and 54 percent had to shut down programs. Despite the 2021 policy decision to increase funding for mental health/SUD services, "they don't begin to fill the gaping hole created by the recession" (Zakaria, 2021).

One key component of mental health and recovery from SUD is social support, so the lockdown triggered drug use even among those with years of recovery. The slogan "connection is the opposite of addiction" stresses the critical role of social support. Two months after the 2020 lockdown started in West Virginia, one clinic director noted that four of his clients had died and many others had stopped treatment. "Addiction makes you want to be alone. A large part of recovery is establishing a face-to-face connection—in person, not on a video. For the large majority of this population, in my opinion, the covid restrictions—everything shutting down—is far more dangerous than covid" (Jamison, 2021). As seen in Illustration 9.1, social isolation can be wrenching.

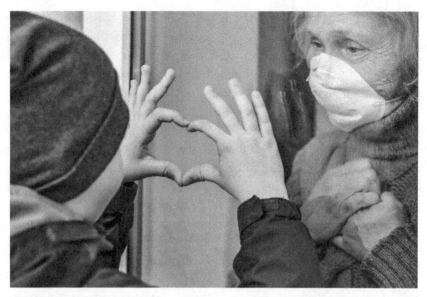

Illustration 9.1 Social isolation caused by COVID-19 (Shutterstock number in picture).

By July 2020, several communities had reported a sharp rise in overdose deaths. One expert stated that "One of the most important things we tell people to do is don't get isolated, get out of your environment or place where you are using and/or drinking and go meet up with other people working on recovery.... Now we have this pandemic, which has literally forced people to do the opposite" (Wan & Long, 2020). Another expert expressed concern about those just starting their recovery: "For newer people that need that human connection, it seems to be pretty difficult. As they say, 'An addict alone is in bad company'... I think there are going to be a lot of people who don't get a chance to get clean" (Moyer, 2020).

In a BBC newsclip titled "The epidemic within the pandemic," one interviewee states that "Quarantine is not easy. And if you just got out of rehab suffering from addiction and have mental health (issues), it's a death sentence." The sister of an overdose victim notes that "meetings, clubs, churches, all of these places were no longer available to us. I've seen people relapse that have 15 years clean" (Barrau & Miller, 2021).

Another reason for the rise in overdose deaths is that the pandemic affected the drug supply, which resulted in more fentanyl-contaminated drugs on the street. One expert stated that "Now, dealers package opioids together haphazardly, mixing dangerous clumps of fentanyl unevenly with fillers, (called the) 'Chocolate-Chip Cookie Syndrome.' You might get too many chocolate chips in your bag. You never know how much fentanyl you're actually getting" so "getting slightly more fentanyl than expected can mean the difference between life and death" (Nissen, 2021). Dr. Volkow, who was cited earlier, said that "70 percent of cocaine overdose deaths and 50 percent of methamphetamine overdose deaths also involved fentanyl. In many cases, users are unaware that their drugs are laced with the powerful painkiller, which can halt breathing even if a minute amount is ingested. In other cases, users knowingly take multiple drugs" (Bernstein & Achenbach, 2021).

How much did the pandemic affect the global drug trade? According to the research brief titled "COVID-19 and the drug supply chain: From production to trafficking to use" (United Nations Office on Drugs and Crime, 2021), the results were mixed. Obviously, the lockdown affected worldwide production, such as the poppy lancers unable to cross the border from Pakistan to Afghanistan for the seasonal production of opium. Synthetic drugs, though, were not as affected by the lockdown because often the necessary chemicals could be easily obtained or produced.

Drug trafficking went through an abrupt shift because of the interruption of commercial air travel. Couriers could no longer fly on airlines to smuggle in drugs, so some traffickers turned to maritime routes. Heroin shortages appeared in many countries, thus resulting in an increased use of synthetic drugs such as fentanyl and substitutes such as benzodiazepines (e.g., Xanax). This shortage has also led to more intravenous drug use and shared needles, which pose serious risks to the drug users (United Nations Office on Drugs and Crime, 2021).

The policy responses to the opioid crisis during the pandemic stressed telehealth over in-person visits, besides waiving the Drug Enforcement Agency (DEA) requirement that patients could only receive MAT prescriptions if they met the medical provider in person instead of via televisit (Indian Health Service, no date). It is possible that televisits will continue to be widely used if they are sufficiently reimbursed by the Center for Medicaid and Medicare and other payors.

Noting that "synthetic opioids are the primary driver of the increases in overdose deaths," the CDC recommends several policy initiatives to reduce the rate of overdose deaths, including these:

- Prioritize MAT services for high-risk persons, including those who had had a nonfatal overdose and those who were newly released from incarceration;
- Provide fentanyl test strips and other harm reduction services;
- "Provide messaging to community groups (particularly those providing services to high risk populations), community leaders, school officials, faith-based leaders, parents, students, and others about the changing illicit drug supply and risks for overdose and exposure to highly potent opioids, such as illicitly manufactured fentanyl or counterfeit drugs appearing to be legal prescription medications" (CDC, 2021).

Discussion question

Select one of the CDC recommendations and write three suggestions about how to implement it in your community. Would you expect any community resistance?

Co-use of methamphetamine

Are stimulants, such as methamphetamine (called "meth" in this section), causing a "fourth wave" of the opioid crisis? The first wave involved prescription opioids, while the second was dominated by heroin, and third by fentanyl. Recently polysubstance use, especially the combination of opioids and meth, has resulted in a rise in overdose deaths (Ciccarone, 2021). In 2019, nearly one-third of overdose deaths were caused by both opioids and stimulants (Lopez, et al., 2021).

Speedballs and goofballs are two names for the co-use of opioids and meth when they are injected together. Sometimes users administer the substances on separate occasions: "It's kind of like having a cup of coffee in the morning to wake up and a glass of wine in the evening to wind down—or using meth on Monday to get to work and heroin on Friday to ease into the weekend" (Dembosky, 2018). When heroin users could not afford their drug of choice, they turned to meth as a cheap substitute. Those who worked extra hours to pay for their opioid use used meth for energy. Also, doctors began to prescribe fewer opioids so pain pills were harder to find on the street—and meth was usually available. (Dembosky, 2018).

Besides these factors, meth can enhance the opioid high (Lopez, et al., 2021). Another reason for meth's popularity is its enhancement of sexual desire and performance. When I was interning in a public health agency, the term used for meth's effect on males was "crystal dick." One drug counselor told me that the sexual arousal can be so intense that "heterosexual men will have sex with other hetero men if they're on meth" and that "no other drug has the same effect" (Childs, 2021). In my practice experience, I had talked to meth users who were reluctant to give up the drug because they could have sex for hours.

Despite the perceived benefits of using meth, its destructive power can be crushing. Extreme paranoia can be misdiagnosed as paranoid schizophrenia because the symptoms are so similar. In 2016, for example, almost half of the emergency psychiatric visits at San Francisco General Hospital One were caused by meth use. One woman in recovery described an episode in which she jumped out of her friend's car when she thought somebody was following them. "'I literally ran a mile. I went through water, went up a tree . . . I was literally running for my life.'" She went into a stranger's house to ask for help, then entered another house to sleep in. "'But then I woke up and stole her car. I was crazy. Meth causes people to act completely insane'" (cited in Dembosky, 2019).

Another woman in recovery had started with opioid painkillers, then heroin, then meth. She described her SUD "'like God tells you that if you take another breath, your children will die. . . . You do everything you can not to take a breath. But eventually you do. That's what it's like. Your brain just screams at you'" (Vestal, 2019).

Discussion question

Dembosky (2019) writes of how the public attention on opioids has resulted in more funding for opioid use disorder (OUD), which leaves other drug programs underfunded. Suggest how to avoid competition between opioid and meth treatment programs to create more equitable funding.

When combined with opioids, the health risks of using meth are indeed disturbing. Meth use is connected to users increasing the frequency and amount of their use of opioids, thus increasing their risk of fatal overdose. Co-morbid physical and psychological conditions, such as mental illness, are more common (Lopez, et al., 2021). In one study, one-third of the polysubstance users had a severe mental illness—a 55 percent increase over those who only used opioids (Shearer, et al., 2020).

Transactional sex (i.e., trading sex for drugs) is also more likely, thus increasing the risks of HIV/AIDS and other sexually transmitted infections. Shared needles are more common among those who co-use, thus resulting in more HIV/AIDS and hepatitis C infections. On the other hand, people have used meth to decrease the use of opioids and the risk of overdose (Lopez, et al., 2021).

Another disturbing aspect of this co-use is its correlation with homelessness. The article titled "Residential eviction predicts initiation of or relapse into crystal methamphetamine use among people who inject drugs: a prospective cohort study" (Damon, et al., 2019) describes how being evicted can cause a newly homeless person to start using meth or to relapse. Drug use leading to eviction may cause a person with OUD to start using meth to stay awake and alert on the streets or in the shelter (Daniulaityte, et al., 2020).

Discussion question

If you were a homeless advocate, what alternatives would you suggest to a homeless person who is taking meth as a survival tactic?

Although OUD alone causes distress in the community, co-using opioids and meth increases the social costs. These costs include:

- 99 percent more overnight hospital stays;
- 46 percent more emergency room visits;
- Doubled rate of homelessness;
- Tripled the rate of more criminal justice involvement (Howell, et al., 2021).

Discussion question

Starting in 2020, the COVID-19 pandemic strained the hospital system (e.g., University Medical Center, 2020). If you were the policymaker allocating funds to hospitals, would you prioritize patients with polysubstance issues or not? Would rationing of care be appropriate during a public health crisis? What ethical argument(s) would you consider?

Unfortunately, MAT may be part of the problem instead of the solution. Anecdotally, I have observed that suboxone clients at my former clinic turned to meth because the MAT does not produce a "ceiling effect" (i.e., inability to get high) for meth. One study based in Dayton, Ohio confirms this observation by stating that Vivitrol, another form of MAT, correlated with meth use. In fact, "the association between Vivitrol treatment participation and greater odds of methamphetamine use has significant implications for substance use treatment delivery strategies, and requires further research to better understand motivational pathways and associated health implications of continued methamphetamine use while in treatment for OUD" (Daniulaityte, et al., 2020).

Discussion questions

> Do you think that the author had a confirmation bias regarding meth use correlated with MAT because of her personal experiences about this topic? Discuss the validity of the above paragraph.
> What are the policy implications for MAT possibly increasing the use of meth among those in opioid treatment programs?

When seeking treatment, polysubstance drug users may face compounded stigma. One interviewee said, "You kind of feel sorry for the opiate addict like, 'Oh, they have pain, and they're covering it up. They're not hurting anybody. They're just sitting there.' Whereas meth, it's like 'That's a psychotic person. That's a dangerous, insane person.'" This has resulted in patients being denied care at an emergency room for non-drug related problems— "It's heartbreaking" (Lopez, et al., 2021).

Recommendations for treating the co-use of methamphetamine and opioids include the following:

> Doctors prescribing off-label medications. This means that although the Food and Drug Administration (FDA) has not approved a medication for a specific condition, doctors should still consider prescribing it. For example, naltrexone has been proven to reduce methamphetamine use (Fogger, 2019);
> Overdose prevention efforts providing Narcan kits to methamphetamine users with the assumption that opioid use is likely (whether

intentional or unintentional, such as fentanyl contamination) (Fogger, 2019);
- Developing "meth only" support groups instead of sending clients to 12-step programs such as AA or NA. "Meth users cannot relate to AA groups. They can only be understood by other meth users" (Childs, 2021).

Discussion questions

- Fogger (2019) describes how off-label prescriptions for persons with polysubstance use may result in harm reduction but not necessarily complete abstinence. Is the treatment still worthwhile if the clients merely reduce their drug use? Write a "pro" argument in favor of harm reduction and a "con" argument stressing that this form of harm reduction is a waste of money.
- In an article about the increased rate of meth overdose deaths in northern Kentucky, a sheriff was asked whether the extraordinary circumstances of the 2020 pandemic lockdown and economic crisis were the primary causes. He replied, "Until we get this socioeconomic problem fixed in the tri-state area, it's a new normal here for us. Unless we get some jobs here and some economic change, unfortunately we're stuck in it" (Culvyhouse, 2021).
  - How would you encourage private companies to move to a depressed area such as northern Kentucky to create more jobs (i.e., capitalist approach)?
  - Would you also encourage more federal spending to stimulate the economy, such as funding for infrastructure (i.e., progressive approach)?
  - Which approach do you prefer, the capitalist or progressive approach? Why?
- In the same article, the local coroner said he had seen victims of fentanyl overdose caused by the contamination of meth or other drugs and pressed pills that were sold as Adderall or less lethal substances. One advocate suggested fentanyl test strips for drug users (Culvyhouse, 2021). If the local officials allowed this form of harm reduction, how would you implement the distribution of fentanyl test strips to the people who need them most?

Fentanyl

In my practice experience, I have met two types of fentanyl users. The first is the one who deliberately uses fentanyl because of the intense high. I have to fight the urge to lunge at them to shake some sense into them—"what the HELL is wrong with you? Why do you want to die?" Fortunately, I have kept my professional demeanor (and my social work license). The other type of fentanyl user is the accidental one, the person whose street drug had been contaminated with this potent synthetic. For example, one woman thought she was merely taking her usual "benzo" (e.g., valium) and expected a low-grade high. Unintentionally exposed to fentanyl, she ended up in the criminal justice system because of her behaviors. Even marijuana, which many would consider to be fairly harmless, can be contaminated with fentanyl. When a client tells me that they are using marijuana, I always ask about whether they trust their supplier because a careless dealer could use the same scale for fentanyl and other street drugs.

Like COVID-19 and the co-use of methamphetamine, fentanyl has emerged as a threat to the health and safety of our society. The mother of an overdose victim who left behind an eight-year-old child said bluntly: "You hear of overdoses all the time, but the difference between what happened to my daughter and all of those stories that I heard about overdose before is that she didn't overdose. She was poisoned" (Inskeep, 2021). Her assertion is backed by the experts who note that the "Mexican drug cartels now cook fentanyl into almost every drug sold on the street, including fake pain pills" (Inskeep, 2021), which are in authentic-looking prescription bottles.

"Poison" is indeed an appropriate word for fentanyl, which is usually 50 times more potent than heroin. According to the DEA, "42% of pills tested for fentanyl contained at least 2 mg of fentanyl, considered a potentially lethal dose" (www.dea.gov/resources/facts-about-fentanyl) and that fentanyl is the main reason for the sharp rise in overdose deaths. Around 75 percent of all drug overdose deaths are due to opioids, with most of them related to fentanyl (Devitt, 2021).

This grim statistic was not at all intended by the inventor. In 1957, a chemist named Paul Janssen invented a synthetic painkiller that is used in medical settings for severe pain. Fentanyl later emerged as a recreational drug called an novel psychoactive substance (NPS), which many opioid users use when they no longer get high from heroin (Westhoff, 2019). For example, some drug users prefer using fentanyl-contaminated and -substituted heroin (FASH) to less potent opioids because the high was stronger. In a Baltimore rapid assessment study, those most at risk were younger males who were homeless and injected drugs (Buresh, et al., 2019). Even names such as "King of Death" (DOJ, 2017) do not deter fentanyl users from seeking the ultimate high.

Besides the high potency of fentanyl and other synthetic opioids, such as carfentanil, other factors are causing the sharp increase in opioid overdose deaths. These include the low cost of fentanyl compared to heroin. Although the street value of heroin had declined by 2018, fentanyl is even cheaper. Producing fentanyl in a lab is much easier than the production of heroin because no poppy plants have to be cultivated and no seeds have to be processed into opiates (Vergano, 2017). Also, fentanyl is highly profitable not only because of its low cost but also because of its easy access from Mexican drug cartels and Chinese labs. "A kilo of heroin nets a dealer $60,000. A kilo of fentanyl? $1.2 million" (Vergano, 2017).

Pill presses play a critical role in fentanyl usage, since dealers use them to make counterfeit tablets that include this dangerous substance. The logos for Percocet, Xanax, and other well-known drugs are pressed onto the tablets, making it difficult to distinguish between the real and counterfeit. For instance, Prince's fatal use of fentanyl could have been accidental because of the counterfeit Vicodin found in his home (Westhoff, 2019). During a DEA sting operation, one investigator found an ingenious solution to the dilemma of selling fake counterfeit tablets (yes, two layers of deception!) to drug traffickers. "He (asked) the only organizations that he knew could make flawless pills: the pharmaceutical companies whose products were being spoofed. 'Drug dealers are using your stamp and killing people,' he told the companies. Would they help put a stop to it? The companies agreed, and sent him thousands of lactose placebos" (Palmer, 2019).

Westhoff (2019) provides an extensive study of this topic in *Fentanyl, Inc.: How Rogue Chemists Are Creating the Deadliest Wave of the Opioid Epidemic*. He describes the three routes of fentanyl into the United States: direct mail from China through the Dark Web (i.e., untraceable websites that are usually able to evade law enforcement), Mexican cartels using Chinese chemicals for production, and the Canadian border. China is the major producer of not only fentanyl, but the precursor chemicals for its production, N-Phenethyl-4-piperidone (NPP) and 4-anilino-N-phenethylpiperidine (ANPP) (Westhoff, 2019). The number of chemical companies in China is estimated between 160,000 and 400,000.

These companies' legal statuses are often uncertain because the laws can be contradictory and confusing (Palmer 2019).

To further complicate the issue, India has become a new player in the fentanyl market. The DEA states that "reporting indicates an Indian national associated with the Sinaloa (Mexico) Cartel initially supplied the organization with fentanyl precursor chemicals, NPP and ANPP, after which a Chinese national also affiliated with the Sinaloa Cartel would synthesize the fentanyl and traffic it from India to Mexico" (Drug Enforcement Agency, 2020). With so many countries involved in the production of fentanyl, it is no wonder that the DEA and other law enforcement agencies are stymied in their efforts to stop the drug flow.

> Addressing the problem is extremely complicated, however, because this is a story that goes well beyond drugs. It's a political story about the clashing of the world's biggest superpowers. It's an economics story about the deception of giant pharmaceutical companies.
>
> And it's forcing us to rethink our assumptions. The drug economy no longer just benefits the producers and dealers. Nowadays it involves the otherwise innocent people who deliver our mail, who program Internet algorithms, who design medicine in chemistry labs, who scrub toilets at drug companies.
>
> More than anything, this is a story of global capitalism run amok. The new-drugs trade is growing for the same reasons the world economy is growing—increasing speed of communications, Internet technology, and shipping; relaxed barriers to trade; and, of course, the ever-present pressure for higher profit margins. And if global capitalism is hard to control, the new-drugs trade is nearly impossible, given that it is peopled by local actors in jurisdictions interacting with far-flung markets and supply chains (Westhoff, 2019, pp. 20–21).

Globally, policymakers have suggested and implemented several policies to address the issue of fentanyl and other synthetic drugs. One ongoing challenge is analogues, synthetics that are "substantially similar" to an illegal drug. For decades, the laws have tried to keep up with the chemists' maddening ability to change just one molecule of a synthetic to make it legal. In 1986, the Federal Analogue Act prohibited psychoactive analogues. This ban, though, was problematic. "Just because chemicals have similar structures doesn't mean they will affect the human body the same way; in fact, quite often the effects can be dramatically different" (Westhoff, 2019, p. 39). Besides, the term "psychoactive" could refer to caffeine and other legal substances.

Another complex policy question is the role of China. For years, China insisted that the source of the fentanyl problem was the United States demand for the drug. Few Chinese citizens use fentanyl or other synthetics, especially since the government has strictly punished users. This logical reasoning is in stark contrast to the U.S. politicians who blame China for their lax enforcement of their laws against fentanyl production for non-medical reasons. "And those quick to blame China should bear in mind that the American doesn't have its clean" with the failure of the War on Drugs (Westhoff, 2019, p. 49).

Brown (2020) suggests some ideas regarding United States–China cooperation in fighting the fentanyl problem including:

➤ "Delink counternarcotics policy and its enforcement from the United States–China global rivalry and encourage broad international cooperation with the United Nations, the European Union, and other countries concerned" (Brown, 2020).
➤ "Mandate that all companies seeking to sell legal fentanyl in the United States institute transparent and verifiable monitoring . . . of their production facilities" (Brown, 2020).

Despite these efforts to stem the flow of fentanyl from China, the product is still arriving in the United States through the mail. "Chinese vendors are often camouflaged by a complex network of corporate entities registered in far-flung cities along China's interior, where they use sophisticated shipping methods to bypass screening measures and where law enforcement scrutiny is often laxer than in bigger cities. . . . Thousands of doses can be shipped together in small, hidden packages" (Feng, 2020).

Harm reduction is another key issue regarding the fentanyl controversy. Although the term "harm reduction" can have several definitions, Westhoff (2019) concludes that "No matter how harm reduction is defined, it springs from the understanding that preventing the use of drugs is impossible and that making sure they are used as safely as possible is a necessity" (Westhoff, 2019, p. 255). For example, he cites the story of Dance Safe, a group of volunteers that went to raves with both health information and drug checking kits. Testing drugs for fentanyl would obviously reduce the rate of overdoses, but government policy prohibited this practice because it allegedly promotes using drugs. In 2003, Congress passed the Rave Act (Illicit Drug Anti-Proliferation Act) that bans groups such as Dance Safe from trying to protect drug users through harm reduction.

Discussion question

The distribution of fentanyl test strips is one harm reduction strategy, especially for dealers who do not want to sell tainted products. One public health expert states, "I see the strips as one avenue. The overdose epidemic right now, in part, is a poisoning epidemic. People are using [fentanyl] without knowing that they're using it. . . . So the more we can have people know whether their drug is poisoned or not, that's a good thing" (Serrano, 2018). If you were advocating for the funding of these test strips, what would you say to a legislator who says, "people who use street drugs deserve what they get"?

Lastly, the term "fentanyl panic" describes how misinformation can fool even the smartest among us. For years, experts believed that casual contact with fentanyl could have devastating effects for law enforcement and other possible victims. This concern has turned out to be unfounded. In 2021, a video showed a police officer allegedly overdosing from an accidental contact with fentanyl. This revived the concern among many, including the Red Cross instructor who was teaching CPR to my group. He suggested that if we suspected fentanyl use, we should not try to help the person in crisis. However, public health experts are fighting back against the myth that just touching or inhaling the powder can cause an overdose. One expert said, "The probability that the deputy shown in that video experienced harm related to opioid exposure is zero percent. Absolutely nothing in that video is consistent with an opioid overdose. . . . The only way to experience intoxication or overdose, from fentanyl or any other opioid, is to take it intentionally" such as through injection (Smith, 2021). At least 400 experts like him sent a petition to the news agencies to demand a more accurate account of the incident.

The consequences of fentanyl panic can be serious because it has "harmed public health through complicating overdose rescue while rationalizing hyper-punitive criminal laws, wasteful expenditures, and proposals to curtail vital access to pain pharmacotherapy" (Beletsky, et al., 2020). Police officers and other first responders may hesitate or even refuse to administer Narcan, while an overdose victim may be designated as a health hazard. This issue is related to the fear of casual contact with HIV-positive persons, who were even criminally prosecuted for spitting at somebody. In the article "Spit does not transmit," the Center for HIV Law and Policy stresses how saliva does not have the virus (factsheet available on www.hivlawandpolicy.org/sites/defa ult/files/Spit%20Does%20Not%20Transmit_0.pdf).

Discussion questions

> Review the DEA's Safety Recommendations for First Responders regarding fentanyl (www.dea.gov/sites/default/files/Publications/Final%20STANDARD%20size%20of%20Fentanyl%20Safety%20Reco mmendations%20for%20First%20Respond....pdf). What would be the most effective way to correct this misinformation?
> In the study regarding fentanyl panic (Beletsky, et al., 2020), the authors did a systematic review of thousands of professional media and social media sources. Only eight percent of the stories regarding casual contact with fentanyl were correct. Suggest a corrective action.

Stigma of SUD

Not only is fentanyl a threat to society's well-being, but the stigma of SUD also poses risks because it stymies recovery efforts. Theories such as social constructionism can deepen the understanding of the stigma of SUD. Social constructionism (also called constructivism) is a motivator for activists, as we see that not everything is set in stone, including oppressive laws and social attitudes. Reality can be subjective when it is defined by a society. This theory is difficult to define because of the variations in meaning among different disciplines (Lynch, 2001). Berger and Luckmann's (1966) seminal work on social constructionism stresses the role of social institutions in creating and transmitting knowledge. In fact, a society can develop its own reality by creating, maintaining, and establishing a hierarchy of institutional fact (Searle, 1995).

Paper money provides one example of social constructionism. Based on its appearance, one piece of green paper is worth more than another piece. The comedian Ryan George states it perfectly: "It was pretty much imaginary to begin with. . . . It's real paper, for sure, but you can't use it to buy anything if no one thinks it's worth anything. . . . I wouldn't say it's worthless, it could have a lot of value to you personally, if you like having tiny pictures of old dead politicians with numbers next to their heads" (George, 2021).

The concept of "race" is also a social construct because the dominant group has both created and maintained the dividing line between groups (Sollors, 2002). One valuable aspect of social constructionism is its opposition to essentialism, which stresses that certain traits are inherent and thus part of a person's essence. For example, the belief that redheads are inherently hot-tempered because of their hair color is essentialist. This type of distorted thinking, of course, can lead to social conflict (Hacking, 1999).

Discussion questions

> Have you ever been judged by somebody who had essentialist leanings? Consider your gender or other aspect of yourself before completing this sentence: "Just because I am (blank) does not mean that I am (blank)." For example, "Just because I am Asian does not mean that I am good at math" or "Just because I am Latino does not mean that I deal drugs."
> How would an essentialist view a person with SUD?

In opposition to essentialism are scholars who assert that "Race is a social construction with no true or absolute biological basis" (Hodson, 2016). Although "race" can be related to physical features such as skin color, "race" is mostly a construct because societies define it differently. For example, countries such as South Africa and Brazil have several racial categories based on skin color while the U.S. slavery system used the "one drop rule" that stated that even one drop of African blood made a person black.

Like "race," "SUD" is a social construct that has multiple connotations. First, the word "substance" in SUD can be defined as a "any psychoactive compound with the potential to cause health and social problems, including addiction" that can be legal or illegal (McLellan, 2017).

This definition is a social construct that is subject to change. Caffeine, for instance, is a psychoactive compound as proven by my consumption of a Coke while writing this section. The long lines at the local Starbucks confirm the addictive power of caffeine—but how harmful is it? I once knew a man who was writing an entire book about the evils of caffeine. In our writing group, he would glare at me while I sipped my soda. I would posit, though, that most people would not rate caffeine as harmful as opioids.

The shifting legal status of marijuana, based on the increased public acceptance of this substance, is another social construct. As different states determine the legality of its medical and recreational use (e.g., see the map of marijuana legality by state on https://disa.com/map-of-marijuana-legality-by-state), drug counselors such as myself must grapple with the question of whether marijuana "counts" as a substance during a discussion of a client's SUD.

The second part of the SUD term, "use disorder," is not the same as "misuse" although I have seen drug counselor job postings use the term "substance misuse." (As stated earlier, "addiction" is commonly used but has a more negative connotation compared to SUD.) Experts differentiate between substance use, misuse, and use disorder. "Substance use" implies little or no harm, while "substance misuse" applies to binge drinking and other harmful situations. SUD, though, can be defined as a "prolonged, repeated use of any of these substances at high doses and/or high frequencies" that results in a "separate, independent, diagnosable illness that significantly impairs health and function and may require special treatment" (McLellan, 2017).

Of course, this distinction between substance "use," "misuse," and "use disorder" is culture-dependent. Alcoholics Anonymous (AA), for example, simply states that an alcoholic is somebody who identifies with the First Step: "We admitted we were powerless over alcohol—that our lives had become unmanageable" (retrieved from www.alcohol.org/alcoholics-anonymous/). Some would argue that a person was either "clean" or not, much like a woman who is either pregnant or not pregnant. Also constructed is the debate on whether SUD is primarily an illness as asserted by medical experts or a moral condition that causes "defects of character" (AA Sixth Step).

A social construct, then, can be based in reality (e.g., a person's drug use) but still be affected by society's changing definitions of this form of prejudice and discrimination (Hacking, 1999). Although prejudice and discrimination may lead to stigma, social awareness can decrease or even eliminate it. Stigma is defined by Goffman (1963) as a spoiled identity, which means that a person is somehow not "normal" or accepted by society because of a physical handicap, sign of "immoral" or nonconformist behavior, or membership to a certain group. This concept is a clear example of social constructionism because society determines which conditions deserve to be stigmatized.

For instance, I am old enough to remember life before the LGBTIA+ acronym, when gay men were called "homos" and lesbians called "lesbos" on a regular basis. The BTIA+ populations were mostly invisible, except for a TV character who was a male soldier dressed as a woman trying to get a psychiatric discharge (i.e., Corporal Klinger on *MASH*). Now social acceptance of transgender rights has increased; one research report states that 73 percent of survey respondents supported anti-discrimination laws to protect transgender persons (Williams Institute, 2019). Also, pansexuality and gender fluidness have become more mainstream (Hinsliff, 2019).

With this encouraging news, reducing the stigma related to SUD and related issues such as mental illness and poverty is possible. A critical element in viewing SUD as a social construct is whether a person believes that the condition is a medical illness or a moral failing. As brain scans and other solid evidence shows, SUD is not caused by a failure of willpower. Researchers have noted findings such as these: "Structural MRI studies have demonstrated that chronic drug exposure can enlarge or shrink some regions of the brain" (Fowler, et al., 2007). Activists can use this kind of research-based information to challenge the social construct of the "addict" who simply does not care about others.

Stigma is also related to deviance, which is a constructed reality determined by people in power (Pfuhl and Henry, 1993). For instance, society rarely viewed drunk driving as a serious crime until the Mothers Against Drunk Driving named this activity as a deviance and lobbied for new laws. On the other hand, my deviant behaviors include refusing to drink alcohol under any circumstances. (Yes, a deviant is writing this book!) For years, people have encouraged me to drink and even mocked me when I refused the beverage. My deviance evoked the "What is wrong with you?" attitude that could be understood by many persons with SUD.

Discussion questions

- Have you ever deviated from the norm? If so, would you call yourself a "deviant"? Why or why not? What does that word imply to you? This reaction is related to the concept of labels, another component of stigma.
- Public health workers use the term "sex workers" instead of "prostitutes" during their outreach efforts. Do you think that changing the label decreases the stigma at all?

Perceived controllability is another aspect of stigma. Did the person with SUD cause their own problem, or were there factors outside of their control? A parallel to SUD is HIV/AIDS, since controllability is related to people's judgment of an HIV-positive person's level of responsibility in becoming infected. If people judge that the situation was controllable, then they may think that "they should have worn a condom" or "they shouldn't have been shooting up drugs." Homophobia also affects the judgment of controllability. Anger and refusal to help the HIV-positive person may result (Wemer, 1993). If the HIV-positive person allegedly became infected through a stigmatized behavior, society is more likely to blame them. In contrast, an HIV-positive wife would receive far less blame than her husband, who may have participated in "deviant" behaviors (i.e., homosexual sex or intravenous drug use).

These reactions to HIV-positive persons resemble the reactions to persons with OUD when news reports of OUD stressed the person's use of opioids starting with prescribed medications, not recreational use. This stress implies the perception of noncontrollability, which usually ends in sympathy and even offers to help.

Another social construct is the "addictive personality" myth. Once I was counseling an SUD client who said she was buying a few extra lottery tickets. She sighed, "I am just an addictive personality." I challenged her with the blunt statement that there is no such thing as an "addictive personality." She had the bad habit of buying lottery tickets, but I had my own bad habits. Bad habits are not addictions.

In fact, SUD is not caused by an "addictive personality" because persons with SUD have no common personality trait. "In reality, anyone can experience addiction—including goal-oriented people who have a large network of friends, plenty of confidence, and a reputation of honesty" (Raypole, 2019). This does not mean that some persons are not at higher risk of developing an SUD than others due to genetics or environment, nor the fact that drug use can cause similar behaviors such as impulsivity. The harm of this myth is that some may consider their recovery from SUD to be impossible because of their "addictive personality."

As social constructionism illuminates the untruths behind established beliefs, such as the addictive personality, its usefulness extends to the fight against oppression. The Anti-Oppression Network defines oppression as "the use of power to disempower, marginalize, silence or otherwise subordinate one social group or category, often in order to further empower and/or privilege the oppressor" (retrieved from https://theantioppressionnetwork.com/what-is-anti-oppression/). Oppression, though, is not inevitable because it is based on the fluid nature of human relationships.

> Oppression takes place in the social arena in the form of interactions between people. Consequently, oppression is socially constructed through people's actions with and behaviours towards others. Its interactive nature means that oppressive relations are not deterministic forces with preordained outcomes. They have to be constantly reproduced in everyday life encounters and routines for them to endure. Thus, resistance to oppression can always take place.
>
> Oppressors attack identity—its formation and reformation—at its core, by depicting a socially constructed status as natural and immutable and, crucial to an oppressive framing of it, as inferior to that held by them. The unalterability of identity posed in negative terms is central to an oppressive framing of people's sense of who they are individually and collectively (Domenelli, 2002, p. 9–10).

This passage demonstrates how activists can challenge the perceived identities of persons with SUD. Instead of accepting the fatalistic belief that "addictive personalities" will probably never recover, we can reframe their identities. Persons with SUD do not have a "natural and immutable" identity as self-destructive losers—each person is unique and worthy of high-quality services. Reasserting the dignity and worth of all persons, a key social work value, will enable us to fight the stigmas related to the opioid crisis.

Viewed in this light, social constructionism provides us with the theoretical structure needed for thoughtful activism. "SUD," a social construct created by medical experts, is an effective tool for diagnosis and treatment. Stigma, though, is a social construct with fewer benefits for those grappling with the opioid crisis. Questioning the origins of a current social construct can lead us to build new and better constructs for the future.

Discussion question

Consider a time when you or somebody you know had been stigmatized. Besides the emotional impact of rejection, were there other implications of that stigma?

10
Advocacy and the opioid crisis

Introduction

Congratulations! If you have made it this far into the book, then you must have true grit (unless you skipped the first nine chapters, of course.) Besides having true grit, you should by now have rejected the "doom and gloom" mentality for a more hopeful attitude. Thoughtful activism requires us to view interrelated social problems without feeling like we need to hide our heads under pillows and whimper. The Jewish text called the Talmud states: "Do not be daunted by the world's grief. Do justly now, love mercy now, walk humbly now. You are *not* obligated to complete the work, but neither are you free to abandon it" (quote retrieved from www.goodreads.com/quotes/7480295-the-talmud-states-do-not-be-daunted-by-the-enormity).

To avoid being daunted by the world's grief, remember that you are not alone. Pick your niche and become part of a coordinated effort to alleviate the pain of others. The goal of this chapter is to help readers shift from the "Where do I even begin?" question to the "What do I do next?" question. First, select one issue and commit to it. Margaret Burnham, a long-time civil rights activist, stated during the Black Lives Matter movement that: "And then it's also to appreciate that this is a long road, and everyone has to figure out how they're going to walk it. You have to figure out the battle you're going to take. Which is the battle where you think you can be most effective? . . . . You've got to pick a battle" (Thomsen, 2020).

The second recommendation is that readers should appreciate the unexpected nature of politics and history. In the early 1980s, I graduated early from college to devote myself to the antinuclear weapons cause. Ronald Reagan's actions and words made many of us fear that he would send bombs to destroy the Soviet Union and, ultimately, the world. One of my first political protests was outside of Rocky Flats, a facility that made the triggers for nuclear bombs. Hundreds of us held hands in a human chain around the fence. On one side, I held the hand of a young woman with purple spiked hair—in the 1980s, this was more shocking than today. On my other side was a Catholic sister, one of those social activist nuns who are so fearless. We were united in our goal to freeze the production of nuclear weapons because the U.S had more than enough to blow up the world several times over.

Six years later, the Berlin Wall came down in 1989. The Soviet Union did the unthinkable by dissolving shortly after, which drastically decreased the threat of nuclear annihilation. New global problems have come to the forefront, of course; climate change, wealth disparity, and persistent racism are but only three. However, my experience as a "freezenik" (the derogatory nickname for advocates for a nuclear arms freeze because we were allegedly dupes of the evil Soviets) has made me immune from despair. Unexpected events such as pandemics can be disastrous, but others—such as the end of the nuclear arms race—can generate a season of optimism.

This chapter focuses on cases of successful advocacy regarding the opioid crisis, besides suggestions for further actions. Unfortunately, proposed solutions such as the Good Samaritan laws can result in tricky complications. Any reader hoping for this chapter to contain only sunny good news should remember that activism is a marathon that requires a long-term, heartfelt commitment.

A community fights back

In the book *Death in Mud Lick: A Coal Country Fight against the Drug Companies That Delivered the Opioid Epidemic* (2020), journalist Eric Eyre describes the devastation created by a flood of opioid pills in rural West Virginia. In the pharmacy in Kermit, West Virginia (population 382), nine million opioid pills were sold in just two years. Customers drove hundreds of miles to this pharmacy to pay cash for their prescriptions, knowing that no questions would be asked. Three corporations were involved in shipping 85 percent of the pain pills to this area: Amerisource Bergen, Cardinal Health, and McKesson Corporation. Through the early 2000s, the Drug Enforcement Agency (DEA) did little to slow down this flood of opioids despite public outcry.

The book's focus, though, is not on the consequences of this avoidable tragedy but on the activism conducted by the author, lawyers, citizens who lost family members to overdoses, and others to fight the corporate malfeasance. Not only were lawsuits awarded, but congressional hearings resulted from their work. Lessons for advocates include the following:

- Build a good team. No single person could have accomplished so much by themselves. The task may seem overwhelming, but effective teamwork can combine each member's strengths and experience.
- Do your research. If you know who the players are, then you can understand the power structure. In West Virginia, the new attorney general was married to a Cardinal Health lobbyist. This obvious conflict of interest undermined the state's efforts to hold the drug companies accountable.
- Use the local media. In an era of small newspapers vanishing from the scene, advocates must recognize the importance of local media and support them. Media coverage is a valuable tool because professional reporters know how to research and write an in-depth story. Although social media outlets can also be useful, advocates should recognize the need to be taken seriously by professional reporters.
- Develop different strategies. Filing lawsuits against the pharmacies was one strategy, which involved the civil court system. The advocates also sent information about the pharmacies to the DEA, an agency under the Department of Justice. Law enforcement and civil suits, then, were two ways to address one issue.
- Fight for transparent government. For decades, the Freedom of Information Act (FOIA) has enabled citizens to access information about government activities. The book describes how difficult it was for the advocates to obtain data from the DEA, forcing them to go to court. The judge ruled in favor of them, quoting: "Democracies die behind closed doors" (Eyre, 2020, p. 247).
- Be prepared to fight the stigma. Local leaders who opposed the lawsuits opined that overdose victims and other opioid users were "criminals, felons, street dealers, a pox on the community—(they) had zero right to sue" (Eyre, 2020, p 47). "Criminals... shouldn't be allowed to use the courts to profit from criminal activity. The addicts admitted they broke the law. They took more drugs than prescribed. They sold prescription painkillers on street corners and in pharmacy parking lots. They were junkies" (Eyre, 2020, p. 48).

Discussion questions

- Provide an example of using the local media in your community. How would you persuade a reporter to consider your cause to be newsworthy?

- Write a short response to the stigmatizing statements by the local leaders. How could you persuade them to support your cause?

Innovation: Linking the legal and medical systems

In rural areas such as eastern Kentucky, poverty appears as a constant. Nikki King, an advocate for persons with substance use disorder (SUD), shares the story of a child in school who was asked what he was going to do when he grew up. He said that he was planning to "draw" on the government for benefits, besides selling "Oxy's" on the street for income. Due to entrenched poverty, the concept of drug courts is unrealistic because of the lack of resources. Not enough medical providers who can prescribe medication assisted treatment (MAT). Not enough counselors, with the ratio of only one counselor for 2000 persons in some rural counties. Not enough money.

In 2018, King was at an opioid forum when she decided that the current treatment options for probationers in her county were insufficient. "I think we can do better" (Macy, 2020). Working with the county judges, she created Courts Addiction and Drug Services (CADS), which provides MAT, nine hours of group therapy a week, and social support, such as job assistance. She recruited a therapist, besides a nurse practitioner, to administer the MAT.

> After taking the training course to prescribe buprenorphine, (the nurse practitioner) went from thinking of the addicted as 'druggies' to seeing them as people with a legitimate disease, not unlike diabetics who struggle to keep their blood sugar under control" (Macy, 2020).

CADS is innovative because it directly links the courts with treatment—literally under one roof. King has used the conference room down the hall from the courtrooms, decorating its walls with posters. The success rate is high enough to garner national attention, and she is planning to expand the program to another county.

King's advocacy for CADS includes the following components:

- Collaboration with judges and other parties, making sure that they also have an ownership in the project;
- Recruitment of qualified staff despite the barriers of long distance (e.g., the psychiatrist has to commute 90 miles one way);

- Creative problem-solving when Medicaid stated that they were going to stop their payments because the services were provided in a nonmedical setting. King and her allies walled off part of the conference room, thus allowing a local hospital to pay a monthly rent of $25 to the courthouse;
- Knowledge of the Medicaid program, which is the major payor;
- Connections with local employers to encourage them to hire the clients.

Discussion questions

- One client had a strong record of recovery, then used methamphetamine once due to a heavy work schedule. If you were the judge, would you send him back to jail or let him stay in the CADS program with stricter requirements?
- If you were King, would you accept a $300,000 grant from Purdue Pharmaceuticals although they were one of the companies that had saturated Kentucky with prescribed opioids? Why or why not?
- While considering the grant from Purdue, review the Code of Ethics for Social Work (available on https://www.socialworkers.org/About/Ethics/Code-of-Ethics/Code-of-Ethics-English), especially the Value of Integrity and the Principle that "social workers behave in a trustworthy manner." Does that principle apply to this ethical dilemma? Or does the Value of Service, with the principle of the primary goal of helping people and addressing social problems, override this concern?

Policy case study one: Good Samaritan laws

On June 16, 2011, my sister is buried in a spot overlooking a beach and beautiful waterfront, where gorgeous sunsets grace the sky. She is buried where we used to play as children, where my brother learned to walk, in the garden next to our summer home. I am the one who digs her grave.

> After the funeral, a few of my cousins . . . stick around. They tell me that my cousin Chris . . . had said he did all he could to save Allison the night she died. Apparently, he and Dusty had discovered my sister in a similar condition a few weeks after phoning my parents, passed out and not responsive,

but this time she wasn't breathing and had a very weak pulse. Apparently, Chris had said that he and Dusty had frantically tried to look on the internet how to revive a person who has overdosed on heroin. Once they realized they weren't making progress, they removed all the illegal narcotic paraphernalia from their small home out of fear of getting into trouble, and then dialed 911. But by that time, it was too late. . . .

In what appears to be a direct result of Allison's death, a "Good Samaritan" law will be created, basically protecting anyone calling the police in similar situation from being charged with a crime (Bush, 2018, pp. 132–135).

For years, the Drug Policy Alliance and other advocacy groups have called for Good Samaritan laws throughout the nation. As of 2017, 40 states and the District of Columbia have enacted several variations of this concept to encourage drug users to call 911 if they are with somebody who has overdosed. The sooner an overdose victim receives medical care, the more likely they will survive. One advocacy group, the Network for Public Health Law, states that Good Samaritan laws have resulted in a 15 percent reduction in deaths (Lieberman & Davis, 2023).

On an intuitive level, the Good Samaritan policy makes perfect sense. A drug user fearing arrest for drug possession and other reasons would be reluctant to call 911. In a compelling scene from the 1996 movie *Trainspotting* (an excellent portrayal of heroin addiction), the drug dealer pays a cabdriver to pick up a customer who had overdosed. The customer lies in a collapsed heap by the side of the road. The drug dealer and cabdriver haul him into the cab, then later the cabdriver dumps him out of the cab at the hospital entrance before speeding away. A Good Samaritan law could improve the emergency services needed by overdose victims such as these.

Discussion questions

Despite this policy's good intentions, every policy has complications beyond its initial purpose. These complications include the following:

> ▸ Persons who call 911 may be protected from drug possession charges, but what about other offenses? For example, some states have expanded

the legal immunity to parole/probation violations. Would you advocate for this protection?
- Vermont provides immunity for those who are involved in drug sales (Drug Policy Alliance, n.d.a). Would you support or oppose this expansion of immunity?
- Child welfare is another concern. Should a parent be protected from any involvement with child protective services if they call 911 for an overdose? This poses an ethical dilemma of whether an immediate crisis (the overdose victim) is more critical than the possibility of ignoring child maltreatment.
- What if the caller has any immigration issues? Should they be immune from Immigration and Customs Enforcement or related agencies?
- Indiana links its Good Samaritan law to naloxone (Narcan) access. To gain immunity for possession charges, the person must first obtain the naloxone before the overdose, administer it, call 911, and stay at the scene to provide information to the EMT and police (The Network for Public Health Law, n.d.). Do you agree with these provisions?
- A Good Samaritan law is probably ineffective if not enough people even know about it. Look up your state's Good Samaritan law (or a neighboring state). Design a public awareness campaign to inform people that they will not be arrested for drug possession if they call 911 for an overdose victim. How would you reach the intended audience—the drug users?
- The author cited the Drug Policy Alliance as a source. According to its website, their mission statement says: The Drug Policy Alliance (DPA) is the nation's leading organization of people who believe the war on drugs is doing more harm than good. In our vision of tomorrow, people are not punished simply for what they put into their bodies but only for harm done to others. (Drug Policy Alliance, 2017). Do you think that this agency's mission may hinder the efforts to promote Good Samaritan laws since critics might accuse this agency of just trying to decriminalize drugs? If you opposed decriminalization, would you still ally yourself with this group for the goal of strong Good Samaritan laws?

Box 10.1 describes the communication tactics that activists can use on behalf of their groups.

Box 10.1 Communication tactics

Sara Falconer, an organizer for prisoners, recommends these tactics for advocates:

- Understand your goal, including knowing your target audience. Think about the age range, political leanings, and other traits of this audience. For example, a publisher would advertise a feminist book on a left-leaning website because that is the desired audience. Also consider the goal of the message—is it to spread information or to encourage people to contact their legislators?
- Knowing your audience means knowing how to talk to them. As the social work saying goes, start where the client is. If you are reaching out to a broad audience, do not use technical jargon or talk down to them.
- Tell stories because "People connect with personal stories, versus numbers or facts or arguments. If you can tell them about a particular person, or share somebody's voice with them, it's so much more effective" (McBay, 2019, p. 373).
- "Be specific, concise, direct. Then repeat" (McBay, 2019, p. 373).
- Avoiding overwhelming the person by presenting one problem at a time.
- Use signs and logos that will have an impact. The Black Lives Matter protesters, for example, often held signs showing the faces of Breonna Taylor and other victims of police violence.
- It may take time to "build trust and creditability" (McBay, 2019, p. 376), but it is essential to "make sure that the people most affected by your campaign are included" (McBay, 2019, p. 377). This advice is congruent with Alinsky's model of community organizing by amplifying the voice of the neighborhood.
- Don't let the opponent set the terms for discussion. The Patriot Act of 2001, for example, made it difficult for critics to speak out without being called unpatriotic. Experts may diminish the activists by calling them irrational or naïve or even immoral (Adapted from McBay, 2019, pp. 370–380).

> **Discussion question**
> Black Lives Matter sparked much criticism, including from Carol Swain, an African American law professor. "No, I don't like what I see. It's pure Marxism. It talks about state violence, genocide. All of those are buzzwords that are quite destructive. We need to look at the credibility of the witnesses, we need to not rush to judgment" (Diaz, 2016). Another critic was Tucker Carlson of Fox News: "Black Lives Matter now enjoys almost complete immunity from criticism. This is unprecedented for an American political movement but Black Lives Matter is more powerful than that. It has singlehandedly revised our moral framework" (Creitz, 2020).
>
> ➢ How would you counteract these attempts to set the terms for discussion?

Policy case study two: Drug-induced homicide laws

No Good Samaritan law would be effective if people are afraid of being prosecuted for drug-induced homicide. The moral question is whether a drug seller should be held responsible for a person's overdose. A related issue emerged in 1995 when Carroll O'Connor, a television actor, stated publicly that his son's cocaine dealer was responsible for his son's suicide. When he first got the phone call from the police, "The thought went through my head: 'At last it's happened—everything I've ever been afraid of.'" Later he called the dealer "a partner in murder," which resulted in a slander lawsuit (Deutsch, 1997).

As the drug crisis continues to worsen, the question of the dealer's liability becomes salient. Just last week, a client told me about being sold "wasp spray" methamphetamine that was more dangerous than his regular meth. He was so enraged that he said he wanted to beat up the dealer. In other cases in my practice experience, drug users are being exposed to fentanyl-contaminated substances, such as cocaine and even marijuana.

On their website, the advocacy group Drug Induced Homicide asks in big letters: "Why are drug dealers getting away with murder?" In their brief to policymakers, they demand a "paradigm shift" to regard some overdose deaths as not accidents but homicides. The website also includes a section that features the photos and descriptions of overdose victims (Drug Induced Homicide, n.d.). In one recent case, a mother of an overdose victim sued the medical examiner to rule her daughter's death as a homicide instead of an accident to reduce the stigma. "The fact is that Teper did not die by choice. She was murdered by someone who delivered her fentanyl" (Main, 2020a). After the mother lost her case, she stated, "Murder is murder!" (Main, 2020b).

As of 2019, at least half of U.S. states have enacted laws on drug-induced homicide (Health in Justice, 2019). Illinois is one state that has implemented the Drug-Induced Homicide policy, one that "doesn't address whether the person delivering the drug must know that it could be deadly" (Main, 2020A). In August 2020, the Illinois State Attorney announced the conviction of Keith Lang because he had sold heroin to a woman who shared it with a male friend who died. He could serve from 6 to 30 years in prison (Illinois State Attorney's Office, 2020).

Some legal experts question the wisdom of this policy. The Northeastern Law School's Health in Justice Action Lab, for example, studied the news reports of drug-induced homicide prosecutions to find that

> a majority of prosecutions are being brought against individuals who do not fit the characterization of a 'dealer' at all, such as friends, family, and co-users of the overdose decedent. In cases that do involve organized drug distribution, the defendants are typically low-level dealers" (Health in Justice, n.d.).

Stark racial disparities also appear in the sentencing decisions, with persons of color receiving a median of over eight years and only five years for whites. The study concludes that this policy has slowed down the volume of drug trades.

Another legal expert points out that the deterrence theory may not work because it requires a rational actor (Gorga, 2020). Because the dealer is often a drug user themselves, the "visceral urge" to use drugs may override any fear of punishment (i.e., deterrence). The first part of the article title is "Retribution, not a solution," which indicates the author's opinion. Gorga also discusses the history of the War on Drugs as a backdrop for the drug-induced homicide policy. In one scenario, two roommates may occasionally sell drugs but do not consider themselves to be dealers. (Based on my practice experience, I agree with the author's premise that many drug users may casually sell drugs but would never consider themselves dealers.) The roommates pool their money to buy the next fix. One roommate goes out to purchase the drug, which causes a fatal overdose for the other roommate. North Carolina law would consider this death to be a drug-induced homicide.

Besides legal experts, what do incarcerated drug users think about this policy? Researchers (Peterson, et al., 2019) conducted a qualitative study of this population (40 men in a Rhode Island facility) regarding this question. The article title starts with "One guy goes to jail, two people are ready to take his spot," which indicates the perceived futility of stopping the drug trade by prosecuting dealers for homicide. One key point is their stress on the drug user's autonomy regarding the decision to start using drugs and continuing to take them. One man noted, "Me, a drug addict—I know how it is; so I wouldn't want my dealer—say I OD'd. I wouldn't want my dealer to go to jail for me buying a bag off him, because it was my choice; it was my option. It was my option, to go to him and cop the drugs" (Peterson, et al., 2019, no page). Box 10.2 presents another dilemma, protecting mothers in treatment.

Discussion questions

- After reading this section, discuss the arguments for and against this policy. Which factor (e.g., the parents' grief) should dominate the debate?
- The author tried to present a balanced discussion of this policy. Discuss whether it was balanced enough. If not, what would you have done differently?

Box 10.2 Protecting mothers in treatment

As discussed in Chapter 5, pregnant women and new mothers face a dilemma when seeking treatment. When an Ohio state representative and his wife took in the infant daughter of their great niece, they did not expect this family issue to become a political issue, However, the infant's mother had been forbidden contact with her because she had been diagnosed with neonatal abstinence syndrome. State Representative Doug Green said, "Mom, who was staying with us, was kicked to the curb. She had to leave home because the court prohibited her from contacting the baby. I, to this day, scratch my head as to why" (Balert, 2015).

Inspired by this incident, Green co-sponsored Maiden's Law (named after the infant) to allow mothers to stay in contact with their infants if they had started treatment within the first 20 weeks of pregnancy. As long as the mother stays in treatment, she would be able to keep the child unless there are safety concerns. Green stressed that "The goal for Maiden's

> Law is to provide healthier outcomes for children who are born to addicted mothers" (Balert, 2015). The bill passed—and Maiden's mother was able to achieve sobriety and become an addiction counselor.

Homelessness and SUD: One advocate's view

Like Seattle as discussed in Chapter 2, Denver has experienced a rise in homelessness partially caused by the high cost of housing. According to Denver's Department of Housing Stability, housing costs rose 60 percent, while wages rose only five percent (www.denvergov.org/Government/Departments/Department-of-Housing-Stability). SUD is also a factor, but one advocate who has worked with the homeless in Denver for 20 years stated that "substance use is easy to demonize, since it is easy to blame the individual. We ignore the systemic problems of housing costs and low wages. Substance use gets more attention, as it reinforces the homelessness" (Wallington, 2021).

In Advocate's practice experience, he estimated that SUD was the primary cause of homelessness for around 30 percent of the population. However, the substance use has usually intersected with mental illness, family violence, trauma background, lost jobs, broken relationships—and most of all, unaddressed childhood trauma. These individual factors, of course, overlap with the scarcity of affordable housing. As one political party once called itself, "The rent is too damned high!" (website: https://rentistoodamnhigh.org). Once-affordable neighborhoods in Denver have become gentrified, which means that low-income residents can no longer afford the higher rents or property taxes. These residents either move outside of the city or end up on the streets.

Advocate also noted that there were two homeless populations: visible and invisible. Perhaps the most visible persons are those living in camps in parks and other public spaces. "Now that the camps are so visible, the homeless are no longer out of sight, out of mind." When the COVID-19 lockdown of 2020 closed down the downtown library, the largest (if unofficial) day shelter in the city, the persons spent their days in the nearby Civic Center Park. The city responded with sweeps of the park to address an alleged rat problem. The persons who were ordered out of the park later told the advocate that they had never seen any rats.

Besides COVID-19, the opioid crisis has adversely affected the homeless persons in Denver. Fentanyl has been the drug of choice, with methamphetamine also "highly prevalent." Unlike the recreational use of methamphetamine, the use of fentanyl is mostly for maintenance purposes to avoid withdrawal symptoms. Fentanyl use is also associated with a rise in crime because gangs have reaped so much profit from it. Overdoses are another concern; as the manufacturers have no uniform standards, the "tiniest amount can be fatal."

Despite these challenges, Advocate expressed hope about these two policy ideas:

- Harm reduction, which "has come a long way but can still be a hard sell." The policy of providing clean needles to drug users has become commonplace in Denver. Safe injection sites are more controversial, since critics believe that they would promote drug use. The response to this objection is: "Where else do you want them to inject themselves, a McDonald's bathroom?" Another controversial measure is the effort to persuade users to smoke/inhale their drugs instead of injecting them, which reduces the rate of Hepatitis C, HIV, and other bloodborne diseases.
- Authorized tent camps and tiny home villages, which are part of the Colorado Village Collaborative. Although this temporary housing is a "stopgap measure," it is still better than shelters for those who want their own living spaces.

Discussion questions

- Advocate estimated that SUD was primarily responsible for 30 percent of the homeless crisis. How would you conduct a research study to confirm this anecdotal observation? For example, would you survey the staff of homeless shelters or other experts? If you asked the homeless persons themselves, how would you protect their dignity and privacy?
- If you were testifying at a state hearing on behalf of homeless programs, how would you respond to a legislator who says, "They're all just addicts and want to die anyway. I don't think we should waste any more money on them!"?
- Consider the persons who are homeless but do not appear so—the "invisible" ones. Do you think that agencies should conduct more outreach to the invisible homeless, or focus their work on those living in camps and shelters?

- Look up the website of the Colorado Village Collaborative (www.coloradovillagecollaborative.org/). In your opinion, what is this group's strongest advantage?
- If you were the owner of a business that is near a vacant lot that will be an authorized homeless camp, would you support or oppose this action? How could the Colorado Village Collaborative persuade a potential neighbor of a camp?

More policy suggestions for homelessness in Denver

Besides Advocate's suggestions for harm reduction and authorized tent camps/tiny home villages, Denver's Department of Housing Stability has initiated some programs that deserve consideration by other communities. One high priority is to decrease the stigma related to homelessness because it "is a context that people are living in, it is not who a person is" (Executive Director Britta Fisher cited in video on www.denvergov.org/Government/Departments/Department-of-Housing-Stability). Every unhoused person has their individual story, so there is no "typical" homeless person.

Another priority is Housing First, which combines services with rapid rehousing. Moving persons from crisis shelters (also called bridge housing) to stable housing results in better outcomes. Persons can store their belongings and know that they have a bed to sleep in that night, which reduces stress and allows them to work on their goals, such as recovery and employment. Despite the stereotype of a homeless man who prefers to live outside on his own, only one out of 300 persons refused the housing and 85 percent remained housed two years later.

Employment remains a challenge for many unsheltered persons, so Denver set up a day labor program that allowed workers to earn wages for housing and develop some work experience. The article title "More than 100 homeless people landed regular jobs after Denver hired them to perform day labor" provides a promising direction for this program (I'm From Denver, 2021).

Although the city has taken these actions to reduce the number of unhoused persons, unauthorized (i.e., illegal) tent cities still exist. Mayor Michael Hancock has vowed to clear out these camps because "House keys have much more power to change a life than tents" (Contreras, 2021). Instead of police enforcement, though, he was using civilian enforcement teams such as city crews to do "sweeps" of the camps. He proposed buying more motels/hotels, besides authorizing more legal camps regardless of the neighborhoods' responses.

Discussion questions

- Does your community have a Housing First approach to homelessness, or does it stress crisis shelters?
- Should a Housing First facility accept active drug users or should it refuse them shelter? What is a strong argument for and against requiring complete sobriety including alcohol?
- Discuss the implications of the Denver mayor's determination to do "sweeps" of unauthorized camps. Sweeps such as these involve confiscation of "personal property including tents, bedding, papers, clothing, medications, etc." (National Coalition of the Homeless website: https://nationalhomeless.org/issues/civil-rights/). What civil rights issues are involved, besides possible medical consequences and/or trauma?

Box 10.3 "It's a marathon"

Vicki Deisner, a social justice advocate, has lobbied all over the country and D.C. on behalf of the environment and animal welfare. When asked about making policy change, she compared it to running a marathon so "you have to be extremely committed and persistent." Taking the long-range approach is also critical. For example, environmental politics have shifted considerably since the 1970s when the Environmental Protection Agency (EPA) was formed in response to disasters, such as the Cuyahoga River catching fire in 1969. The Clean Water Act (1972) was an easy law for people to understand because nobody wants to drink polluted water. Because the EPA had focused on corporate regulations, the average person made few if any sacrifices.

Decades later, battling with the reality of climate change does require the average person to make sacrifices without any tangible reward such as a glass of clean water or a park trail. People must consider their "carbon footprint" (defined here as the environmental impact) in their daily lives such as food choices, transportation, and using plastic. The trade-off for these sacrifices is abstract, while the idea of climate change is so massive that many people choose to ignore it.

Discussion question

Like climate change, the opioid issue can seem huge and overwhelming. People may also feel that they are making sacrifices for no good reason. How would you increase the sense of self-efficacy of people who want to ignore climate change or the opioid crisis?

Deisner also believes that incremental change is the best strategy because ideologues (e.g., the radical left or right) must be balanced with pragmatists such as herself. For example, an advocate may state the desire to shut down all puppy mills in Ohio. Since puppies are legally classified as an agricultural product, this is not a realistic goal. Instead, Deisner has tried to improve the dogs' living conditions as an incremental change toward the future goal of banning puppy mills.

As founder of the Ohio Animal Advocates group, Deisner has strong feelings about the meat industry and other forms of animal abuse. However, she carefully uses the less controversial term "animal welfare" instead of "animal rights" in her approach to politicians. This group focuses on common ground issues that usually involve human welfare. One example is the link between animal abuse and family violence, since abusers often injure or kill pets before attacking family members. This troubling connection has resulted in state legislation that requires cross-reporting of animal abuse and domestic violence/child abuse/elder abuse. Deisner hopes that an issue like this will build a broad coalition of stakeholders, a coalition that will support more far-reaching reforms, such as improving conditions for farm animals.

For anyone starting a new advocacy group, Deisner recommends the following:

- Research the issue, including "what is possible";
- Consider the political atmosphere: "don't assume people will agree with you on any issue, you should assume people won't";
- Research the individual politicians before your meetings so you can present your idea in the most effective way;
- Bring professional people to the table, such as program developers and marketing experts;
- Develop the skills of the volunteers.

Keeping one's emotional balance is essential work for any advocate. "If you want to make a difference on any small issue, you're going to have to become aware. You have to grapple with tragedy, but stay focused on the end goal. Follow your compass. The whole point of your work is to end the tragedy or at least make a dent" (Deisner, 2021).

Discussion question
What was one key point in this section that you want to remember? Write a paragraph describing how this point will help you with your advocacy.

Harm reduction

The Housing First approach is but one example of how the harm reduction philosophy remains a strong component of the opioid issue. As described earlier, harm reduction focuses on reducing the harm done by drug use without first requiring total abstinence. Examples of harm reduction include needle exchange programs and syringe cleaning kits (Smye, et al., 2011). Box 10.3 describes how activists can increase their effectiveness.

If methadone clinics have evoked controversy for decades, a new form of harm reduction has evoked even more. Supervised (or safe) injection sites allow persons to use intravenous drugs under medical supervision. They "are clean indoor environments where people can consume pre-obtained drugs with trained health professionals present to ensure safe injection methods, respond in the event of an overdose, and provide counseling and referrals to vital social services and treatment options (Cohen, 2018). Insite Supervised Injection Site, based in Vancouver, Canada, reported more than 3.6 million visits from 2003 to 2019. "There have been 48,798 clinical treatment visits and 6,440 overdose interventions without any deaths" (statistics retrieved from www.vch.ca/public-health/harm-reduction/supervised-consumption-sites/insite-user-statistics). Based on such startling results, cities such as Denver have considered safe injection sites to reduce the number of overdose deaths (Kenney, 2018).

Not surprisingly, public opposition to these sites has stymied efforts in the United States to replicate the success of other countries' programs. The War on Drugs' criminalization of street drugs directly contradicts this harm reduction measure. Opponents would stress that these sites endorse and even encourage drug use, besides bringing undesirable people into the sites' neighborhoods (Cohen, 2018).

In response to this opposition, one hospital used outreach to help community members better understand what the sites were like. In response to the question in the article title "Do mock-ups, presentations of evidence, and Q&As help participants voice their opinions during focus groups and interviews about supervised injection services?" (Kryszajtys, et al., 2021), the answer was affirmative. People were able to visit a site mock-up that included a waiting room, assessment room, and of course an injection room. Having seen what the physical spaces would look like, one person said "the mock-up helped them experience the additional rooms in a concrete way. . . . 'I did not realize you had to have a chill space, an assessment space. Obviously, you need the safe injection space . . . they're not part of my life, right?'" (Kryszajtys, et al., 2021). Participants expressed interest in learning more about the sites after this educational experience, an indication that it is possible to reduce opposition to these sites.

Discussion questions

- Would you be comfortable living one block away from a methadone clinic? Why or why not?
- Do you agree with the idea of safe injection sites? Is your community considering this idea?

Jobs and sober housing

Recovery from SUD can be arduous on several levels, especially regarding employment and housing. This section will discuss initiatives that are assisting persons to reintegrate into the community despite any records of felonies, evictions, and other barriers to social acceptance.

The good news is that employers have recognized the need to hire and retain persons in recovery not for humanitarian but for business purposes. In Ohio, for example, an estimated one-third to one-half of the workforce decline was caused by the opioid crisis (Rembert, et al., 2017). Now "recovery-friendly workplaces" is the term used by the "Building a Healthy

& Productive Workforce by Supporting Employees in Recovery" training modules for employers. The training stresses that:

> SUD is a brain disease and a treatable medical condition like heart disease;
> In the past, persons with SUD have been judged as "weak-willed and lazy" before researchers used brain scans that showed physical changes;
> The disease may involve relapses and remissions;
> Employees in recovery are "productive, safe, and grateful" www.odjfs.state.oh.us/tutorials/OWD/WorkforeProf/Building-a-Healthy-and-Productive-Workforce/story_html5.html).

This employer education effort is a public–private partnership that includes the Ohio Department of Job and Family Services, the Ohio Chamber of Commerce, Anthem Insurance, and the module developer (Working Partners). The Opioid Toolkit emphasizes that employers need a "dose of reality" to confront the worker shortage and its impact on the state's economy.

Discussion questions

Does your local area have a similar initiative to help employers develop a plan to hire and retain persons with SUD? If not, would contacting the Chamber of Commerce or similar entity be your first step?

Besides work, housing is a necessity for persons in recovery. This book's sections about the homeless should not mislead the reader into thinking that most persons with SUD are living on the streets. Persons in recovery, though, may need a living environment free from substance use—a difficult challenge for those residing with active users. Sober living houses are one option for recovery. Usually long-term and run by a manager, these houses can promote recovery through peer support (Polcin, Mahoney, & Mericel, 2021).

While maintaining their sobriety, residents often recognize the need for looking out for their peers. For example, one resident reported that "One of the things that I think is completely awesome is when somebody is having a bad day around here and you can kind of see . . . . You kind of feel it, the aura . . . . There [are] people that step up that ask you, hey, what's going on?" (Polcin & Korcha, 2015). Trauma-informed care has also emerged as a trend in sober living houses, especially for women who have experienced domestic and/or sexual violence. Because lifetime victimization is often co-morbid with SUD, addressing past traumas during the recovery journey is critical (Edwards, et al., 2017).

Community resistance to sober living houses in their neighborhoods, though, plays a role in this policy solution to the opioid crisis. At a meeting in Chicago about a proposed sober living house, one homeowner stated that that "They bring problems and their addictions to our nice family neighborhood." Another neighbor concerned about the possible impact on house values noted that "Nobody is going to want to live next door to a bunch of junkies." However, another neighbor stated that "I think a community that values supporting one another should create every opportunity for folks struggling to get back on their feet and succeed" (Vivanco, 2017).

Discussion questions

- If you had been the presenter for the proposed sober living house at the Chicago meeting, which points would you emphasize: required 30 days sobriety before being admitted, house management to ensure rules are followed, required work or volunteering during the day so there would be no loitering, enforcement of curfews, random drug testing, and zero tolerance for substance use?
- If you had been advocating for these houses, how would you build on the neighbor's statement of support about communities helping those in recovery?
- Look up the website National Alliance for Recovery Residences (www.narronline.org). Do you consider this website to be an effective advocacy tool? Why or why not?

Conclusion

The other day, I talked to someone who had just found out that she had been cheated by a big corporation. She said that at first she felt apathetic and even fatalistic about the bad news, then she became angry. Instead of backing down, she decided to find a lawyer to help her fight for her rights. Healthy anger about an injustice can compel us to such positive actions.

"I'm going to get feisty!" she promised me.

Get feisty. Show off your ornery side (but not too ornery, please!) Not everybody is going to like your advocacy work, so get used to it. Misinformed people may sneer at persons with SUD and their advocates, so resist the temptation to sneer back at them. Respect and kindness should remain the bedrock of our advocacy.

Besides embracing your inner feistiness, consider the possibility of becoming a policy geek. Hopefully, the readers who had once shuddered at the idea of macro social work are reconsidering their aversion. Micro social work, direct practice with clients, is inseparable from the other levels. For example, I was counseling clients with OUD (micro level) while researching compliance regulations for my agency (mezzo level) and writing this book (macro level). Seeing the interconnectedness of all three levels is essential for social workers. My policy work has not decreased my effectiveness as a counselor, since these roles reinforce each other.

Policy is also about the stories of your clients and others who deserve to be heard. The stories of mothers in recovery, for instance, can draw people into the issue as well as hard data such as housing statistics. Recognizing the humanity of others helps us to find common ground instead of stigmatizing the outsiders.

Whether or not you will identify as a policy geek, consider the words of Whitney M. Young, Jr. This social worker helped to lead the civil rights movement, marching alongside Martin Luther King, Jr. and John Lewis. As director of the National Urban League, he connected business leaders with the Black/AA communities that needed economic investments. (www.britannica.com/biography/Whitney-M-Young-Jr). He once wrote, "I am not anxious to be the loudest voice or the most popular. But I would like to think that at a crucial moment, I was an effective voice of the voiceless, an effective hope of the hopeless" (www.goodreads.com/quotes/738442-i-am-not-anxious-to-be-the-loudest-voice-or#).

As we refuse to be daunted by the world's grief, may we emerge as an effective voice of the voiceless. Joyful transformation awaits us all.

References

(No author). (1859). Freedom and slavery. (1859, December 6). The Spectator. http://www2.vcdh.virginia.edu/teaching/vclassroom/proslavewsht2.html

(No author). (2017). Veterans and opioid addiction. Military Officers Association of America. www.moaa.org/Content/Publications-and-Media/Features-and-Columns/Health-Features/Veterans-and-Opioid-Addiction

(No author). (2018). Chairman Johnson releases report on how Medicaid has helped to fuel the opioid epidemic. Homeland Security and Governmental Affairs. www.hsgac.senate.gov/media/majority-media/chairman-johnson-releases-report-on-how-medicaid-has-helped-to-fuel-the-opioid-epidemic-/

(No author). (2018). Grandparents raising grandchildren as opioid epidemic takes toll. CBSNews. www.cbsnews.com/news/grandparents-raising-grandchildren-amid-opioid-epidemic/

(No author). (2019). Photos: Look back at historic Dow Chemical anti-Vietnam War protests at UW-Madison. Wisconsin State Journal. https://madison.com/wsj/news/local/education/university/photos-look-back-at-historic-dow-chemical-anti-vietnam-war-protests-at-uw-madison/collection_ac29edf2-674e-584b-998c-ad64a88da0e5.html#1

(No author). (2021). Jim Crow laws. History.com. www.history.com/topics/early-20th-century-us/jim-crow-laws

Adamo, C. G. (2019). *Rules for defeating radicals: Countering the Alinsky strategy*. Self-published.

Adams, M. (2017). How #NoHateInMyHoller became the war cry for Appalachia. 100 Days in Appalachia. www.100daysinappalachia.com/2017/08/nohateinmyholler-became-war-cry-appalachia/

Agarwal, P., Bailey, B., Hall, J., Devoe, M., & Wood, D. (2018). Factors associated with maternal drug use and the severity of neonatal abstinence syndrome. *International Public Health Journal, 10*(3), 265–274.

Alexander, B. (2017). *Glass house: The 1% economy and the shattering of the all-American town*. St. Martin's Press.

Alexander, G. C., Stoller, K. B., Haffajee, R. L., & Saloner, B. (2020). An epidemic in the midst of a pandemic: Opioid use disorder and COVID-19. *Annals of Internal Medicine, 173*(1), 57–58.

Alexander, M. (2012). *The new Jim Crow: Mass incarceration in the age of colorblindness*. New Press.

Alinsky, S. (1971). *Rules for radicals: A practical primer for realistic radicals*. Vintage Books.

Allam, H., & Urquhart, J. (2020). 'I am antifa': One activist's violent death became a symbol for the right and left. NPR. www.npr.org/2020/07/23/893533916/i-am-antifa-one-activist-s-violent-death-became-a-symbol-for-the-right

All Home. (2020). Count us in: Seattle/King County point-in-time count of individuals experiencing homelessness. https://regionalhomelesssystem.org/wp-content/uploads/2020/07/Count-Us-In-2020-Final.pdf

Althauser, D. (2019). Custody and recovery: Law versus legend. Presentation at North Community Counseling Centers by director of Family and Youth Law Center at Capital University Law School.

Amaya, B. (2015). I was human trafficked for 10 years. We can do more to stop it. Ted Talks series. www.youtube.com/watch?v=U_kXuQHZmWs

American Civil Liberties Union. (n.d.). Banking on bondage: Private prisons and mass incarceration. www.aclu.org/banking-bondage-private-prisons-and-mass-incarceration

American Civil Liberties Union. (2021). Over-jailed and un-treated: How the failure to provide treatment for substance use in prisons and jails fuels the opioid epidemic. www.aclu.org/sites/default/files/field_document/20210625-mat-prison_1.pdf

American Presidency Project. (n.d.). Voter turnout in presidential elections. University of California-Santa Barbara. www.presidency.ucsb.edu/statistics/data/voter-turnout-in-presidential-elections

American Security News Reports. (2018). Republican Governor's Association: Wisconsin Governor Scott Walker signs new legislation to combat opioid crisis. https://americansecuritynews.com/stories/511389649-republican-governor-s-association-wisconsin-governor-scott-walker-signs-new-legislation-to-combat-opioid-crisis

Ames, D., Erickson, Z., Youssef, N. A., Arnold, I., Adamson, C. S., Sones, A. C., ... Koenig, H. G. (2019). Moral injury, religiosity, and suicide risk in US veterans and active duty military with PTSD symptoms. *Military Medicine, 184* (3–4), e271–e278.

Anonymous. (2021). Phone interview with a medical professional.

Applied Survey Research. (2016). City of Seattle 2016 homeless needs assessment. City of Seattle. www.documentcloud.org/documents/3480319-City-of-Seattle-Homeless-Needs-Assessment-March.html

Arditti, J. A., Molloy, S., Spiers, S., & Johnson, E. I. (2019). Perceptions of nonresident father involvement among low-income youth and their single parents. *Family Relations, 68*(1), 68–84.

Aseltine, E. D., & Antunes, M. J. L. (2021). Tribal healing to wellness courts. In E. M. Ahlin & A. S. Douds (Eds.), Taking *problem-solving courts to sca*le: Diverse *applications of the specialty court model* (pp. 195–210). Lexington Books.

Associated Press. (2013). 'Crack baby' scare overblown, teen research says. www.news-press.com/story/news/nation/2013/05/27/crack-baby-research/2362959/

Associated Press. (2020). California Supreme Court allows murder charge in stillborn fetus case. *LA Times*. www.latimes.com/california/story/2020-12-24/california-supreme-court-allows-murder-charge-after-fetus-is-stillborn

Bachhuber, M. A., Roberts, C. B., Metraux, S., & Montgomery, A. E. (2015). Screening for homelessness among individuals initiating medication-assisted treatment for opioid use disorder in the Veterans Health Administration. *Journal of Opioid Management, 11*(6), 459–462.

Baird, S. (2014). Stereotypes of Appalachia obscure a diverse picture. NPR. www.npr.org/sections/codeswitch/2014/04/03/298892382/stereotypes-of-appalachia-obscure-a-diverse-picture

Balch, O. (2021). Mars, Nestlé, and Hershey to face child slavery lawsuit in US. The Guardian. www.theguardian.com/global-development/2021/feb/12/mars-nestle-and-hershey-to-face-landmark-child-slavery-lawsuit-in-us

Balert, J. (2015). Bill would protect addicted mothers who seek treatment. *Cincinnati Enquirer.* www.cincinnati.com/story/news/local/2015/09/02/bill-protect-addicted-mothers-seek-treatment/71585328/

Bardasi, E., & Wodon, Q. (2010). *Working long hours and having no choice: Time poverty in Guinea.* The World Bank.

Barrau, K., & Miller, M. (2021). The epidemic within the pandemic. BBC. www.bbc.com/news/av/world-us-canada-57786542

Battle, B. P. (2018). Deservingness, deadbeat dads, and responsible fatherhood: Child support policy and rhetorical conceptualizations of poverty, welfare, and the family. *Symbolic Interaction, 41*(4), 443–464.

Baumer, E. (1994). Poverty, crack, and crime: A cross-city analysis. *Journal of Research in Crime and Delinquency, 31*(3), 311–327.

Bebinger, M. (2018). Latinos are hit especially hard by the opioid crisis in Mass. But why? WBUR. www.wbur.org/commonhealth/2018/05/03/latino-opioid-overdose-deaths

Beckerman, A. (2017). Charting a course: Meeting the challenge of permanency planning for children with 2 incarcerated mothers. In C. Hairston (Ed.), *Children with parents in prison: Child welfare policy, program, and practice issues* (pp. 45–62). Taylor & Francis.

Bedford, K. (2016). Boston's Methadone Mile. *Boston Globe.* www3.bostonglobe.com/news/bigpicture/2016/07/16/boston-methadone-mile/cLqxOAY7X9tHiooOGuATAI/story.html?arc404=true

Bedrick, B. S., O'Donnell, C., Marx, C. M., Friedman, H., Carter, E. B., Stout, M. J., & Kelly, J. C. (2020). Barriers to accessing opioid agonist therapy in pregnancy. *American Journal of Obstetrics & Gynecology MFM, 2*(4), 100225.

Beletsky, L., Seymour, S., Kang, S., Siegel, Z., Sinha, M. S., Marino, R., . . . Freifeld, C. (2020). Fentanyl panic goes viral: The spread of misinformation about overdose risk from casual contact with fentanyl in mainstream and social media. *International Journal of Drug Policy, 86,* 102951.

Belknap, J. (2014). *The invisible woman: Gender, crime, and justice.* Stamford. CT: Cengage Learning.

Bennis, P. (2013). February 15, 2003. The day the world said no to war. Institute of Policy Studies. https://ips-dc.org/february_15_2003_the_day_the_world_said_no_to_war/

Berger, P. L., & Luckmann, T. (1966). *The social construction of reality: A treatise on the sociology of knowledge.* Anchor Books.

Bernstein, L., & Achenbach, J. (2021). Drug overdose deaths soared to a record 93,000 last year. *Washington Post.* www.washingtonpost.com/health/2021/07/14/drug-overdoses-pandemic-2020/

Blackford, M. (2019). Phone interview with drug counselor.

Blakey, J. M., & Hatcher, S. S. (2013). Trauma and substance abuse among child welfare involved African American mothers: A case study. *Journal of Public Child Welfare, 7*(2), 194–216.

Blight, D. W. (2018). *Frederick douglass: Prophet of freedom.* Simon & Schuster.

Bluvas, E. (2022). Coverage for opioid addiction treatment varies dramatically across the nation's Medicaid programs. Arnold School of Public Health. www.sc.edu/study/colleges_schools/public_health/about/news/2022/opioid_use_disorder_medications_medicaid_andrews.php#.Y_klBHbMLIU

Boppre, B., & Boyer, C. (2021). "The traps started during my childhood": The role of substance abuse in women's responses to adverse childhood experiences (ACEs). *Journal of Aggression, Maltreatment & Trauma, 30*(4), 429–449.

Botzet, A. M., McIlvaine, P. W., Winters, K. C., Fahnhorst, T., & Dittel, C. (2014). Data collection strategies and measurement tools for assessing academic and therapeutic outcomes in recovery schools. *Peabody Journal of Education, 89*(2), 197–213.

Bowden, M. (2013). 'Idiot', 'Yahoo', 'Original Gorilla': How Lincoln was dissed in his day. The Atlantic. www.theatlantic.com/magazine/archive/2013/06/abraham-lincoln-is-an-idiot/309304/

Bowers, J., & Abrahamson, D. (2020). Kicking the habit: The opioid crisis and America's addiction to prohibition. CATO Institute. www.cato.org/policy-analysis/kicking-habit-opioid-crisis-americas-addiction-prohibition?queryID=f816d053b5e545de7fadebe2c6dde8a7

Braden, M., Watson, L., Gilbert, T., & Enos, J. (2019). Too poor to pay: How Arkansas's offender-funded justice system drives poverty and mass incarceration. Lawyer's Committee for Civil Rights Under Law (report). https://indd.adobe.com/view/f3b39ab5-1da5-409e-97a6-a0b060d2f578

Brain, J. (n.d.). The abolition of slavery in Britain. Historic UK. www.historic-uk.com/HistoryUK/HistoryofBritain/Abolition-Of-Slavery/

Breines, J. G., & Ayduk, O. (2015). Rejection sensitivity and vulnerability to self-directed hostile cognitions following rejection. *Journal of Personality, 83*(1), 1–13.

Brenner, L. A., Ignacio, R. V., & Blow, F. C. (2011). Suicide and traumatic brain injury among individuals seeking Veterans Health Administration services. *The Journal of Head Trauma Rehabilitation, 26*(4), 257–264.

Brewer, S. (2018). Tribes lead the battle to combat a national opioid crisis. High Country News (Wyoming). www.hcn.org/articles/tribal-affairs-tribes-lead-the-battle-to-combat-a-national-opioid-crisis

Bride, B. E., Smith Hatcher, S., & Humble, M. N. (2009). Trauma training, trauma practices, and secondary traumatic stress among substance abuse counselors. *Traumatology, 15*(2), 96–105.

Brittany, P. B. (2018). Deservingness, deadbeat dads, and responsible fatherhood: Child support policy and rhetorical conceptualizations of poverty, welfare, and the family. *Symbolic Interaction, 41*(4), 443–464.

Brown, D. (2018). 'Barbaric': America's cruel history of separating children from their parents. Washington Post. www.washingtonpost.com/news/retropolis/wp/2018/05/31/barbaric-americas-cruel-history-of-separating-children-from-their-parents/

Brown, J. P. (2018). Opioid abuse and elder justice. Dep't of Just. J. Fed. L. & Prac, 66, 159.

Brown, V. F. (2020). Fentanyl and geopolitics: Controlling opioid supply from China. Brookings. www.brookings.edu/research/fentanyl-and-geopolitics-controlling-opioid-supply-from-china/

Buckner, J. C., Mezzacappa, E., & Beardslee, W. R. (2003). Characteristics of resilient youths living in poverty: The role of self-regulatory processes. *Development and Psychopathology, 15*(1), 139–162.

Bump, P. (2016). Steve Bannon once suggested only property owners should vote. What would that look like? Washington Post. www.washingtonpost.com/news/the-fix/wp/2016/11/28/steve-bannon-once-suggested-only-property-owners-should-vote-what-would-that-look-like/

Bump, P. (2021). Party polarization hit a high under Trump. Can Biden reel it back? Washington Post. www.washingtonpost.com/politics/2021/01/20/party-polarization-hit-high-under-trump-can-biden-reel-it-back/

Burden, M., Kingston, A., Wallace, M. A., Busse, J. W., Casademont, J., Chadaga, S. R., . . . Albert, R. K. (2019). Opioid utilization and perception of pain control in hospitalized patients: A cross-sectional study of 11 sites in 8 countries. *Journal of Hospital Medicine*, *14*(12), 737–745.

Buresh, M., Genberg, B. L., Astemborski, J., Kirk, G. D., & Mehta, S. H. (2019). Recent fentanyl use among people who inject drugs: Results from a rapid assessment in Baltimore, Maryland. *International Journal of Drug Policy*, *74*, 41–46.

Burke, E. (1790). *Reflections on the French Revolution*, excerpt. https://allenbolar.files.wordpress.com/2014/08/burke-edmund-1790-reflections-on-the-french-revolution-excerpt.pdf

Bush, N. (2018). *One by one: A memoir of love and loss in the shadows of opioid America*. Apollo Publishers.

Calcaterra, S. L., Bach, P., Chadi, A., Chadi, N., Kimmel, S. D., Morford, K. L., . . . Samet, J. H. (2019). Methadone matters: What the United States can learn from the global effort to treat opioid addiction. *Journal of General Internal Medicine*, *34*, 1039–1042.

Caldwell, E. (2021). Many Hispanics died of COVID-19 because of work exposure. Medical Xpress. https://medicalxpress.com/news/2021-04-hispanics-died-covid-exposure.html

Campbell, R. M. (2011). The myth of Appalachian whiteness: Stereotyping and racism from the perspective of a white Appalachian woman. The Urban Appalachian Coalition. https://uacvoice.org/wp-content/uploads/2011/10/workingpaper21.pdf

Cappelli, P., Barankay, I., & Lewin, D. (2018). How the Great Recession changed American workers. Wharton (University of Pennsylvania). https://knowledge.wharton.upenn.edu/article/great-recession-american-dream/

Cappello, O. (2021).Powerful contraception, complicated programs: Preventing coercive promotion of long-acting reversible contraceptives. Guttmacher Institute. www.guttmacher.org/gpr/2021/05/powerful-contraception-complicated-programs-preventing-coercive-promotion-long-acting

Carew, A. M., & Comiskey, C. (2018). Treatment for opioid use and outcomes in older adults: A systematic literature review. *Drug and Alcohol Dependence*, *182*, 48–57.

Carlson, K. F., Nelson, D., Orazem, R. J., Nugent, S., Cifu, D. X., & Sayer, N. A. (2010). Psychiatric diagnoses among Iraq and Afghanistan war veterans screened for deployment-related traumatic brain injury. *Journal of Traumatic Stress*, *23*(1), 17–24.

Carrasco, J. (2021). Latinos grapple with opioid overdose rise as pandemic triggers surge in U.S. use. NBC News. www.nbcnews.com/news/latino/latinos-grapple-opioid-overdose-rise-covid-pandemic-triggers-surge-us-rcna415

Carrega, C. (2020). 'Because they can get away with it': Why African Americans are blamed for crimes they didn't commit: Experts. ABC News. https://abcnews.go.com/US/african-americans-blamed-crimes-commit-experts/story?id=70906828

Case, A., & Deaton, A. (2015). Rising morbidity and mortality in midlife among white non-Hispanic Americans in the 21st century. *Proceedings of the National Academy of Sciences*, *112*(49), 15078–15083. www.pnas.org/content/112/49/15078

Casey Foundation. (2019). The Child Abuse Prevention and Treatment Act. https://caseyfamilypro-wpengine.netdna-ssl.com/media/CAPTA-Paper_web.pdf

CDC. (n.d.). Opioid overdose. www.cdc.gov/drugoverdose/epidemic/index.html

CDC. (2020). Interim guidance on unsheltered homelessness and coronavirus disease 2019 (COVID-19) for homeless service providers and local officials. www.cdc.gov/coronavirus/2019-ncov/community/homeless-shelters/unsheltered-homelessness.html

CDC. (2021). Increase in fatal drug overdoses across the United States driven by synthetic opioids before and during the COVID-19 pandemic. https://emergency.cdc.gov/han/2020/han00438.asp

Cesur, R., Sabia, J. J., & Bradford, W. D. (2019). *Did the war on terror ignite an opioid epidemic?* (No. w26264). National Bureau of Economic Research.

Chavkin, W. (2001). Cocaine and pregnancy—time to look at the evidence. *Jama*, 285(12), 1626–1628.

Chhatre, S., Cook, R., Mallik, E., & Jayadevappa, R. (2017). Trends in substance use admissions among older adults. *BMC Health Services Research*, 17(1), 1–8.

Child Welfare Information Gateway. (2019). Parental Substance Use as Child Abuse—Texas. www.childwelfare.gov/resources/parental-substance-use-child-abuse-texas/

Child Welfare Organization. (2019). CAPTA Fact Sheet. Child Welfare Organization. www.childwelfare.gov/pubPDFs/about.pdf

Childs, T. (2021). In-person interview with drug counselor on August 6, 2021.

Children's Defense Fund. (2017). Fifth National Grandrally Brings Hundreds of Grandparents and Other Relatives Raising Children to the U.S. Capitol. Children's Defense Fund. www.childrensdefense.org/2017/fifth-national-grandrally-brings-hundreds-of-grandparents-and-other-relatives-raising-children-to-the-u-s-capitol/

Choi, S. (2019). Improving children-parents visitation for families with substance abuse problems in child welfare. *Journal of Social Science for Policy Implications*, 7(1), 1–6.

Ciccarone, D. (2021). The rise of illicit fentanyls, stimulants and the fourth wave of the opioid overdose crisis. *Current Opinion in Psychiatry*, 34(4), 344–350.

City of Seattle. (2017). Complaint filed by city attorney. City of Seattle. www.seattle.gov/Documents/Departments/CityAttorney/OpioidLitigation/SeattleComplaint-Opioid.pdf

Clay, R. A. (2020). Are you experiencing compassion fatigue? American Psychological Association. www.apa.org/topics/covid-19/compassion-fatigue

Cleveland Clinic. (2018). The Opioid Epidemic: What can we learn from Europe? Cleveland Clinic. https://consultqd.clevelandclinic.org/the-opioid-epidemic-what-can-we-learn-from-europe

Cohen, J. (2018). Supervised injection facilities face obstacles, but that shouldn't stop them. Health Affairs. www.healthaffairs.org/do/10.1377/hblog20181127.121405/full/

Cohen, S. (1972). *Moral panics and folk devils*. London: MacGibbon & Kee, 9.

Coles, C.D. (1993). Saying "Goodbye" to the "Crack Baby." *Neurotoxicology and Teratology*, 15, 290–292.

Conner, K. O., & Rosen, D. (2008). "You're nothing but a junkie": Multiple experiences of stigma in an aging methadone maintenance population. *Journal of Social Work Practice in the Addictions*, 8(2), 244–264.

Contreras, O. (2021). More safe outdoors spaces, encampments 'not an option' as Mayor Hancock lays out strategy to fight homelessness. Denver 7 ABC. https://www.denver7.com/news/local-news/more-safe-outdoors-spaces-encampments-not-an-option-as-mayor-hancock-lays-out-strategy-to-fight-homelessness

Cooley, P. (2020). 10 people died of overdoses in Columbus in 24 hours. *The Columbus Dispatch*. https://www.dispatch.com/story/lifestyle/public-safety/2020/02/01/10-people-died-overdoses-in/1781729007/

Creitz, J. (2020). Tucker: Black Lives Matter 'enjoys almost complete immunity from criticism.' Fox News. www.foxnews.com/media/tucker-carlson-black-lives-matter-dangerous-moment

Culvyhouse, H. (2021). Meth, fentanyl, isolation driving local OD deaths. *Daily Independent*. https://news.yahoo.com/meth-fentanyl-isolation-driving-local-204600589.html?fr=yhssrp_catchall

Damon, W., McNeil, R., Milloy, M. J., Nosova, E., Kerr, T., & Hayashi, K. (2019). Residential eviction predicts initiation of or relapse into crystal methamphetamine use among people who inject drugs: A prospective cohort study. *Journal of Public Health, 41*(1), 36–45.

Daniulaityte, R., Silverstein, S. M., Crawford, T. N., Martins, S. S., Zule, W., Zaragoza, A. J., & Carlson, R. G. (2020). Methamphetamine use and its correlates among individuals with opioid use disorder in a midwestern US city. *Substance Use & Misuse, 55*(11), 1781–1789.

Daoust, R., Paquet, J., Moore, L., Gosselin, S., Gélinas, C., Rouleau, D. M., . . . Morris, J. (2018). Incidence and risk factors of long-term opioid use in elderly trauma patients. *Annals of Surgery, 268*(6), 985–991.

Davidson, J. (2018). Unseen face of the opioid epidemic: Drug abuse among the elderly grows. Washington Post. www.washingtonpost.com/news/powerpost/wp/2018/05/25/unseen-face-of-the-opioid-epidemic-drug-abuse-among-the-elderly-grows/

Davis, D. R. (2013). Harm reduction. Encyclopedia of Social Work. https://oxfordre.com/socialwork/view/10.1093/acrefore/9780199975839.001.0001/acrefore-9780199975839-e-171

Declan, L. (2021). Dear adults: If you're not fighting for trans kids' rights, please start. Huffington Post. www.huffpost.com/entry/transgender-kids-rights_n_6091acdfe4b0ccb91c37327d

Deisner, V. (2021). In-person interview on July 22, 2021.

Dell, M. (2019). Escaping the pain of human trafficking. TEDx Talks. www.youtube.com/watch?v=NcyYBhVDFHM

Dembosky, A. (2018). Meth in the morning, heroin at night: Inside the seesaw struggle of dual addiction. NPR. www.npr.org/sections/health-shots/2019/06/17/730803759/meth-in-the-morning-heroin-at-night-inside-the-seesaw-struggle-of-dual-addiction

Dembosky, A. (2019). Meth vs. opioids: America has two drug epidemics, but focuses on one. *NPR* story on KHN. https://khn.org/news/meth-vs-opioids-america-has-two-drug-epidemics-but-focuses-on-one/

Demeril, M. (n.d.). Seattle's "Hooverville": The failure of effective unemployment relief in early 1930s Seattle. University of Washington. https://depts.washington.edu/depress/hooverville_seattle.shtml

Department of Justice. (2014). Convicted sex trafficker sentence to more than 30 years in prison. www.justice.gov/opa/pr/convicted-sex-trafficker-sentenced-more-30-years-prison

Deutsch, J. (1997). An emotional O'Connor describes his son's suicide to jurors. AP News. https://apnews.com/article/dea6a1afc5df44c5847fe81164015817

Devega, C. (2020). Historian Anthony Harkins on the real story of white poverty and "Hillbilly Elegy." Salon. www.salon.com/2020/12/27/historian-anthony-harkins-on-the-real-story-of-white-poverty-and-hillbilly-elegy/

Devitt, M. (2021). Drug overdose deaths reached new high in 2020, says CDC. American Academy of Family Physicians. www.aafp.org/news/health-of-the-public/20210806overdosedeaths.html

Diamond, C. (2020). I was sex trafficked for years. Brothels are hidden in plain sight. TEDx Talks. www.youtube.com/watch?v=Rg6xCRemYw4

REFERENCES

Diaz, D. (2016). African-American professor Carol Swain slams Black Lives Matter. CNN. www.cnn.com/2016/07/09/politics/carol-swain-black-lives-matter-smerconish/index.html

Dickson-Gomez, J., Convey, M., Hilario, H., Corbett, A. M., & Weeks, M. (2008). Structural and personal factors related to access to housing and housing stability among urban drug users in Hartford, Connecticut. *Contemporary Drug Problems*, 35(1), 115–152.

Dodge, B. (2019). Democratic primary candidates addressed the opioid crisis for the first time Tuesday night. Here's why that matters. *Newsweek*. www.newsweek.com/candidates-addressed-opioid-first-time-matters-left-out-1465701

DOJ. (2017). "King of Death" dealer pleads guilty to heroin and fentanyl distribution. Department of Justice. www.justice.gov/usao-edva/pr/king-death-dealer-pleads-guilty-heroin-and-fentanyl-distribution

Domenelli, L. (2002). *Anti oppressive social work theory and practice*. Palgrave Macmillan.

Doubek, J. (2017). Conspiracy theorist Alex Jones apologizes for promoting 'Pizzagate'. NPR. www.npr.org/sections/thetwo-way/2017/03/26/521545788/conspiracy-theorist-alex-jones-apologizes-for-promoting-pizzagate

Doucet, B., & Philp, D. (2016). In Detroit 'ruin porn' ignores the voices of those who still call the city home. *The Guardian*. www.theguardian.com/housing-network/2016/feb/15/ruin-porn-detroit-photography-city-homes

Drash, W., & Blau, M. (2016). In America's drug death capital: How heroin is scarring the next generation. CNN. https://edition.cnn.com/2016/09/16/health/huntington-heroin/index.

Drug Enforcement Agency. (2020). Fentanyl flow to the United States. www.dea.gov/sites/default/files/2020-03/DEA_GOV_DIR-008-20%20Fentanyl%20Flow%20in%20the%20United%20States_0.pdf

Drug Induced Homicide (n.d.). Why are drug dealers getting away with MURDER? https://druginducedhomicide.org/

Drug Policy Alliance.. (n.d.b). Vision and mission. Drug Policy Alliance. www.drugpolicy.org/about-us#vision-mission

Dube, S. R. (2020). Twenty years and counting: The past, present, and future of ACEs research. In G. J. G. Asmundson & T. O. Afif (Eds.), *Adverse Childhood Experiences* (pp. 3–16). Academic Press.

Eason, J. M. (2017). *Big house on the prairie: Rise of the rural ghetto and prison proliferation*. University of Chicago Press.

East Tennessee State University and NORC at the University of Chicago. (2019). Creating a culture of health in Appalachia: Disparities and bright spots. Appalachian Regional Commission. www.arc.gov/wp-content/uploads/2020/06/HealthDisparitiesRelatedtoOpioidMisuseinAppalachiaApr2019.pdf

Eckert, B. (2017). How big pharma wrings more profits from opioid addicts. Class Action. www.classaction.com/news/big-pharma-profits-opioid-epidemic/

Edelman, M. W. (n.d.). Ending child poverty: The legacy of Senator Edward M. Kennedy. John F. Kennedy Library. www.jfklibrary.org/events-and-awards/forums/past-forums/transcripts/ending-child-poverty-the-legacy-of-senator-edward-m-kennedy

Edwards, K. M., Murphy, S., Palmer, K. M., Haynes, E. E., Chapo, S., Ekdahl, B. A., & Buel, S. (2017). Co-occurrence of and recovery from substance abuse and lifespan victimization: A qualitative study of female residents in trauma-informed sober living homes. *Journal of Psychoactive Drugs*, 49(1), 74–82.

Ella Baker Center for Human Rights. (2015). Who pays? The true cost of incarceration on families. https://ellabakercenter.org/wp-content/uploads/2022/09/Who-Pays-exec-summary.pdf

Enos, G. (2021). Stigmatizing comments about medication can derail treatment. *Alcoholism & Drug Abuse Weekly, 33*(38), 1–8.

Esposito, L. (2015). How social workers help your health. U.S. News and World Report. https://health.usnews.com/health-news/patient-advice/slideshows/how-social-workers-help-your-health?slide=9

Esposito, L. (2016). The countless ways poverty affects people's health. U.S. News and World Report. https://health.usnews.com/health-news/patient-advice/articles/2016-04-20/the-countless-ways-poverty-affects-peoples-health

Evans, W. N., Garthwaite, C., & Moore, T. J. (2018). *Guns and violence: The enduring impact of crack cocaine markets on young black males* (No. w24819). National Bureau of Economic Research.

Eyre, E. (2020). *Death in Mud Lick: A coal country fight against the drug companies that delivered the opioid epidemic*. Simon and Schuster.

Farrell, G., Tilley, N., & Tseloni, A. (2014). Why the crime drop? *Crime and Justice, 43*(1), 421–490.

Felitti, V. J., Anda, R. F., Nordenberg, D., & Williamson, D. F. (1998). Adverse childhood experiences and health outcomes in adults: The Ace study. *Journal of Family and Consumer Sciences, 90*(3), 31.

Feng, E. (2020). 'We are shipping to the U.S.': Inside China's online synthetic drug networks. NPR. www.npr.org/2020/11/17/916890880/we-are-shipping-to-the-u-s-china-s-fentanyl-sellers-find-new-routes-to-drug-user

Fill, M. M. A., Miller, A. M., Wilkinson, R. H., Warren, M. D., Dunn, J. R., Schaffner, W., & Jones, T. F. (2018). Educational disabilities among children born with neonatal abstinence syndrome. *Pediatrics, 142*(3), e20180562.

Finno-Velasquez, M., & Dettlaff, A. J. (2018). Challenges to family unity and opportunities for promoting child welfare in an increasingly punitive immigration landscape. *Advances in Social Work, 18*(3), 727–744.

Finno-Velasquez, M., Seay, K. D., & He, A. S. (2016). A national probability study of problematic substance use and treatment receipt among Latino caregivers involved with child welfare: The influence of nativity and legal status. *Children and Youth Services Review, 71*, 61.

Flake, J. (2017). Text of Senate speech. www.azcentral.com/story/news/politics/arizona/2017/10/24/sen-jeff-flake-senate-speech-full-text/794958001/

Flores, T. L. (2019). *The slave across the street: A human trafficking survivor's spiritual journey of healing*. Ampelon Publishing.

Fogger, S. A. (2019). Methamphetamine use: A new wave in the opioid crisis? *Journal of Addictions Nursing, 30*(3), 219–223.

Fowler, J. S., Volkow, N. D., Kassed, C. A., & Chang, L. (2007). Imaging the addicted human brain. *Science & Practice Perspectives, 3*(2), 4.

Friedberg, B. (2020). The dark virality of a Hollywood blood-harvesting conspiracy. Wired. www.wired.com/story/opinion-the-dark-virality-of-a-hollywood-blood-harvesting-conspiracy/

Friedman, M. J. (n.d.). History of PTSD in veterans: Civil War to DSM-5. Department of Veterans Affairs. www.ptsd.va.gov/understand/what/history_ptsd.asp

Friend, C. (n.d.). Social contract theory. Internet Encyclopedia of Philosophy. https://iep.utm.edu/soc-cont/

Frost, N. A., & Gross, L. A. (2012). Coercive mobility and the impact of prison-cycling on communities. *Crime, Law and Social Change, 57*(5), 459–474.

Fugett, K. (2020). War has ripple effects. New York Times. www.nytimes.com/2020/01/17/opinion/war-has-ripple-effects.html

Gabbatt, A. (2019). Golden escalator ride: The surreal day Trump kicked off his bid for president. The Guardian. www.theguardian.com/us-news/2019/jun/13/donald-trump-presidential-campaign-speech-eyewitness-memories

Ganeva, T. (2015). Woman thrown in jail for having an addiction while pregnant. *AlterNet*. www.alternet.org/2015/01/woman-thrown-jail-having-addiction-while-pregnant/

Gannon, M., Short, V., LaNoue, M., & Abatemarco, D. (2021). Prevalence of adverse childhood experiences of parenting women in drug treatment for opioid use disorder. *Community Mental Health Journal, 57*(5), 872–879.

Gautney, H. (2011). What is Occupy Wall Street? The history of leaderless movements. Washington Post. www.washingtonpost.com/national/on-leadership/what-is-occupy-wall-street-the-history-of-leaderless-movements/2011/10/10/gIQAwkFjaL_story.html

Gavin, K. (2019). As opioids kill more veterans, study shows treatment needs. University of Minnesota Health Blog. https://labblog.uofmhealth.org/rounds/as-opioids-kill-more-veterans-study-shows-treatment-needs

Generations United. (2017). In loving arms: The protective role of grandparents and other relatives in raising children exposed to trauma. www.gu.org/app/uploads/2018/05/Grandfamilies-Report-SOGF-2017.pdf

George, R. (2021). The human sacrifice call center. Video. www.youtube.com/watch?v=76sX2tZSx9g

Ghandnoosh, N. (2021). A second look at injustice. Sentencing Project. https://www.sentencingproject.org/reports/a-second-look-at-injustice/

Gilmore, R. G. (2007). *Golden gulag: Prisons, surplus, crisis, and opposition in globalizing California*. University of California Press.

Gluck, F. (2019). A glimmer of hope in SW Florida's opioid crisis, even as addictions continue. *Fort Myers News-Press*. www.news-press.com/story/news/local/2019/06/28/infant-opioid-exposures-dropping-southwest-florida-offering-hope/1370975001/

Glynn, T. R., & van den Berg, J. J. (2017). A systematic review of interventions to reduce problematic substance use among transgender individuals: A call to action. *Transgender Health, 2*(1), 45–59.

Goedel, W. C., Shapiro, A., Cerdá, M., Tsai, J. W., Hadland, S. E., & Marshall, B. D. (2020). Association of racial/ethnic segregation with treatment capacity for opioid use disorder in counties in the United States. *JAMA Network Open, 3*(4), e203711–e203711.

Goffman, E. (1963). Stigma: Notes on the management of spoiled identity. Simon & Schuster.

Goldberg, B. (2017). Opioid abuse crisis takes heavy toll on U.S. veterans. Reuters. www.reuters.com/article/us-usa-veterans-opioids-idUSKBN1DA1B2

Gone, J. P. (2013). Redressing First Nations historical trauma: Theorizing mechanisms for indigenous culture as mental health treatment. *Transcultural Psychiatry, 50*(5), 683–706.

Gonyea, D., & Montanaro, D. (2015) Trump on his plan to ban Muslims: 'Not politically correct, but i don't care'. NPR. www.npr.org/2015/12/08/458875362/trump-on-his-plan-to-ban-muslims-not-politically-correct-but-i-don-t-care

Gonzales, R., Anglin, M. D., Beattie, R., Ong, C. A., & Glik, D. C. (2012). Understanding recovery barriers: Youth perceptions about substance use relapse. *American Journal of Health Behaviors*, 36, 602–614.

Gorga, J. M. (2020). Retribution, not a solution: Drug-induced homicide in North Carolina. *Campbell Law Review*, 42, 161.

Gotbaum, R. (2018). School-based counselors help kids cope with fallout from drug addiction. NPR. https://radio.wosu.org/post/school-based-counselors-help-kids-cope-fallout-drug-addiction#stream/0

Grassley, C. (2018). Senate passes landmark criminal justice reform. Press release. www.grassley.senate.gov/news/news-releases/senate-passes-landmark-criminal-justice-reform

Grassley, C. (2023). Durbin, Grassley Reintroduce Criminal Justice Reform Bills. Press release. www.grassley.senate.gov/news/news-releases/durbin-grassley-reintroduce-criminal-justice-reform-bills

Grawert, A. (2020). What is the First Step Act—And what's happening with it? Brennan Center. www.brennancenter.org/our-work/research-reports/what-first-step-act-and-whats-happening-it

Greef, R. (2018a). Introduction. In R. Greeff (Ed.), *Fostering kinship: An international perspective on kinship foster care* (pp. 1–3). Routledge.

Greef, R. (2018b). Kinship, fostering, and obligations of the state. In R. Greeff (Ed.), *Fostering kinship: An international perspective on kinship foster care*. Routledge.

Guzman, J. (2022). Ohio AG warns of rise in 'Frankenstein opioiods' more dangerous than fentanyl. The Hill. https://thehill.com/changing-america/well-being/prevention-cures/3460077-ohio-ag-warns-of-rise-in-frankenstein-opioids-more-dangerous-than-fentanyl

Hacking, I. (1999). *The social construction of what?* Harvard University Press.

Halperin, J. H., & Blistein, D. (2019). *Opium*. Hatchette Books.

Han, B. H. (2018). Aging, multimorbidity, and substance use disorders: The growing case for integrating the principles of geriatric care and harm reduction. *International Journal on Drug Policy*, 58, 135.

Harris, L. H., & Wolfe, T. (2014). Stratified reproduction, family planning care and the double edge of history. *Current Opinion in Obstetrics and Gynecology*, 26(6), 539–544.

Hart, J. P., & Stough-Hunter, A. N. (2017). *Pathways to pacifism and antiwar activism among US veterans: The role of moral identity in personal transformation*. Lexington Books.

Harwood, J. (2008). Meet John McCain, centrist. CNBC. www.cnbc.com/2008/04/03/meet-john-mccain-centrist.html

Hassan, A. (2019). Hate-crime violence hits 16-year high, F.B.I. reports. *New York Times*. www.nytimes.com/2019/11/12/us/hate-crimes-fbi-report.html

Hauslohner, A. (2019). During first two years of 'Muslim ban,' Trump administration granted few waivers. Washington Post. www.washingtonpost.com/immigration/during-first-two-years-of-muslim-ban-trump-administration-granted-few-waivers/2019/09/24/44519d02-deec-11e9-8dc8-498eabc129a0_story.html

Hayes, C. M., Sufrin, C., & Perritt, J. B. (2020). Reproductive justice disrupted: Mass incarceration as a driver of reproductive oppression. *American Journal of Public Health*, 110(S1), S21–S24.

Hayward, S. F. (2013). Reagan, conservative statesman. Heritage Foundation. www.heritage.org/political-process/report/ronald-reagan-conservative-statesman

He, A. S. (2015). Examining intensity and types of interagency collaboration between child welfare and drug and alcohol service providers. *Child Abuse & Neglect, 46*, 190–197.

Health in Justice Action Lab and Legal Science (n.d.). Drug-induced homicide. www.healthinjustice.org/drug-induced-homicide

Health in Justice Action Lab and Legal Science. (2019). Drug-induced homicide laws. http://pdaps.org/datasets/drug-induced-homicide-1529945480-1549313265-1559075032

Health Resources and Services Administration (HRSA). (n.d.). Who Was Ryan White? https://hab.hrsa.gov/about-ryan-white-hivaids-program/about-ryan-white-hivaids-program

Hefling, K. (2018). Cash-strapped schools struggle to help children of opioid epidemic. Politico. www.politico.com/story/2018/06/18/opioid-epidemic-childen-schools-649564

Hendy, H. M., Black, P., Can, S. H., Fleischut, A., & Aksen, D. (2018). Opioid abuse as maladaptive coping to life stressors in U.S. adults. *Journal of Drug Issues, 48*(4), 560–571.

Hinsliff, G. (2019). The pansexual revolution: How sexual fluidity became mainstream. *The Guardian*. www.theguardian.com/society/2019/feb/14/the-pansexual-revolution-how-sexual-fluidity-became-mainstream

History.com. (2018). Hoovervilles. www.history.com/topics/great-depression/hoovervilles

History.com. (2019). The War on Drugs. www.history.com/topics/crime/the-war-on-drugs

History.com. (2020). Trail of Tears. History.com. www.history.com/topics/native-american-history/trail-of-tears

Hodson, G. (2016). Race as a social construction. *Psychology Today*. www.psychologytoday.com/us/blog/without-prejudice/201612/race-social-construction#

Holder, J. (2022). Tracking coronavirus vaccinations around the world. New York Times. www.nytimes.com/interactive/2021/world/covid-vaccinations-tracker.html

Horwitt, S. D. (1992*). Let them call me rebel: Saul Alinsky: His life and legacy*. First Vintage Books.

House Committee on Oversight and Reform. (2015). Mikulski and Cummings introduce the REBUILD Act to address systemic poverty in urban areas. Press release. https://oversightdemocrats.house.gov/news/press-releases/mikulski-and-cummings-introduce-the-rebuild-act-to-address-systemic-poverty-in

Howard University. (n.d.). A Brief History of Civil Rights in the United States: The War on Drugs and Mass Incarceration. https://library.law.howard.edu/civilrightshistory/blackrights/massincarceration

Howard, D. L. (2019). Effective treatment of opioid use disorder among African Americans. In *Effective Prevention and Treatment of Substance Use Disorders for Racial and Ethnic Minorities*. IntechOpen.

Howell, B. A., Bart, G., Wang, E. A., & Winkelman, T. N. (2021). Service involvement across multiple sectors among people who use opioids, methamphetamine, or both, United States—2015–2018. *Medical Care, 59*(3), 238–244.

Hughes, M., & Tucker, W. (2018). Poverty as an adverse childhood experience. *North Carolina Medical Journal, 79*(2), 124–126.

Huhn, A. S., Strain, E. C., Tompkins, D. A., & Dunn, K. E. (2018). A hidden aspect of the US opioid crisis: Rise in first-time treatment admissions for older adults with opioid use disorder. *Drug and Alcohol Dependence*, *193*, 142–147.

Human Rights Campaign. (2020). Coming out, living authentically as transgender or non-binary. https://hrc-prod-requests.s3-us-west-2.amazonaws.com/ComingOut-TNB-Resource-2020.pdf?mtime=20201009121132&focal=none

Humphreys, K. (2018). How Medicaid can strengthen the national response to the opioid epidemic. *American Journal of Public Health*, *108*(5), 589.

Hunt, B. D., Locklear, L., Bullard, C., & Pacheco, C. (2020). "Do you live in a teepee? Do you have running water?" The harrowing experiences of American Indians in North Carolina's urban K-12 schools. *The Urban Review*, 1–19.

Illingworth, A. (2020). Edmund Burke, the father of conservatism. The Burkean. www.theburkean.co.uk/edmund-burke-the-father-of-conservatism/

International Labor Organization. (2018). Ending forced labour by 2030: A review of policies and programmes. www.ilo.org/wcmsp5/groups/public/---ed_norm/---ipec/documents/publication/wcms_653986.pdf

I'm From Denver. (2021). More than 100 homeless people landed regular jobs after Denver hired them to perform day labor. https://imfromdenver.com/more-than-100-homeless-people-landed-regular-jobs-after-denver-hired-them-to-shovel-mulch-and-perform-other-day-labor/

Indian Children Welfare Act Guide. (n.d.). Indian Children Welfare Act. https://icwaguide.tribalinformationexchange.org/index.html

Indian Health Service (n.d.). Opioids and the COVID-19 pandemic addressing the opioid crisis during the COVID-19 pandemic. www.ihs.gov/opioids/covid19

Inskeep, S. (2021). Fentanyl is one reason why the U.S. drug addiction crisis is roaring back. NPR. www.npr.org/2021/10/19/1047223109/fentanyl-is-one-reason-why-the-u-s-drug-addiction-crisis-is-roaring-back

Isenberg, N. (2016). *White trash: The 400-year untold history of class in America*. Penguin Books.

Jaffe, C. (2017). Melting the polarization around climate change politics. *Georgetown Environmental Law Review*, *30*, 455.

Jalali, M. S., Botticelli, M., Hwang, R. C., Koh, H. K., & McHugh, R. K. (2020). The opioid crisis: A contextual, social–ecological framework. *Health Research Policy and Systems*, *18*(1), 1–9.

Jamison, P. (2018a). The opioid epidemic and its effect on African Americans. Washington Post. www.washingtonpost.com/graphics/2018/local/opioid-epidemic-and-its-effect-on-african-americans/

Jamison, P. (2018b) 'Pure incompetence.' Washington Post. www.washingtonpost.com/graphics/2018/local/dc-opioid-epidemic-response-african-americans/?itid=lk_inline_manual_10

Jamison, P. (2021). They'd battled addiction together. Then lockdowns became a 'recipe for death.' Washington Post. www.washingtonpost.com/dc-md-va/2021/07/29/west-virginia-addiction-overdose-lockdown

Jarvis, M. (2020). Challenges in outpatient and residential treatment. ASAM. https://elearning.asam.org/products/supporting-addiction-treatment-during-covid-19-nam-asam-collaboration#tab-product_tab_content

Johnson, L., & Byrd, W.C. (2020). Searching for the real Appalachia in Netflix's 'Hillbilly Elegy.' Washington Post. www.washingtonpost.com/nation/2020/11/20/searching-real-appalachia-netflixs-hillbilly-elegy/

Johnson, V. E., & Carter, R. T. (2020). Black cultural strengths and psychosocial well-being: An empirical analysis with Black American adults. *Journal of Black Psychology*, 46(1), 55–89.

Jojack, B. (2018). "No hate in my holler" march is a window into West Virginia's political divide. Salon. www.salon.com/2018/02/10/no-hate-in-my-holler-march-a-window-into-west-virginias-political-divide_partner/

Jones, C. M. (2018). Testimony from Christopher M. Jones, PharmD., M.P.H. on opioids in Indian Country: Beyond the crisis to healing the community before Committee on Indian Affairs. Health and Human Services. https://www.govinfo.gov/content/pkg/CHRG-115shrg32784/pdf/CHRG-115shrg32784.pdf

Joshi, P., Shah, N. K., & Kirane, H. D. (2019). Medication-assisted treatment for opioid use disorder in older adults: An emerging role for the geriatric psychiatrist. *The American Journal of Geriatric Psychiatry*, 27(4), 455–457.

Judiciary Committee. (2021). Durbin, Lee introduce Smarter Sentencing Act. Senate Committee on the Judiciary. www.judiciary.senate.gov/press/dem/releases/durbin-lee-introduce-smarter-sentencing-act

Justice, C. (2020). Small group of protesters gather in Dr. Amy Acton's neighborhood. News5 Cleveland. www.news5cleveland.com/news/continuing-coverage/coronavirus/local-coronavirus-news/small-group-of-protesters-gather-in-dr-amy-actons-neighborhood

Kaiser Family Foundation. (2023). Status of state Medicaid expansion decisions: Interactive map. KFF. www.kff.org/medicaid/issue-brief/status-of-state-medicaid-expansion-decisions-interactive-map/

Kane, P. (2018). What democrats can learn from the centrists who got Bill Clinton to the White House. Washington Post. www.washingtonpost.com/lifestyle/magazine/what-democrats-can-learn-from-the-centrists-who-got-bill-clinton-to-the-white-house/2018/01/02/07380834-db56-11e7-b1a8-62589434a581_story.html

Kenney, A. (2018). Supervised drug-use site for heroin, other substances wins support of Denver City Council. Denver Post. www.denverpost.com/2018/11/19/supervised-drug-use-denver-city-council/

Khan, H., & Taylor, C. (2009). Ted Kennedy's legislative accomplishments. ABC News. https://abcnews.go.com/Politics/TedKennedy/story?id=7787098

Khindaria, B. (2019). Drug users are biggest casualties of global war on drugs says UNAIDS. Newstex. http://ezproxy.fiu.edu/login?url=https://search-proquest-com.ezproxy.fiu.edu/docview/2251594088?accountid=10901

Kidd, J. D., Goetz, T. G., Shea, E. A., & Bockting, W. O. (2021). Prevalence and minority-stress correlates of past 12-month prescription drug misuse in a national sample of transgender and gender nonbinary adults: Results from the US Transgender Survey. *Drug and Alcohol Dependence*, 219, 108474.

Kime, P.(2019). Combat troops at higher risk for opioid, heroin addiction, study says. Military Times. www.militarytimes.com/pay-benefits/2019/10/14/combat-troops-at-higher-risk-for-opioid-heroin-addiction-study-says/

King County (2020). Point-in-Time count estimates a 5 percent increase in people experiencing homelessness, newly updated data dashboards reveal more people receiving shelter and services. King County (WA). https://kingcounty.gov/elected/executive/constantine/news/release/2020/July/01-homeless-count.aspx

Klein, A. (2018). What's in the new federal opioid legislation to help schools. Education Week. http://blogs.edweek.org/edweek/campaign-k-12/2018/10/opioid-schools-congress-mental-health-education.html?print=1

Klepper, D., & Swenson, A. (2022). Trump openly embraces, amplifies QAnon conspiracy theories. AP News. https://apnews.com/article/technology-donald-trump-conspiracy-theories-government-and-politics-db50c6f709b1706886a876ae6ac298e2

Knight, K. R., Duncan, L. G., Szilvasi, M., Premkumar, A., Matache, M., & Jackson, A. (2019). Reproductive (in)justice—Two patients with avoidable poor reproductive outcomes. *New England Journal of Medicine, 381*, 593–596.

Koob, G. F. (2020). Neurobiology of opioid addiction: Opponent process, hyperkatifeia, and negative reinforcement. *Biological Psychiatry, 87*(1), 44–53.

Kreusi, K., & Mattise, J. (2021). Tennessee governor signs two new anti-trans 'bathroom bills' into law. Time. https://time.com/6049595/tennessee-anti-trans-bathroom-bill/

Kroelinger, C. D., Rice, M. E., Cox, S., Hickner, H. R., Weber, M. K., Romero, L., . . . Barfield, W. D. (2019). State strategies to address opioid use disorder among pregnant and postpartum women and infants prenatally exposed to substances, including infants with neonatal abstinence syndrome. *Morbidity and Mortality Weekly Report, 68*(36), 777.

Kryszajtys, D. T., Rudzinski, K., Chan Carusone, S., Guta, A., King, K., & Strike, C. (2021). Do mock-ups, presentations of evidence, and Q&As help participants voice their opinions during focus groups and interviews about supervised injection services? *International Journal of Qualitative Methods, 20*, 16094069211033439.

LaBrecque, L. The CARES act has passed: Here are the highlights. Forbes.www.forbes.com/sites/leonlabrecque/2020/03/29/the-cares-act-has-passed-here-are-the-highlights/?sh=4e8d0c5c68cd

Lageson, S. E. (2020). *Digital punishment: Privacy, stigma, and the harms of data-driven criminal justice.* Oxford University Press.

LaGrotta, C. (2020). Treatment of opioid use disorder in the elderly. *Current Treatment Options in Psychiatry*, 1–13.

Lane, C. (2021). Here's some hope for supporters of criminal justice reform. Washington Post. www.washingtonpost.com/opinions/heres-some-hope-for-supporters-of-criminal-justice-reform/2021/03/30/d41a1d72-9194-11eb-9668-89be11273c09_story.html

Leahey, A. (2022). Expanded child tax credit likely isn't coming back. Now What? Bloomberg News. https://news.bloombergtax.com/tax-insights-and-commentary/expanded-child-tax-credit-likely-isnt-coming-back-now-what

Lecher, C. (2015). Criminal charges. The Verge. www.theverge.com/a/prison-phone-call-cost-martha-wright-v-corrections-corporation-america

Lederer, L. J., & Wetzel, C. A. (2014). The health consequences of sex trafficking and their implications for identifying victims in healthcare facilities. *Annals of Health Law, 23*(1), 61.

Lee, B. (2020). Not-so-grand strategy: America's failed war on drugs in Colombia. Harvard International Review. https://hir.harvard.edu/americas-failed-war-on-drugs-in-colombia/

Lee, H., & Wildeman, C. (2013). Things fall apart: Health consequences of mass imprisonment for African American women. *The Review of Black Political Economy, 40*(1), 39–52.

Lee, N. (2021). America has spent over a trillion dollars fighting the war on drugs. 50 years later, drug use in the U.S. is climbing again. CNBC. www.cnbc.com/2021/06/17/the-us-has-spent-over-a-trillion-dollars-fighting-war-on-drugs.html

Lemann, L. (2020). The republican identity crisis after Trump. New Yorker. www.newyorker.com/magazine/2020/11/02/the-republican-identity-crisis-after-trump

Lembke, A. (2016). *Drug Dealer, MD.* Random House.

Leonard, N. (2018a). After losing their children and parents to addiction, families rebuild a new normal. Press of Atlantic City. www.pressofatlanticcity.com/news/breaking/after-losing-their-children-and-parents-to-addiction-families-rebuild/article_d48b6794-b2c1-5288-980f-d5fd127a6c6b.html

Leonard, N. (2018b). How EMS in South Jersey fight responder fatigue amid opioid epidemic. Press of Atlantic City. www.pressofatlanticcity.com/news/how-ems-in-south-jersey-fight-responder-fatigue-amid-opioid/article_738e5cab-42ab-5e19-b68c-9bc738fb2e17.html

Levinson-King, R. (2021). US women are being jailed for having miscarriages. BBC. https://www.bbc.com/news/world-us-canada-59214544

Levi-Minzi, M. A., Surratt, H. L., Kurtz, S. P., & Buttram, M. E. (2013). Under treatment of pain: A prescription for opioid misuse among the elderly? *Pain Medicine, 14*(11), 1719–1729.

Levin, J. (2019). *The queen: The life behind an American myth.* Back Bay Books.

Levitin, M. (2015). The triumph of Occupy Wall Street. The Atlantic. www.theatlantic.com/politics/archive/2015/06/the-triumph-of-occupy-wall-street/395408/

Leza, L., Siria, S., López-Goñi, J. J., & Fernandez-Montalvo, J. (2021). Adverse childhood experiences (ACEs) and substance use disorder (SUD): A scoping review. *Drug and Alcohol Dependence,* 108563.

Lieberman, A., & Davis, C. (2023). *Legal Interventions to Reduce Overdose Mortality: Overdose Good Samaritan Laws.* Network for Public Health Law. www.networkforphl.org/resources/legal-interventions-to-reduce-overdose-mortality-overdose-good-samaritan-laws/

Light, M. T. (2021). The declining significance of race in criminal sentencing: Evidence from US federal courts. *Social Forces, 100*(2), doi:10.1093/sf/soab018

Limbeck, R. (n.d.). He sold my soul. Polaris Project. https://polarisproject.org/survivor-gallery-rachelle-limbeck/

Lin, L. A., Bohnert, A. S., Kerns, R. D., Clay, M. A., Ganoczy, D., & Ilgen, M. A. (2017). Impact of the Opioid Safety Initiative on opioid-related prescribing in veterans. *Pain, 158*(5), 833–839.

Lister, J. J., Greenwald, M. K., & Ledgerwood, D. M. (2017). Baseline risk factors for drug use among African-American patients during first-month induction/stabilization on methadone. *Journal of Substance Abuse Treatment, 78,* 15–21.

LoBianco, T. (2016). Report: Aide says Nixon's war on drugs targeted blacks, hippies. CNN. www.cnn.com/2016/03/23/politics/john-ehrlichman-richard-nixon-drug-war-blacks-hippie/index.html

Lopez, A. M., Dhatt, Z., Howe, M., Al-Nassir, M., Billing, A., Artigiani, E., & Wish, E. D. (2021). Co-use of methamphetamine and opioids among people in treatment in Oregon: A qualitative examination of interrelated structural, community, and individual-level factors. *International Journal of Drug Policy, 91,* 103098.

Lopez, G. (2017). The opioid epidemic has now reached black America. Vox. www.vox.com/science-and-health/2017/12/22/16808490/opioid-epidemic-black-white

Lukes, E. (2020a). *A date with destiny; A sex-trafficking story of survival: From victim to survivor*. Self-published.
Lukes, E. (2020b). *Don't call me destiny; That's not my name: A sex-trafficking story of survival*. Self-published.
Luoma, J. B., Chwyl, C., & Kaplan, J. (2019). Substance use and shame: A systematic and meta-analytic review. *Clinical Psychology Review, 70*, 1–12.
Lynch, M. (2001). The contingencies of social construction. *Economy and Society, 30*(2), 240–254.
Ma, J., Bao, Y. P., Wang, R. J., Su, M. F., Liu, M. X., Li, J. Q., . . . Lu, L. (2019). Effects of medication-assisted treatment on mortality among opioids users: A systematic review and meta-analysis. *Molecular Psychiatry, 24*(12), 1868–1883.
Macy, B. (2018). *Dopesick: Dealers, doctors, and the drug company that addicted America*. Back Bay Books.
Macy, B. (2020). America's other epidemic: A new approach to fighting the opioid crisis as it quietly rages on. Atlantic. www.theatlantic.com/magazine/archive/2020/05/nikki-king-opioid-treatment-program/609085/
Macy, B. (2022). *Raising Lazarus: Hope, justice, and the future of America's overdose crisis*. New York, NY: Little, Brown, and Company.
Main, F. (2020a). Mother of Chicago overdose victim suing to get daughter's death reclassified as homicide. Chicago Sun-Times. https://chicago.suntimes.com/2020/3/6/21162262/heroin-fentanyl-overdose-drug-induced-homicide-valerie-teper-irene-rodik
Main, F. (2020b). Judge rejects Chicago mom's request to reclassify daughter's death 'drug-induced homicide.' Chicago Sun-Times. https://chicago.suntimes.com/politics/2020/3/10/21173545/valerie-teper-drug-induced-homicide-law-illinois-sanjay-tailor-irene-rodik
Malone, S. (2017). Cuts to Medicaid could worsen U.S. opioid crisis, governors warn. Reuters. www.reuters.com/article/us-usa-governors-opioids-idUSKBN19Y2XH
Manhapra, A., Stefanovics, E., & Rosenheck, R. (2021). The association of opioid use disorder and homelessness nationally in the veterans health administration. *Drug and Alcohol Dependence, 223*, 108714.
Mann, B. (2021a). After 50 years of the War on Drugs, 'What good is it doing for us?' NPR. www.npr.org/2021/06/17/1006495476/after-50-years-of-the-war-on-drugs-what-good-is-it-doing-for-us
Mann, B. (2021b). As opioid deaths surge, Biden team moves to make buprenorphine treatment mainstream. NPR. www.npr.org/2021/04/27/990997759/as-opioid-deaths-surge-biden-team-moves-to-make-buprenorphine-treatment-mainstre
Mannix, A. (2019). In Duluth-Superior, small-town cops face a formidable foe: Mexican cartels. Minneapolis Star-Tribune. www.startribune.com/in-duluth-superior-small-town-cops-face-a-formidable-foe-mexican-cartels/561640682/
Marcellus, L., & Poag, E. (2016). Adding to our practice toolkit: using the ACTS script to address stigmatizing peer behaviors in the context of maternal substance use. *Neonatal Network, 35*(5), 327–332.
Marietta, S. (2020). Meet the artist who sets a standard for social justice work in Appalachia. Moonbow. www.kentuckymoonbow.com/blog/lacy-hale
Masterson, L. (2019). Seniors love Medicare but are pessimistic about its long-term future. Healthcare Dive. www.healthcaredive.com/news/seniors-love-medicare-but-are-pessimistic-about-its-long-term-future/548721/

Matesa, J. (2011). The great suboxone debate. The Fix. www.thefix.com/content/best-kept-secret-addiction-treatment?page=all

Matthews, D. (2014). Everything you need to know about the War on Poverty. Washington Post. www.washingtonpost.com/news/wonk/wp/2014/01/08/everything-you-need-to-know-about-the-war-on-poverty/

Matthews, D. (2016a). Who is Saul Alinsky, and why does the right hate him so much? Vox. www.vox.com/2014/10/6/6829675/saul-alinsky-explain-obama-hillary-clinton-rodham-organizing

Matthews, D. (2016b). Sweden pays parents for having kids—and it reaps huge benefits. Why doesn't the US? Vox. www.vox.com/2016/5/23/11440638/child-benefit-child-allowance

Matthews, S., Dwyer, R., & Snoek, A. (2017). Stigma and self-stigma in addiction. *Journal of Bioethical Inquiry, 14*(2), 275–286.

Mathewson, T. G. (2016). More grandparents are raising grandchildren—Here's how to help them. Hechinger Report. https://hechingerreport.org/parent-substance-abuse-incarceration-drives-increase-in-grandparents-raising-grandchildren/

Mazenko, M. (2021). Lauren Boebert lacks the conscience of a conservative. Denver Post. www.denverpost.com/2021/01/11/lauren-boebert-lacks-the-conscience-of-a-conservative/

McBay, A. (2019). *Full spectrum resistance: Actions and strategies for change* (Vol. 2). Seven Stories Press.

McGreal, C. (2019a). Why were millions of opioid pills sent to a West Virginia town of 3,000? The Guardian. www.theguardian.com/us-news/2019/oct/02/opioids-west-virginia-pill-mills-pharmacies

McGreal, C. (2019b). Capitalism gone wrong: How big pharma created America's opioid carnage. The Guardian. www.theguardian.com/us-news/2019/jul/24/opioids-crisis-big-pharma-drugs-carnage

McLellan, A. T. (2017). Substance misuse and substance use disorders: why do they matter in healthcare? *Transactions of the American Clinical and Climatological Association, 128*, 112.

McVicar, D., Moschion, J., & Van Ours, J. C. (2015). From substance use to homelessness or vice versa? *Social Science & Medicine, 136*, 89–98.

Meier, B. (2018). *Pain killer: An empire of deceit and the origin of America's opioid epidemic.* Random House.

Miller, M. (2000). Nothing's safe when Gore, Bush hunt for 'lockbox' issues. LA Times. www.latimes.com/archives/la-xpm-2000-oct-31-cl-44460-story.html

Miller, M. (2010). Alinsky for the left: The politics of community organizing. Dissent. https://www.dissentmagazine.org/article/alinsky-for-the-left-the-politics-of-community-organizing

Miller, R. J. (2021). *Halfway home: Race, punishment, and the afterlife of mass incarceration.* Hatchette Book Group.

Minnesota Department of Health. (updated 2022). Opioids. www.health.state.mn.us/communities/opioids/prevention/painperception.html

Moore, J. (2018). On Indian Child Welfare Act, time for critics and supporters to talk in earnest. Chronicle of Social Change. https://chronicleofsocialchange.org/icwa/indian-child-welfare-act-time-for-critics-supporters-talk-earnest/32509

Morris-Hafner, B. E. (2019). From felon to law enforcement: A retrospective. In D. Skinner & B. Franz (Eds.), *Not far from me: Stories of opioids and Ohio* (pp. 141–146). Trillium Press.

REFERENCES   233

Moyer, J. W. (2020). Rise in fatal drug overdoses in D.C. region likely tied to pandemic, officials say. Washington Post. www.washingtonpost.com/local/drug-overdose-washington-coronavirus/2020/08/20/2a4c64b8-e0a4-11ea-ade1-28daf1a5e919_story.html

Moyers, B. (1988). What a real president was like. Washington Post. www.washingtonpost.com/archive/opinions/1988/11/13/what-a-real-president-was-like/d483c1be-d0da-43b7-bde6-04e10106ff6c/

Mukhopadhyay, C. C. (2016). Getting rid of the word "causcasian." *Privilege: A Reader*, 21.

Mukosi, L. (2020). A tour of the Healing to Wellness Court. *Fourth World Journal*, 19(N2), 41–49.

Murphy, M. (2014). In prostitution, 'race, class, and sex intersect in the worst of ways to subjugate Native women' *Feminist Current*. https://www.feministcurrent.com/2014/03/19/in-prostitution-race-class-and-sex-intersect-in-the-worst-of-ways-to-subjugate-native-women/.

NAACP (National Association for the Advancement of Colored People). (n.d.). Criminal Justice Fact Sheet. www.naacp.org/criminal-justice-fact-sheet/

Najmabadi, S. (2021). Gov. Greg Abbott signs into law one of nation's strictest abortion measures, banning procedure as early as six weeks into a pregnancy. *Texas Tribune*. www.texastribune.org/2021/05/18/texas-heartbeat-bill-abortions-law/

National Archives. (2016). American Indian urban relocation. www.archives.gov/education/lessons/indian-relocation.html

National Council of Jewish Women (NCJW). (2016). Factsheet on safe harbor laws. www.ncjw.org/wp-content/uploads/2017/07/Fact-Sheet_Safe-Harbor_Updated-2016.pdf

National Institute of Health (2015). NIH analysis shows Americans are in pain. https://nccih.nih.gov/news/press/08112015

National Working Group on Foster Care and Education. (2018). Fostering success in education. file:///C:/Users/user/Downloads/NationalEducationDatasheet2018.pdf

NBC News. (2022). Jan 6 committee shows video of protesters chanting "Hang MikePence." www.nbcnews.com/video/jan-6-committee-shows-video-of-protesters-chanting-hang-mike-pence-142262341584

NCSACW (n.d.). Neonatal abstinence syndrome. https://ncsacw.samhsa.gov/topics/neonatal-abstinence-syndrome.aspx

Needham, B. (2021). Blacks, Hispanics among hardest hit during COVID-19 pandemic, study says. University of Michigan. https://record.umich.edu/articles/blacks-hispanics-among-hardest-hit-during-covid-19-pandemic/

Neilson, J. (2019). More kids are getting placed in foster care because of parents' drug use. NPR. www.wbur.org/npr/741790195/more-kids-are-getting-placed-in-foster-care-because-of-parents-drug-use

Nelson, J. L. (2019). What is Fox News? Researchers want to know. Columbia Journalism School. www.cjr.org/tow_center/fox-news-partisan-progaganda-research.php

Nerenberg, L. (2019). *Elder justice, ageism, and elder abuse*. Springer.

Neutill, R. (2020). Why are so many people ready to let the elderly die? *Refinery 29*. www.yahoo.com/lifestyle/why-many-people-ready-let-195927020.html

Newman, K. (2018). Taking the opioid crisis personally. U.S. News and World Report. www.usnews.com/news/healthiest-communities/articles/2018-05-11/counselor-and-consultant-jamelia-hand-taking-the-opioid-crisis-personally

Neykafh, L. (2015). Why are so many Americans in prison? *Slate*. https://slate.com/news-and-politics/2015/02/mass-incarceration-a-provocative-new-theory-for-why-so-many-americans-are-in-prison.html

Nguyen, T. (2020). How 'antifa' became a Trump catch-all. Politico. www.politico.com/news/2020/06/02/how-antifa-became-a-trump-catch-all-297921

Niayesh, V. (2019). Trump's travel ban really was a Muslim ban, data suggests. Washington Post. www.washingtonpost.com/politics/2019/09/26/trumps-muslim-ban-really-was-muslim-ban-thats-what-data-suggest/

NIDA. (2019). Dramatic increases in maternal opioid use and neonatal abstinence syndrome. National Institute on Drug Abuse. www.opioidlibrary.org/document/dramatic-increases-in-maternal-opioid-use-disorder-and-neonatal-abstinence-syndrome-infographic/

Nirrapil, F. (2020). Despite efforts by Bowser and D.C. Council, opioid deaths hit record this year. Washington Post. www.washingtonpost.com/local/dc-politics/dc-opioid-deaths-2020/2020/12/05/95cfba3a-34c0-11eb-b59c-adb7153d10c2_story.html

Nissen, N. (2021). Dying of loneliness: What COVID-19 has taught us about the opioid epidemic. Good Morning America. www.yahoo.com/gma/dying-loneliness-covid-19-taught-130100328.html

Novak, E. H. (2016). Vagrants, vixens, and victims: Exploring the limitations of human trafficking victim recognition criteria in Texas (Doctoral dissertation, Texas Woman's University). https://twu-ir.tdl.org/bitstream/handle/11274/8767/Novakd2.pdf?sequence=3&isAllowed=y

Obama, B. (2006). *The audacity of hope: Thoughts on reclaiming the American Dream*. Random House.

Oei, J. L., Melhuish, E., Uebel, H., Azzam, N., Breen, C., Burns, L., . . . Feller, J. M. (2017). Neonatal abstinence syndrome and high school performance. *Pediatrics, 139*(2), e20162651.

Office of the State's Attorney. (2020). Keith Lang found guilty of drug-induced homicide. www.mchenrycountyil.gov/Home/Components/News/News/16134/6389

Ohio Bureau of Criminal Investigation. (2022). Nitazenes: Ohio BCI laboratory update. *Public Bulletin, 18*:2. www.ohioattorneygeneral.gov/Files/Briefing-Room/News-Releases/BCI-Bulletin-Vol-18-02-Nitazenes-(Public).aspx

Ollove, K. (2019). The politics of Medicaid expansion have changed. Pew Stateline. www.pewtrusts.org/en/research-and-analysis/blogs/stateline/2019/11/13/the-politics-of-medicaid-expansion-have-changed

Olsen, Y. (2020). Overview of the American Society of Addiction Medicine's COVID-19 response. ASAM. https://elearning.asam.org/products/coordination-across-the-social-safety-net-to-avert-a-crisis-among-patients-with-addiction-nam-asam-collaboration#tab-product_tab_handouts

Om, A. (2018). The opioid crisis in black and white: The role of race in our nation's recent drug epidemic. *Journal of Public Health, 40*(4), e614–e615.

Ondocsin, J., Mars, S. G., Howe, M., & Ciccarone, D. (2020). Hostility, compassion and role reversal in West Virginia's long opioid overdose emergency. *Harm Reduction Journal, 17*(1), 1–11.

Onyekwere, A. (2021). How cash bail works. Brennan Center for Justice. www.brennancenter.org/our-work/research-reports/how-cash-bail-works

Ortiz, A. (2020). Understanding the opioid crisis and impact on African-American and Latinx communities. Webinar presented by MACC (Multi-ethnic Advocates for Cultural Competence) on September 25, 2020.

Ortiz, A. T., & Briggs, L. (2003). The culture of poverty, crack babies, and welfare cheats: The making of the" healthy white baby crisis." *Social Text, 21*(3), 39–57.

OSU Moritz College of Law. (2020). Law student/recent graduate drafting contest: An Ohio "Second Look" statute. https://moritzlaw.osu.edu/depc/wp-content/uploads/sites/115/2020/04/DEPC-OJPC-Law-Student-Contest-Prompt_FINAL-edits-1.pdf

Otiniano Verissimo, A. D., Grella, C. E., Amaro, H., & Gee, G. C. (2014). Discrimination and substance use disorders among Latinos: The role of gender, nativity, and ethnicity. *American Journal of Public Health*, *104*(8), 1421–1428.

Owen, B. (2005). Afterword: The case of the women. In J. Irwin (Ed.), *The warehouse prison: Disposal of the new dangerous class*. Roxbury Press.

Oxford English Dictionary. (n.d.). Definition of policy. www.oed.com/view/Entry/146842?rskey=7DlX6O&result=1#eid

Pacia, D. M. (2020). Reproductive rights vs. reproductive justice: Why the difference matters in bioethics. Harvard Law Petrie-Flom Center. https://blog.petrieflom.law.harvard.edu/2020/11/03/reproductive-rights-justice-bioethics/

Palmer, A. W. (2019). The China connection: How one D.E.A. agent cracked a global fentanyl ring. *New York Times Magazine*. www.nytimes.com/2019/10/16/magazine/china-fentanyl-drug-ring.html

Papenfuss, M. (2023). Arizona columnist rips Kari Lake's 'cuckoo land' delusion of being governor. Huffington Post. www.huffpost.com/entry/kari-lake-neverland-governor-arizona-republic_n_63b9fef9e4b0d6f0b9fb88c3

Parrott, S. (2014). War on poverty: Large positive impact, but more work remains. Center on Budget and Policy Priorities. www.cbpp.org/research/commentary-war-on-poverty-large-positive-impact-but-more-work-remains?fa=view&id=4074

Partnership for Drug-free Kids. (2017). Why you shouldn't use the word "addict." https://drugfree.org/parent-blog/shouldnt-use-word-addict/

Patrick, S. W., Martin, P. R., Scott, T. A., Michael Richards, M. D., & Cooper, W. O. (2018). Barriers to accessing treatment for pregnant women with opioid use disorder in Appalachian states. *Substance Abuse*, 40(3), 356–362.

Pattillo, M., Western, B., & Weiman, D. (2004). Introduction. In M. Pattillo, B. Western, & D. Weiman (Eds.), *Imprisoning America: The social effects of mass incarceration* (pp. 1–20). Russell Sage Foundation.

Pauly, B., Goldstone, I., McCall, J., Gold, F., & Payne, S. (2007). The ethical, legal and social context of harm reduction. Canadian Nurse, *103*, 19–23.

Paybarah, A. (2021). Judge dismisses murder charge against California mother after stillbirth. *New York Times*. www.nytimes.com/2021/05/20/us/chelsea-becker-stillbirth-murder-charges-california.html

PBS. (n.d.). Napalm and the Dow Chemical Company. PBS. www.pbs.org/wgbh/americanexperience/features/two-days-in-october-dow-chemical-and-use-napalm/

Pennsylvania Support Alliance. (2016). Recovering families: A tool for parents in recovery. www.cwla.org/wp-content/uploads/2016/08/C8-%E2%80%93-Recovering-Families.pdf

Peterson, M., Rich, J., Macmadu, A., Truong, A. Q., Green, T. C., Beletsky, L., Pognon, K., & Brinkley-Rubinstein, L. (2019). "One guy goes to jail, two people are ready to take his spot": Perspectives on drug-induced homicide laws among incarcerated individuals. *International Journal of Drug Policy*, *70*, 47–53.

Pettit, B. (2012). *Invisible men: Mass incarceration and the myth of black progress*. Russell Sage Foundation.

Pfaff, J. F. (2017). *Locked in: The true causes of mass incarceration and how to achieve real reform*. Basic Books.

Pfuhl, E. H., & Henry, S. (1993). *The deviance process* (3rd ed.). Aldine DeGruyter.

Pinedo, M. (2020). Deportation of family members of US-Citizen Latinos and misuse of prescription drugs: United States, 2019. *American Journal of Public Health, 110*(4), 560–566.

Polaris Project (2017). Human trafficking and the opioid crisis. https://polarisproject.org/wp-content/uploads/2019/10/Human-Trafficking-and-the-Opioid-Crisis.pdf

Polcin, D. L., & Korcha, R. (2015). Motivation to maintain sobriety among residents of sober living recovery homes. *Substance Abuse and Rehabilitation, 6*, 103.

Polcin, D. L., Mahoney, E., & Mericle, A. A. (2021). House manager roles in sober living houses. *Journal of Substance Use, 26*(2), 151–155.

Ports, K. A., Ford, D. C., Merrick, M. T., & Guinn, A. S. (2020). ACEs: Definitions, measurement, and prevalence. In J. G. J. Asmundson & T. O. Afifi (Eds.), *Adverse childhood experiences* (pp. 17–34). Academic Press.

Powell, T. B. (2022). An increase in "Frankenstein opioids" prompts warning from Ohio Attorney General. CBS News. www.cbsnews.com/news/frankenstein-opioids-nitazene-ohio-attorney-general-dave-yost-warning/

Preston, A., & Bennett, M. (2003). The history of methadone and methadone prescribing. In J. Strang, & G. Tober (Eds.), *Methadone matters: Evolving community methadone treatment of opiate addiction* (pp. 13–21). CRC Press.

Quinones, S. (2015). *Dreamland: The True Tale of America's Opiate Epidemic*. New York, NY: Bloomsbury Press.

Rabuy, B., & Kopf, D. (2016). Detaining the poor: How money bail perpetuates an endless cycle of poverty and jail time. Prison Policy. www.prisonpolicy.org/reports/incomejails.html

Radel, L., Baldwin, M., Crouse, G., Ghertner, R., & Waters, A. (2018). Substance use, the opioid epidemic, and the child welfare system: Key findings from a mixed methods study. ASPE Brief, Health and Human Services. https://aspe.hhs.gov/system/files/pdf/258836/SubstanceUseChildWelfareOverview.pdf

Rank, M. R., & Hirschl, T. A. (2015). The likelihood of experiencing relative poverty over the life course. *PLoS One, 10*(7), e0133513.

Rathbone, C. (2006). *A world apart: Women, prison, and life behind bars*. Random House.

Ray, M. (n.d.). Fox News. Encyclopedia Brittanica. www.britannica.com/topic/Fox-News-Channel

Ray, R. (2020). What does 'defund the police' mean and does it have merit? Brookings. www.brooking.edu/blod/fixgov/2020/06/19/what-does-defund-the-police-mean-and-does-it-have-merit

Raypole, C. (2019). What is an addictive personality? Healthline. www.healthline.com/health/addictive-personality-traits#harmful-effects

Reckdahl, K. (2016). Housing authority eliminates ban of ex-offenders. Shelterforce. https://shelterforce.org/2016/07/06/housing-authority-eliminates-ban-of-ex-offenders/

Recto, P., McGlothen-Bell, K., McGrath, J., Brownell, E., & Cleveland, L. M. (2020). The role of stigma in the nursing care of families impacted by neonatal abstinence syndrome. *Advances in Neonatal Care, 20*(5), 354.

Rembert, M. H., Betz, M. R., Feng, B., & Partridge, M. D. (2017). *Taking measure of Ohio's opioid crisis*. Ohio State University Press.

Reneau, A. (2020a). *Child sex trafficking organizations set the record straight on QAnon*. Upworthy. www.upworthy.com/child-sex-trafficking-organizations-debunk-qanon-conspiracies

Reneau, A. (2020b). *If you really want to #SaveTheChildren, stop spreading QAnon conspiracy theories.* Upworthy. www.upworthy.com/save-the-children-stop-the-qanon-conspiracies

Rigg, K. K., & Nicholson, H. L. (2019). Prescription opioid misuse among African-American adults: A rural-urban comparison of prevalence and risk. *Drug and Alcohol Dependence, 197,* 191–196.

Rimmerman, C. (1998). *ACT UP.* The Body website www.thebody.com/author/craig-a-rimmerman

Roberson, L. N. (2017). She leads a lonely life: When sex trafficking and drug addiction collide. *Wake Forest L. Rev., 52,* 359.

Rodriguez, R. M. (2008, June). (Dis) unity and diversity in post-9/11 America. Sociological Forum, *23*(2), 379–389.

Romero, D. (2022). 'Holi-Drag Storytime' for children canceled because of right-wing protesters. NBC News. www.nbcnews.com/news/us-news/holi-drag-storytime-children-canceled-right-wing-protesters-rcna59990

Roy, A. (2016). Transcending Obamacare: Achieving Truly Affordable, Patient-Centered, Near-Universal Coverage. Testimony to U.S. Congress. https://docs.house.gov/meetings/IF/IF14/20160511/104905/HHRG-114-IF14-Wstate-RoyA-20160511.pdf

Salisbury-Afshar, E. (2020). Enhanced risks for unsheltered populations with SUD during the COVID 19 pandemic. ASAM. https://elearning.asam.org/products/coordination-across-the-social-safety-net-to-avert-a-crisis-among-patients-with-addiction-nam-asam-collaboration#tab-product_tab_handouts

SAMHSA. (2017). Report reveals that about 1 in 8 children lived with at least one parent who had a past year substance use disorder. Substance Abuse and Mental Health Services Administration. www.samhsa.gov/newsroom/press-announcements/201708241000

SAMHSA. (2020a). The opioid crisis and the Black/African American population: An urgent issue. https://store.samhsa.gov/sites/default/files/SAMHSA_Digital_Download/PEP20-05-02-001_508%20Final.pdf

SAMHSA. (2020b). The opioid crisis and the Hispanic/Latino population: An urgent issue. https://store.samhsa.gov/sites/default/files/pep20-05-02-002.pdf?utm_medium=email&utm_source=transaction#:~:text=In%202018%2C%201.7%20million%20Hispanic,misuse%20in%20the%20past%20year

Sampson, R. J. (2011). The incarceration ledger: Toward a new era in assessing societal consequences. *Criminology & Public Policy, 10,* 819.

Sanders, S. (2020). The surprising legacy of Occupy Wall Street in 2020. NPR. www.npr.org/2020/01/23/799004281/the-surprising-legacy-of-occupy-wall-street-in-2020

Santoro, T. N., & Santoro, J. D. (2018). Racial bias in the US opioid epidemic: A review of the history of systemic bias and implications for care. *Cureus, 10*(12).

Saunders, J. B., Jarlenski, M. P., Levy, R., & Kozhimannil, K. B. (2018). Federal and state policy efforts to address maternal opioid misuse: Gaps and challenges. *Women's Health Issues, 28*(2), 130–136.

Savansky, B. (2020a). Groups call for police to be removed from Seattle Navigation Team. *Seattle PI.* www.seattlepi.com/seattlenews/article/Groups-call-for-police-to-be-removed-from-Seattle-15397978.php

Savansky, B. (2020b). Seattle to suspend work of team that sweeps homeless encampments, connects residents to resources. *Seattle PI.* www.seattlepi.com/seattlenews/article/seattle-to-suspend-homeless-encampment-sweep-team-15612785.php

Sawhill, I. V., & Pulliam, C. (2019). Six facts about wealth in the United States. Brookings Institute. www.brookings.edu/blog/up-front/2019/06/25/six-facts-about-wealth-in-the-united-states/

Sawyer, W., & Wagner, P. (2020). Mass incarceration: The whole pie 2020. Prison Policy Initiative. www.prisonpolicy.org/reports/pie2020.html

Saylor Academy. (n.d.). The traditional political spectrum. https://learn.saylor.org/mod/page/view.php?id=17382

Scherlen, R. (2012). The never-ending drug war: Obstacles to drug war policy termination. *PS: Political Science & Politics, 45*(1), 67–73.

Schneiberg, E. (2021). These are the states trying to stop trans kids from playing sports. Human Rights Campaign. www.hrc.org/news/these-are-the-states-trying-to-stop-trans-kids-from-playing-sports

Schnell, M. (2022). Pelosi says she 'absolutely' draws parallel between husband's attack, Jan. 6. The Hill. https://thehill.com/homenews/house/3724219-pelosi-says-she-absolutely-draws-parallel-between-husbands-attack-jan-6/

School Food Programs. (n.d.). School food programs. State University. https://education.stateuniversity.com/pages/2395/School-Food-Programs.html

Schor, E. L., & Johnson, K. (2021). Child health inequities among state Medicaid programs. *JAMA Pediatrics, 175*(8), 775–776.

Schwab, K. (2022). How much of our labor force has been lost to COVID-19? Marketplace. www.marketplace.org/2022/01/24/how-much-labor-force-has-been-lost-covid-19/

Seal, K. H., Bertenthal, D., Barnes, D. E., Byers, A. L., Gibson, C. J., Rife, T. L., . . . Chronic effects of Neurotrauma Consortium Study Group. (2018). Traumatic brain injury and receipt of prescription opioid therapy for chronic pain in Iraq and Afghanistan veterans: Do clinical practice guidelines matter? *The Journal of Pain, 19*(8), 931–941.

Searle, J. R. (1995). *Construction of social reality*. Free Press.

Serrano, A. (2018). $1 Fentanyl test strip could be a major weapon against opioid ODs. Scientific American. www.scientificamerican.com/article/1-fentanyl-test-strip-could-be-a-major-weapon-against-opioid-ods/

Serres, C. (2018). Opioid epidemic is driving thousands of Minnesota children into foster care. Star Tribune. www.startribune.com/opioid-epidemic-is-driving-thousands-of-minnesota-children-into-foster-care/501714932/

Serwer, A. (2020). The next reconstruction. The Atlantic. www.theatlantic.com/magazine/archive/2020/10/the-next-reconstruction/615475/

Seunagel, G. (2017). Why did President Trump win the election? USA Herald. https://usaherald.com/president-trump-win-2016-election/

Shapiro, D. (1978). *Appalachia on our mind: The southern mountains and mountaineers in the American consciousness, 1870–1920*. University of North Carolina Press.

Shared Justice. (2017). Aging out of foster care: 18 and on your own. http://www.sharedjustice.org/most-recent/2017/3/30/aging-out-of-foster-care-18-and-on-your-own

Shearer, R. D., Howell, B. A., Bart, G., & Winkelman, T. N. (2020). Substance use patterns and health profiles among US adults who use opioids, methamphetamine, or both, 2015–2018. *Drug and Alcohol Dependence, 214*, 108162.

Shelley, L. (2012). The relationship of drug and human trafficking: A global perspective. *European Journal on Criminal Policy and Research, 18*(3), 241–253.

Shihipar, A. (2019). The opioid crisis isn't white. New York Times. www.nytimes.com/2019/02/26/opinion/opioid-crisis-drug-users.html

Singletary, M. (2019). How the opioid crisis is leading to elder financial abuse. Washington Post. www.washingtonpost.com/business/2019/06/17/how-opioid-crisis-is-leading-elder-financial-abuse/

Smith, A, Stoklosa, H, Corrigan, C, & Foley, L. (2016). The intersection of substance abuse and human trafficking. Paper presented at: Office for Victims of Crime Human Trafficking Regional Training Forum. Providence, RI; August 24, 2016

Smith, C., Morse, E., & Busby, S. (2019). Barriers to reproductive healthcare for women with opioid use disorder. *The Journal of Perinatal & Neonatal Nursing*, 33(2), E3–E11.

Smith, J. (n.d.). A tarpaper Carthage: Interpreting Hooverville. University of Washington. https://depts.washington.edu/depress/hooverville_seattle_tarpaper_carthage.shtml

Smith, P. A. (2021). A myth that lingers on: Casual contact with fentanyl causes overdoses. Washington Post. www.washingtonpost.com/outlook/fentanyl-police-overdose-myth-san-diego-video/2021/08/13/5be44ec0-fbb3-11eb-8a67-f14cd1d28e47_story.html

Smye, V., Browne, A. J., Varcoe, C., & Josewski, V. (2011). Harm reduction, methadone maintenance treatment and the root causes of health and social inequities: An intersectional lens in the Canadian context. *Harm Reduction Journal*, 8(1), 1–12.

Sollors, W. (2002). What race are you? In J. Perlmann & M. C. Waters (Eds.), *The new race question: How the census counts multiracial individuals* (pp. 263–268). Russell Sage.

Sopela, B., & Yurcaba, J. (2021) Biden to transgender Americans: 'We've got your back.' NBC News. www.nbcnews.com/feature/nbc-out/biden-transgender-americans-your-president-has-your-back-n1265836

Sorrell, T. R. (2020). Mexican traditional medicine: Application of a traditional and complementary medicine system to improve opioid use treatment in Latinos. *Journal of Holistic Nursing*, 38(4), 384–399.

Sperling, G. (2021). Will Biden's tax plan discourage work? We already know the answer. Politico. www.politico.com/news/magazine/2021/02/10/biden-tax-plan-work-child-tax-credit-labor-sperling-468183

Stanford Encyclopedia of Philosophy (2005). Collective responsibility. Stanford University. https://plato.stanford.edu/entries/collective-responsibility/#:~:text=The%20notion%20of%20collective%20responsibility,for%20having%20caused%20such%20harm.

Stanford Encyclopedia of Philosophy (2018). Common good. Stanford University. https://plato.stanford.edu/entries/common-good/

Stanford Law School Three Strikes Project (n.d.). Three strikes basics. Stanford Law School. https://law.stanford.edu/three-strikes-project/three-strikes-basics/

Starecheski, L. (2015). Take the ACE quiz—And learn what it does and doesn't mean. NPR. www.npr.org/sections/health-shots/2015/03/02/387007941/take-the-ace-quiz-and-learn-what-it-does-and-doesnt-mean

Steele, H., Bate, J., Steele, M., Dube, S. R., Danskin, K., Knafo, H., Nikitiades, A., Bonuck, K., Meissner, P., & Murphy, A. (2016). Adverse childhood experiences, poverty, and parenting stress. *Canadian Journal of Behavioural Science*, 48(1), 32–38. https://doi.org/10.1037/cbs0000034

Sterling, V. (2018). Special considerations for opioid use in elderly patients with chronic pain. *US Pharmacist*, 43(3), 26–30.

Stevens-Watkins, D. (2020). Opioid-related overdose deaths among African Americans: Implications for research, practice and policy. *Drug and Alcohol Review*, 39(7), 857–861.

Stoklosa, H. (2016A). Anti-trafficking policy developments impacting health care providers. Office on Trafficking Persons. www.acf.hhs.gov/otip/resource/stoklosa

Stoklosa, H., Stoklosa, J. B., & MacGibbon, M. (2017). Human trafficking, mental illness, and addiction: avoiding diagnostic overshadowing. *AMA Journal of Ethics*.

Stoll, S. (2017). Ramp hollow: The ordeal of Appalachia. Hill and Wang.

Strain, M. R. (2021). Biden's child tax credit has a fatal flaw. American Enterprise Institute. www.aei.org/op-eds/bidens-child-tax-credit-has-a-fatal-flaw/

Strang, J., & Tober, G. (2003). Methadone: Panacea or poison? In J. Strang, & G. Tober (Eds.), *Methadone matters: Evolving community methadone treatment of opiate addiction* (pp. 3–12). CRC Press.

Strang, J., & Tober, G. (Eds.). (2003). *Methadone matters: Evolving community methadone treatment of opiate addiction*. CRC Press.

Sufrin, C. (2017). *Jailcare: Finding the safety net for women behind bars*. University of California Press.

Swanson, C. (2021). Denver mayor says "unsanctioned encampments" aren't an option for homeless. Denver Post. www.denverpost.com/2021/06/30/denver-homelessness-strategy-hancock/

Sykes, S. (2020). 8 million Americans slipped into poverty amid coronavirus epidemic, new study says. NBC News. www.nbcnews.com/news/us-news/8-million-americans-slipped-poverty-amid-coronavirus-pandemic-new-study-n1243762

Szalavitz, M., & Rigg, K. K. (2017). The curious (dis) connection between the opioid epidemic and crime. *Substance Use & Misuse, 52*(14), 1927–1931.

Taifa, N. (2021). Race, mass incarceration, and the disastrous War on Drugs. Brennan Center for Justice. www.brennancenter.org/our-work/analysis-opinion/race-mass-incarceration-and-disastrous-war-drugs

Tanner, M. D. (2019). A libertarian perspective on the modern welfare state. Libertarianism. www.libertarianism.org/columns/libertarian-perspective-modern-american-welfare-state

TeamEBONY. (2014). Black girls for sale. Ebony Magazine. https://www.ebony.com/black-girls-human-trafficking-993/

Teaster, P. B., Lindberg, B. W., & Gallo, H. B. (2020). Assessing the federal response to elder abuse, while the opioid crisis rages on. *Generations, 43*(4), 73–79.

Temple, J. (2015). *American pain: How a young felon and his ring of doctors unleashed America's deadliest drug epidemic*. Rowan & Littlefield.

Terkel, A., & Ahmed, A. S. (2021). Looking back on 20 years at war in Afghanistan. Huffington Post. www.huffpost.com/entry/looking-back-on-20-years-at-war-in-afghanistan_n_6092b882e4b05af50dca9a64

Thaler, S. (2021). 'I've seen more death than ever': ICU nurse tells news crew she is QUITTING due to 'compassion fatigue' because of the number of sick and dying who failed to get their shots. Daily Mail. www.dailymail.co.uk/news/article-9888511/Nurse-tells-MSNBC-crew-QUITS-compassion-fatigue-COVID-19-pandemic.html

The Justice Collaborative. (2020). New report tackles role of 'jail churn' in fueling COVID-19 crisis behind bars. https://thejusticecollaborative.com/2020/04/new-report-jail-churn-covid-19-crisis/

The Network for Public Health Law. (n.d.). Legal interventions to increase access to naloxone in Indiana fact sheet. www.networkforphl.org/wp-content/uploads/2020/01/Overdose-Prevention-Indiana-Fact-Sheet.pdf

REFERENCES 241

Thomas, T. (2019). Seattle is dying because liberalism is killing it. American Thinker. www.americanthinker.com/articles/2019/04/seattle_is_dying_because_liberalism_is_killing_it.html

Thomsen, I. (2020). How do today's Black Lives Matter protests compare to the civil rights movement of the 1960s? Northeastern University. https://news.northeastern.edu/2020/06/04/how-do-todays-black-lives-matter-protests-compare-to-the-civil-rights-movement-of-the-1960s/

Tilly, J., Skowronski, S., & Ruiz, S. (2017). The opioid health emergency and older adults. Administration of Community Living. https://theconsumervoice.org/uploads/files/general/ACL_Issue_Brief_-_Opioid_Abuse_and_Older_Adults_-_Dec2017.pdf

Tipps, R. T., Buzzard, G. T., & McDougall, J. A. (2018). The opioid epidemic in Indian Country. *The Journal of Law, Medicine & Ethics, 46*(2), 422–436.

Traube, D. E., He, A. S., Zhu, L., Scalise, C., & Richardson, T. (2015). Predictors of substance abuse assessment and treatment completion for parents involved with child welfare: One state's experience in matching across systems. *Child Welfare, 94*(5), 45–66.

Tribal Epicenters. (n.d.). AASTEC Fact Sheet: The opioid crisis: Impact on Native American communities. https://tribalepicenters.org/wp-content/uploads/2018/03/AASTEC-opioids-fact-sheet.pdf

Tyler, N. A., Winkleman, N. V., Kozhimannil, K. B., Davis, M. M., & Patrick, S. W. (2018). Incidence and costs of neonatal abstinence syndrome among infants with Medicaid: 2004–2014. *Pediatrics*, e20173520 DOI: 10.1542/peds.2017-3520

UNICEF (United Nations Children's Fund). (n.d.). Convention on the Rights of the Child. https://www.unicef.org/child-rights-convention/convention-text

United Nations Office on Drugs and Crime. (2009). Global report on trafficking of persons. www.unodc.org/documents/Global_Report_on_TIP.pdf

United Nations Office on Drugs and Crime. (2021). COVID-19 and the drug supply chain: From production to trafficking to use. www.unodc.org/documents/data-and-analysis/covid/Covid-19-and-drug-supply-chain-Mai2020.pdf

University Medical Center. (2020). The impact of COVID-19 on hospitals. University of Alabama. https://umc.ua.edu/the-impact-of-covid-19-on-hospitals/

U.S. Congress. (1978). Report No. 1386 on establishing standards for the placement of Indian children in foster or adoptive homes, to prevent the breakup of Indian families, and for other purposes. U.S. House of Representatives. www.narf.org/nill/documents/icwa/federal/lh/hr1386.pdf

U.S. Department of Health and Human Services (n.d.). Children and family services review information portal. https://training.cfsrportal.acf.hhs.gov/section-2

U.S. Department of Health and Human Services (n.d.). Concept and history of permanency in U.S. child welfare. www.childwelfare.gov/topics/permanency/overview/history/

U.S. Department of Health and Human Services. (2018). Transcript: Human trafficking and the opioid crisis webinar. Administration for Children and Families (ACF). https://www.acf.hhs.gov/media/3439

Valdez, A., Cepeda, A., Frankeberger, J., & Nowotny, K. M. (2022). The opioid epidemic among the Latino population in California. *Drug and Alcohol Dependence Reports, 2*, 100029.

Vaughn, M. G., Fu, Q., Perron, B. E., Bohnert, A. S., & Howard, M. O. (2010). Is crack cocaine use associated with greater violence than powdered cocaine use? Results from a national sample. *American Journal of Drug and Alcohol Abuse, 36*(4), 181–186.

Vergano, D. (2017). This drug is cheaper and more powerful than heroin—And may be killing way more people. Buzzfeed. www.buzzfeednews.com/article/danvergano/fentanyl-by-the-numbers

Vergano, D. (2018). Nobody really knows what is causing the overdose epidemic, but here are a few theories. Buzzfeed. www.buzzfeednews.com/article/danvergano/whats-causing-the-opioid-crisis#.oujxYM7rG

Vestal, C. (2019). Cheap and powerful 'meth 2.0' is ravaging communities and slowly killing its victims. USA Today. www.usatoday.com/story/news/health/2019/11/02/meth-use-surges-stronger-cheaper-drugs-imported-mexico/4124765002/

Vivanco, L. (2017). Some neighbors oppose sober-living home proposed in Uptown's Buena Park. Chicago Tribune. www.chicagotribune.com/news/breaking/ct-sober-living-home-buena-park-met-20170712-story.html

Walker, F. X. (2006). Creative solutions to life's challenges. NPR. www.npr.org/templates/story/story.php?storyId=5298083

Wall Street Journal Opinion (2008). Capitalism encourages more personal responsibility. Wall Street Journal. www.wsj.com/articles/SB122420450801243221

Waller, C. (2020). Enhanced risks for criminal justice populations with SUD during the COVID 19 pandemic. ASAM. https://elearning.asam.org/products/coordination-across-the-social-safety-net-to-avert-a-crisis-among-patients-with-addiction-nam-asam-collaboration#tab-product_tab_handouts

Wallington, M. (2021). Phone interview on May 23, 2021 with the Homeless Navigator with the Lakewood, Colorado police.

Wan, W., & Long, H. (2020). 'Cries for help': Drug overdoses are soaring during the coronavirus pandemic. Washington Post. www.washingtonpost.com/health/2020/07/01/coronavirus-drug-overdose/

Wang, L. (2021). Biden is opposing a promising step toward buprenorphine deregulation. Filter. https://filtermag.org/biden-administration-buprenorphine-deregulation/

Wang, S. C., Chen, Y. C., Lee, C. H., & Cheng, C. M. (2019). Opioid addiction, genetic susceptibility, and medical treatments: a review. *International Journal of Molecular Sciences*, *20*(17), 4294.

Wang, Z., Lohrmann, D. K., Buu, A., & Lin, H. C. (2021). Resilience as a mediator between adverse childhood experiences and prescription opioid misuse among US adults. *Substance Use & Misuse*, *56*(4), 484–492.

Washington Post graphic. (2020). 2020 turnout is the highest in over a century. Washington Post. www.washingtonpost.com/graphics/2020/elections/voter-turnout/

Weimer, M. (2020). Challenges for providing addiction treatment in hospitals during COVID-19. ASAM. https://elearning.asam.org/products/supporting-addiction-treatment-during-covid-19-nam-asam-collaboration#tab-product_tab_content

Weiss, E. (n.d.). Housing access for people with criminal records. National Low Income Housing Coalition. https://nlihc.org/sites/default/files/2016AG_Chapter_6-6.pdf

Wemer, B. (1993). AIDS from an attributional factor. In J. B. Pryor & G. D. Reeder (Eds.), *The social psychology of AIDS* (pp. 287–302). Lawrence Erlbaum Associates.

Westhoff, B. (2019). *Fentanyl, Inc.: How rogue chemists are creating the deadliest wave of the opioid epidemic*. Atlantic Monthly Press.

Whelan, A. (2018). The opioid overdose crisis is hitting all of Philadelphia, new data show. Philadelphia Inquirer. www.inquirer.com/philly/health/addiction/the-opioid-overdose-crisis-is-hitting-all-of-philadelphia-new-data-show-20180620.html

White, R. C., Jr. (2009). *A. Lincoln: A biography*. Random House.

Whittle, P., & Sharp, D. (2016). Maine governor's claim that 90 percent of drug dealers are 'black or Hispanic' is unsubstantiated. PBS. www.pbs.org/newshour/nation/maine-governors-claim-90-percent-drug-dealers-black-hispanic-unsubstantiated

Wilkerson, I. (2020). *Caste: The origins of our discontents*. Random House.

Williams Institute. (2019). Public opinion of transgender rights in the United States. UCLA School of Law. https://williamsinstitute.law.ucla.edu/publications/public-opinion-trans-rights-us/

Williamson, K. (2020). *Big white ghetto: Dead broke, stone-cold stupid, and high on rage in the dank woolly wilds of the "Real America"*. Regnery Publishing.

Winship, S. (2021). The conservative case against child allowances. American Enterprise Institute. www.aei.org/wp-content/uploads/2021/03/The-conservative-case-against-child-allowances.pdf?x91208&x91208

Winstanley, E. L. (2020). The bell tolls for thee & thine: Compassion fatigue & the overdose epidemic. *International Journal of Drug Policy, 85*, 102796.

Wong, C. M. (2017). Newly unearthed tapes reveal the Reagan administration's shocking response to HIV/AIDS: "When AIDS was funny" shows how the White House treated the epidemic like a joke in the 1980s. Huffington Post. www.huffpost.com/entry/ronald-reagan-aids-crisis_n_565e002ae4b08e945fecef1d

WSYX/WTTE. (2020). Opioid overdose rates increasing among Latino community. ABC6. https://abc6onyourside.com/features/sinclair-cares/opioid-overdose-rates-increasing-among-latino-community

Yan, G. W. (2016). The invisible wound: Moral injury and its impact on the health of Operation Enduring Freedom/Operation Iraqi Freedom veterans. *Military Medicine, 181*(5), 451–458.

Young, Y., Johnson, B., Bidorini, C., & Williamson, E. (2019). Let's talk about race and human trafficking. Love146. https://love146.org/lets-talk-about-race-and-human-trafficking/

Zakaria, F. (2021). "What in the world is going on?" Fareed looks at the opioid crisis. CNN. www.cnn.com/videos/tv/2021/03/14/exp-gps-0314-last-look-covid-opioids.cnn

Zeledon, I., West, A., Antony, V., Telles, V., Begay, C., Henderson, B., Unger, J.B., & Soto, C. (2020). Statewide collaborative partnerships among American Indian and Alaska Native (AI/AN) communities in California to target the opioid epidemic: Preliminary results of the Tribal Medication Assisted Treatment (MAT) key informant needs assessment. *Journal of Substance Abuse Treatment, 108*, 9–19.

Zidan, K. (2020). Far-right and white supremacist groups are training for violence in the US. Right Wing Watch. www.rightwingwatch.org/post/far-right-and-white-supremacist-groups-are-training-for-violence-in-the-us/

Zitelmann, R. (2019). China's economic success proves the power of capitalism. Forbes. www.forbes.com/sites/rainerzitelmann/2019/07/08/chinas-economic-success-proves-the-power-of-capitalism/?sh=7de231d63b9d

Zubatov, A. (2021). We are living in the ruins of our civilization. American Greatness. amgreatness.com/2021/02/24/we-are-living-in-the-ruins-of-our-civilization/

Zuckerman, J. (2021). Pandemic brings protests, and guns, to officials' personal homes. Ohio Capital Journal. https://ohiocapitaljournal.com/2021/01/27/pandemic-brings-protests-and-guns-to-officials-personal-homes/

Zurther, A. (2020). RNC 2020: The Republican Party now the Party of Trump. BBC. www.bbc.com/news/election-us-2020-53914829

Index

For the benefit of digital users, indexed terms that span two pages (e.g., 52–53) may, on occasion, appear on only one of those pages.

Figures and boxes are indicated by *f* and *b* following the page number

AARP (American Association of Retired Persons), 98
Abbott, Greg, 103
abolitionism, 55–58
abortion, 103
ACA (Affordable Care Act), 42–43, 76–79
ACE (adverse childhood experiences), 96–98, 115–16
ACS (alternative care sites), 173
activism
　advice for, 54
　thoughtful, 49–51
Acton, Amy, 39
ACTS script, 106
ACT UP (AIDS Coalition to Unleash Power), 3
Adderall, 181
addiction, 11*b*, 127*f*, 128. *See also* substance use disorder (SUD)
　Framework of Addiction, 23–27
　opioid, 6–9, 7*f* (*see also* opioid use disorder [OUD])
　pseudo-addiction, 16–17
　resources for information about, 13
　terminology, 5, 10*b*
　Trainspotting (1996), 198
"addictive personality" myth, 191, 192
adolescents
　Save Our Adolescents from Prostitution (SOAP) project, 106–7
　teens in recovery, 92*b*
Adoption and Safe Families Act, 88–89
adverse childhood experiences (ACE), 96–98, 115–16
advocacy, 193–213
　community, 194–96

components of, 196–97
examples, 36*b*
lessons, 194–95
recommendations, 200*b*, 208*b*
tactics and strategies, 53, 195
Affordable Care Act (ACA), 42–43, 76–79
Affrilachian movement, 69*b*
Afghanistan military service members, 142, 143, 144
African Americans. *See* Blacks/African Americans
age, 23
ageism, 137–38
aging, successful, 137*f*, 137–41
aging out of foster care, 93*b*–94*b*
AIDS. *See* HIV/AIDS
AIDS Coalition to Unleash Power (ACT UP), 3
alcohol abuse, 111–12
alcohol and other drugs (AOD) field, x
Alcoholics Anonymous (AA), 189
alcoholism, 34, 35*b*
Alexander, Michelle, 151–52
Alinsky, Saul, 51, 52–54, 56, 200*b*
alternative care sites (ACS), 173
alt right (alternative right), 45
"America First" campaign, 40
American Association of Retired Persons (AARP), 98
American Conservative Union, 166
American Enterprise Institute, 78
American Pain clinics, 17–18
American Pain Society, 16–17
American Rescue Act ("COVID relief bill"), x
American Rescue Plan, 75, 77*b*

American Society of Addiction Medicine (ASAM), 79, 172
Americans with Disabilities Act, 46
Amerisource Bergen, 194
Amish, 81–82
ANPP (4-anilino-N-phenethylpiperidine), 183–84
Anthem Insurance, 211
"antifa" movement, 39
Anti-Oppression Network, 191–92
antisemitism, 39
Appalachia, x–xi, 24, 26, 68b–69b, 70–71, 103
Arizona, 38
Arkansas, 152
art for social justice, 68b–69b
ASAM (American Society of Addiction Medicine), 79, 172
Asian Americans, 73–74, 123
Auld, Thomas, 56
authorized tent camps, 205

"baby mama drama," 94
Back of the Yards Neighborhood Council (Chicago), 52
bail practices, 153
barriers to recovery, 131
barriers to services, 103, 132–33
Basic Books, 156
benzodiazepines, 19, 176
bias, 12b
Biden, Joe, x, 39–40, 41, 76, 78, 146
bin Laden, Osama, 144
biology, 25–27
Black Lives Matter (BLM) movement, 37, 39, 54–55, 62, 63f, 67, 124, 200b, 201
Blacks/African Americans, 11–12, 63–64, 66, 84, 123–28
　addicts, 127f, 128
　Affrilachian movement, 69b
　case study, 128–29
　in criminal justice system, 168b, 169
　human trafficking, 109
　hypersexualized women, 109
　incarcerated population, 119, 121, 151–52, 160–61
　overdose deaths, 124, 125, 128, 130
　poverty rates, 24, 73–74

sex trafficking, 108–9
welfare queens, 95
women with OUD, 99
Bolivia, 155
Booker, Cory, 76, 165
Boston, Massachusetts, 20
boys, 117
Brackeen v. Bernhardt, 86
Brandy (case study), 6b
Brazil, 188
Bread of Life Mission (Seattle), 29, 30f
bridge housing, 206
Brown, Sherrod, 49
"Building a Healthy & Productive Workforce by Supporting Employees in Recovery" training, 210–11
buprenorphine, 49, 72b, 126, 159
Bureau of Prisons (BOP), 165
Burke, Edmund, 43–44
Burnham, Margaret, 193
Bush, George W., 39–40, 144

CADS (Courts Addiction and Drug Services), 196–97
California, 102, 151, 169
Canada, 107–8
capitalism, 70–73
CAPTA (Child Abuse Prevention Treatment Act), 87
CARA (Comprehensive Addiction and Recovery Act), 49
carceral-therapeutic state, 122
Cardinal Health, 194, 195
CARES Act, 42
Carlson, Tucker, 201
case managers, 34
case plans, 88b
case studies
　Brandy, 6b
　drug-induced homicide laws, 201–3
　Eleana, 118b
　Good Samaritan laws, 197–99
　Maria, 149b
　Oswaldo, 132
　Seattle homeless population, 28–34
　Tess, 72b
　Washington, DC, 128–29
　Yvette, 162

Casey Family Program, 98
caste system, 62–64, 65f
CATO Institute, 48
"Caucasian" term, 84
Center for HIV Law and Policy, 186–87
Center for Human Rights, 161
Center for Law and Social Policy, 76
Centers for Disease Control and
    Prevention (CDC), 33, 136
  recommended initiatives to reduce
    overdose deaths, 176–77
  strategies to prevent ACEs, 97
Centers for Medicare and Medicaid
    Services (CMS), 176
centrists, 42–43
Cherokee, 71
Chicago, Illinois, 52, 148
Child Abuse Prevention Treatment Act
    (CAPTA), 87
child protective services (CPS), 81, 82, 84,
    88b, 199
children
  adverse childhood experiences (ACE),
    96–98, 115–16
  childhood trauma, 15
  child hunger, 2–3
  child labor, 110b
  child maltreatment, 82, 87
  child welfare, 81–98, 83f, 97f, 199
  "crack babies," 99, 101, 102
  drug use, 112
  foster youth, 93b–94b, 94, 98
  human trafficking of, 110, 112, 115–
    16, 117
  Indian Child Welfare Act
    (ICWA), 85–86
  neonatal abstinence syndrome (NAS),
    72b, 99, 101, 102, 104, 105b, 203b
  neonatal opioid withdrawal syndrome
    (NOWS), 101–2, 105b
  nonbinary youth, 117
  in poverty, 73
  rights of, 81–82
  sex trafficking of, 116–17
Children's Defense Fund, 76, 98
child separation policy, 85
Child Tax Credit, 74, 77b
child welfare system, 82–87

China, 19, 183–84, 185
Chocolate-Chip Cookie
    Syndrome, 175–76
chronic pain, 138
Churchill, Winston, 50–51
cisgender (term), 145
Civil Rights Act, 46
Civil War, 57
Clean Water Act, 207b
climate change, 54
Clinton, Bill, 43, 95, 154
Clinton, Hillary, 114b
cocaine, 111, 127–28
  case study, 118b
  "crack babies," 99, 101, 102
  crack cocaine, 67–68, 155
  overdose deaths, 175–76
Code of Ethics for Social Work, 197
coercive mobilization, 160
collective responsibility, 50b
Colombia, 155
Colorado, 152
Colorado Village Collaborative, 205, 206
Columbus, Ohio, 148
common good, 50b
communication tactics, 200b
community advocacy, 194–96
community factors, 26, 27
community norms, 26
community organizing, 52, 53
compassion fatigue, 105b–6b
Comprehensive Addiction and Recovery
    Act (CARA), 49
Congressional Budget Office
    (CBO), 75–76
Congressional Social Work Caucus, 76
conservatives, 43–44
conspiracy theories, 114b–15b
corruption, 113
Coulter, Ann, 157
counselors, 4b, 11b, 92b, 132–33
Courts Addiction and Drug Services
    (CADS), 196–97
COVID-19, ix–x, 12–13, 33, 130, 158–59
  American Rescue Act ("COVID relief
    bill"), x
  conspiracy theories about, 114b
  COVID-19 Safer Detention Act, 167

COVID-19 (*cont.*)
  government response, 42
  impact of, 64, 171–77, 175*f*, 179, 204–5
  lockdown caused by, 62, 174–76, 175*f*
  long COVID, ix, 171
  overdose deaths during, 172, 175–76
  in prison, 173
  social isolation caused by, 160, 175*f*
  "Stay Safe Ohio" program, 39
"crack babies," 99, 101, 102
crack cocaine, 67–68, 155
"crackers," 65–66
criminal justice, 31, 148–70, 158*f*
  case study, 149*b*
  co-use of methamphetamine and, 179
  criminalization of drug use, 125
  criminalization of pregnancy, 100*f*, 100–4
  criminalization of street drugs, 209–10
  digital punishment, 163*b*
  Fair Sentencing Act, 168*b*
  mass incarceration, 12, 150–53, 156*b*–57*b*, 160–61, 162–65
  racial disparity in sentencing, 168*b*
  re-entry programs, 173
  sentencing reform, 165
  Smarter Sentencing Act, 168*b*
  women in prison, 119–22, 149*b*
crisis shelters, 206
crystal dick, 178
crystal methamphetamine, 179
cultural poverty, 60–61
"culture in crisis," 70
culture of poverty, 60–61

Dance Safe, 185–86
Dark Web, 183–84
day labor programs, 206
DEA (Drug Enforcement Agency), 17, 176, 183–84, 194, 195
deadbeat dads, 95–96
Deisner, Vicki, 208–9
DeLauro, Rosa, 77*b*
Democratic Party, 40, 49
Democratic Whip Task Force on Poverty, Income Inequality, and Opportunity, 76
Denver, Colorado, 204–5, 206–7, 209
depression, 24–25

despair, 20–21
Detroit, Michigan, 69
deviant behavior, 190
Dickens, Charles, 59
digital punishment, 163*b*
Dillon's Rule, 71
Douglass, Frederick, 55*f*, 55–58
drug abuse. *See also* substance use disorder (SUD); *specific drugs*
  case studies, 118*b*
  co-use of methamphetamine, 177–81
  COVID-19 and, 176
  criminalization of, 125, 158*f*
  human trafficking and, 111–12, 113
  intergenerational, 125
  language regarding, 63
  parenting and, 82
  and treatment in prisons/jails, 158–59
drug cartels, 19, 155, 182, 183, 184
drug charges, 157
drug counselors, 4*b*, 11*b*
drug crimes, 168*b*
Drug Enforcement Agency (DEA), 17, 176, 183–84, 187, 194, 195
Drug Induced Homicide, 201–2
drug-induced homicide laws, 201–3
drug overdose, 15–16
Drug Policy Alliance, 198, 199
drug tests, 91
drug trafficking, 113, 159, 176, 183–84
Duluth, Minnesota, 19
Durbin, Dick, 168*b*

Eagleton, Terry, 157
Earned Income Tax Credit (EITC), 74, 77*b*, 78
Eason, John, 148
economic disparities, 31
Economist, 156
education, 27
Ehrlichman, John, 154
EITC (Earned Income Tax Credit), 74, 77*b*, 78
elder justice, 140
Elder Justice Act, 140, 141
Eleana (case study), 118*b*
election deniers, 38
Ellison, Ralph, 123

employment, 151, 181, 206, 210–12
Environmental Protection Agency (EPA), 207b
Equality Act, 147
essentialism, 188
ethical dilemmas, 197, 199
ethnicity, 23, 84–86
European Union (EU), 72–73
evidence-based medicine, 136
extremists, 41–42
Eyre, Eric, 194

Fair Recruitment, 110–11
Fair Sentencing Act, 168b
Falconer, Sara, 200b
Family First Services Act, 87
Family Opportunity Act, 46
far left, 46–48
far right, 44–45
FASH (fentanyl-contaminated and -substituted heroin), 182–83
fathers, 94–96
Federal Analogue Act, 184–85
Federal Poverty Line (FPL), 61
fentanyl, 14, 130, 182–87
  Chocolate-Chip Cookie Syndrome, 175–76
  -contaminated drugs, 12–13, 19, 125, 182–83
  homeless use and, 204–5
  overdose deaths, 12b, 175–76, 177, 181
  Safety Recommendations for First Responders (DEA), 187
  test strips, 177, 181, 186
  in Washington, DC, 128
fentanyl panic, 186–87
financial abuse, 140
financial costs, 161
financial disparities, 31
financial poverty, 60. *See also* poverty
First Step Act, 165
First Step Implementation Act, 165–66
Flake, Jeff, 40
Flores, Theresa, 106–7
Florida, 17
Floyd, George, 54–55, 62
food stamps, 94–95, 162
forced labor, 110b, 112

Fordham University, 156
foster care, 99
foster youth, 93b–94b, 94, 98
Fox News, 28–29, 30–31, 201
FPL (Federal Poverty Line), 61
Framework of Addiction, 23–27
Frankenstein opioids, 171
Franklin County (Ohio) Children's Services, 93b
Freedom of Information Act (FOIA), 195
French Revolution, 43
Fudge, Marcia, 73, 76
funding, 178

Gates, Bill, 114b
Generations United, 90
genetics, 25–27
geography, 24, 26
George, Ryan, 187–88
global drug trade, 19, 155, 176, 182, 183, 184
Goffman, Erving, 5
good, common, 50b
Good Samaritan laws, 129, 194, 197–99
goofballs, 177
GOP (Grand Old Party). *See* Republican Party
Gore, Al, 39–40
grandparents, 89–91, 140
GrandRally: Building a Community of Hope, 89–90
Great Britain, 57–58
Great Depression, 2, 34b, 36, 52
Great Recession, 62
Green, Doug, 203b
gun control, 41

Hale, Lacy, 68b–69
hallucinogens, 113
Hancock, Michael, 206–7
Hand, Jamelia, 84
Hanks, Tom, 114b
Harkins, Anthony, 70
Harlem, New York, 55f
harm reduction, 181, 209–10
  examples, 9, 185–86, 209
  recommended initiatives to reduce overdose deaths, 177
  support for, 8–9, 48, 205

Hayes, Chris, 156
health, social determinants of, 27–28
health care, 27
Healthy Grandfamilies program (West Virginia), 90
Healthy People 2030, 27
hepatitis C, 72*b*
heroin, 4*b*, 6–7, 14
  brown, 19
  case study, 72*b*
  COVID-19 and, 176
  fentanyl-contaminated and -substituted (FASH), 182–83
  human trafficking and, 112
  older adults and, 139
  street value, 183
  synthetic (*see* fentanyl)
  Trainspotting (1996), 198
  women and, 116, 117
Heroin, Opioid Prevention, and Education (HOPE) agenda, 48
hierarchy
  occupational, 64
  power of, 62–68
Hillbilly Elegy (2020), 68*b*, 70
Hinton, Aaron, 154
Hispanic/Latinx, 84–85, 126, 129–32
  case studies, 132
  incarcerated population, 152
  incarcerated women, 119, 121
  opioid misuse, 129–30
  poverty rates, 24, 73–74
  sex trafficking, 108–9
HIV/AIDS, 3–5, 155, 179, 186–87, 191
holistic care, 132
Hollywood, 114*b*
Homelessness Response, 32
homeless (unsheltered) population, 145
  COVID-19 and, 173
  methamphetamine use and, 179
  one advocate's view of, 204–6
  policy suggestions for, 206–7
  root causes of homelessness, 31–32
  Seattle (case study), 28–34, 30*f*
  steps to fight the homeless crisis, 32
  SUD and, 28, 204–6
  visible vs invisible, 204, 205
Hoover, Herbert, 34*b*

Hoovervilles, 34*b*–36*b*, 34, 35*f*
HOPE (Heroin, Opioid Prevention, and Education) agenda, 48
hospital system, 179
House Resolution 1048 (HR1048), 73–76
housing, 31, 32, 164, 205, 206, 211–12
Housing Authority of New Orleans, 162
Housing First, 206, 207
Housing Opportunity Extension Act, 162
human trafficking, 99–100, 106–17, 108*f*
  case study, 118*b*
  international, 113
  risk factors, 115–16
hydrocodone, 22

ICWA (Indian Child Welfare Act), 85–86
IG Publisher, 156
IHS (Indian Health Service), 136
Illicit Drug Anti-Proliferation Act (Rave Act), 185–86
Illinois, 202
ILO (International Labour Organization), 110*b*
immigration, 84–85, 131
Immigration and Naturalization Act, 46
Immigration and Naturalization Service (INS), 42
Immigrations and Customs Enforcement (ICE), 42, 199
incarceration
  bail practices, 153
  COVID-19 and, 173
  drug use and treatment in prisons/jails, 158–59
  mass, 12, 150–53, 160–61
  rapid release programs, 173
  social costs of mass incarceration, 160–61
  of women, 119–22, 149*b*
incarceration ledger, 160
India, 63–64, 184
Indiana, 199
Indian Child Welfare Act (ICWA), 85–86
Indian Health Service (IHS), 136
Indian Relocation Act, 133–34
Indian Removal Act, 71
Infowars, 114*b*
injection drug users, 179, 209–10

innovation, 196–97
Insite Supervised Injection Site (Vancouver, Canada), 209
intergenerational drug use, 125
International Labour Organization (ILO), 110b
interpersonal factors, 26
intravenous drug use, 176
"Invisible Man" motif, 123
Iraq/Afghanistan military service members, 142, 143, 144
Ivory Coast, 110–11

jailcare, 121–22
Janssen, Paul, 182–83
January 6, 2021 attack on the U.S. Capitol, 37–38, 45
Jews, 51
Jim Crow, 151–52
jobs, 210–12
Johnson, Lyndon, 64, 77b
Joliet prison, 52
Jones, Alex, 114b
Journal of the American Medical Association, 101
justice
  criminal, 31, 148–70
  elder, 140
  reproductive, 104
  social, 2–3, 68b–69b, 164b

Kennedy, Edward, 46
Kennedy, John, 77b
Kentucky, 181, 196
King, Nikki, 196–97
King County, Washington, 28–29
Kinsey, Jimmy Cleveland II, 141
kinship providers, 89–91, 98
KOMO, 30–31

Lake, Kari, 38
Lancaster, Ohio, x–xi, 20
Lang, Keith, 202
Latinx population. *See* Hispanic/Latinx
Lee, Barbara, 73, 76
Lee, Mike, 168b
legal system, 196–97
legislation. *See also specific acts*

drug-induced homicide laws, 201–3
Good Samaritan laws, 129, 194, 197–99
marijuana laws, 153, 189
safe harbor laws, 116–17
second look laws, 166–70
Lembke, Anna, 17
LePage, Paul, 63
LGBTIA+ acronym, 190
LGBT+ persons, 117
liberals, 45–46, 49
Libertarian Party, 44–45
Limbeck, Rachelle, 111
Lincoln, Abraham, 57, 66
literature, 69b
Locke, John, 44
Lorde, Audre, 104
Love146, 117

macaroni-and-cheese issues, 80b
machismo, 130
macro issues, 80b
macro social work, 213
Maiden's Law, 203b–4
Mainstream Act, 49
Make America Great Again (MAGA), 37, 38f
Mali, 110
Maria (case study), 149b
marijuana laws, 153, 189
Marxism, 201
mass incarceration, 150–53
  causes, 151, 156b–57b
  financial costs, 161
  personal costs, 12, 162–65
  social costs, 160–61
MAT. *See* medication assisted treatment
McCain, John, 43
MCI-Framingham (Massachusetts), 119–20
McKesson Corporation, 194
media relations, 195
Medicaid, 3, 46, 48, 125–26, 129, 197
  expansion of, 76–79, 77b
  role in the opioid crisis, 76–80
  women and, 103, 104
medical-social framework, 15
medical system, 196–97
Medicare, 1, 22, 39–40, 42, 77b, 140

medication assisted treatment (MAT), x,
    7–9, 125–26, 158–59, 172
  advocacy for, 196
  case studies, 132
  concerns about, 8
  COVID-19 and, 176
  definition of, 10b
  meth use and, 180
  types of, 159
  women and, 103
Medicine Wheel Teaching, 134, 135f
Meier, Barry, 16
mental health, 24–25
mental health counselors, 132–33
mentoring, 94
methadone, 6–8, 9, 99, 125–26, 139, 159
Methadone Mile (Boston), 20
methamphetamine, 14, 19, 102, 180, 204–5
  co-use, 177–81
  crystal, 178, 179
  overdose deaths, 175–76
  social costs of, 179
Mexican drug cartels, 19, 155, 182, 183, 184
Mexican traditional medicine, 132
mezzo social work, 213
micro social work, 213
Middle East, 110b
Mikulski, Barbara, 80b
military personnel, 141–45, 143f
Minneapolis, Minnesota, 133
Model Penal Code, 166
moderates, 43
moral framework, 15
moral injury, 143–45
moral panic, 151
Mothers Against Drunk Driving, 190
mothers in treatment, 203b
mudsills, 64, 66

naloxone (Narcan), 8, 10b, 105b, 131,
    186–87, 199
naltrexone, 159
Narcan (naloxone), 8, 10b, 105b, 131,
    186–87, 199
Narcan kits, 8
narcotics, 8
NAS (neonatal abstinence syndrome),
    72b, 99, 101, 102, 104, 105b, 203b

National Alliance for Recovery
    Residences, 212
National Center for Complementary and
    Integrative Health (NCCIH), 22
National Center on Elder Abuse, 141
National Coalition of the Homeless, 207
National Family Caregiver Support
    Program, 90
National Institute on Drug Abuse, 13
National Institutes of Health (NIH), 22
National Kinship Alliance for Children, 98
National Review, 156
National School Lunch Program, 2
Native Americans, 33, 85, 102–3, 107–8,
    133–36
  Indian Child Welfare Act (ICWA), 85–86
  Indian Health Service (IHS), 136
  Indian Relocation Act, 133–34
  Indian Removal Act, 71
  Medicine Wheel Teaching, 134, 135f
  overdose deaths, 85–86, 133, 136
  poverty rates, 24
  risks for trafficking, 117
  Tribal Healing to Wellness Courts, 134–36
Navigation Teams, 33
NCCIH (National Center for
    Complementary and Integrative
    Health), 22
neighborhoods, 27
neonatal abstinence syndrome (NAS),
    72b, 99, 101, 102, 104, 105b, 203b
neonatal opioid withdrawal syndrome
    (NOWS), 101–2, 105b
neo-Nazis, 68b–69
New Democrats, 43
Newtown Action Alliance, 41
NIH (National Institutes of Health), 22
9/11 attacks, 1, 42
nitrazene, 171
Nixon, Richard, 154
"No Hate in my Holler" slogan, 68b–69
nonbinary persons, 117, 145–47
North Carolina, 110b, 202
North Dakota, 133
novel psychoactive substance
    (NPS), 182–83
NOWS (neonatal opioid withdrawal
    syndrome), 101–2, 105b

NPP (N-Phenethyl-4-piperidone), 183–84
NPS (novel psychoactive substance), 182–83

Obama, Barack, 45–46, 52, 64
Obamacare, 42–43, 76–79
Occupy Wall Street movement, 46–48, 47f
OCF (overdose-related compassion fatigue), 105b
O'Connor, Carroll, 201
Ohio, 20, 39, 210–11
Oklahoma, 80
older adults, 137
   definition of, 138
   grandparents, 89–91, 140
   Medicare beneficiaries, 141
   in prison, 167, 169
   successful aging, 137f, 137–41
Operation Holy Ground, 148
opioid addiction. *See also* opioid use disorder (OUD)
   history of, 6–9
   media portrayals of, 6, 7f
opioid crisis, x–xi
   background, 15–23, 18f
   causes, 14–34
   fourth wave, 177–81
   Medicaid role in, 76–80
   ongoing challenges, 171–92
   political context, 37–58
   racial and ethnic aspects, 84–86
   school responses, 91b
   socio-ecological framework of, 23f, 23–27
   terminology, 19
opioid epidemic. *See* opioid crisis
opioids
   definition of, 10b
   Frankenstein, 171
   neonatal opioid withdrawal syndrome (NOWS), 101–2, 105b
   synthetic, 176 (*see also* fentanyl)
Opioid Safety Initiative, 141–42
Opioid Toolkit, 211
opioid use disorder (OUD), xi, 72–73. *See also* substance use disorder (SUD)
   ACEs and, 97
   case study, 72b
   co-use of methamphetamine, 177–81

COVID-19 complications, ix, 174
   as cycle, 25
   definition of, 10b
   funding for, 178
   in older adults, 141
   in prison, 159
   racialized treatment landscape, 126
   recommended care for, 79
   risk factors, 125, 132, 142, 144–45
   susceptibility to, 25–27
   symptoms of, 138
   in women, 99–122
opium, 6
opium dens, 6, 7f
oppression, 191–92
Oregon, 34b, 35f, 153
Oswaldo (case study), 132
"others," 35b, 64
OUD. *See* opioid use disorder
Our Mutual Friend (Dickens), 59
outreach workers, 34
overdose-related compassion fatigue (OCF), 105b
overprescribing, 17–18, 18f
OxyContin, 8, 16–17, 18, 72–73, 115

pain management, 22, 25, 138–39
parents
   "baby mama drama," 94
   deadbeat dads, 95–96
   drug abuse and parenting, 82
   father's rights and responsibilities, 94–96
   grandparents, 89–91
   incarcerated women, 120
   mothers in treatment, 203b
   in recovery, 86–87
Parents in Recovery program (Pennsylvania), 81
paternity, 94–95
Patriot Act, 200b
PDMP (Prescription Drug Monitoring Program), 18–19
Pelosi, Nancy, 38
Pence, Mike, 38
Percocet, 183
permanency planning, 88–89
permitted villages, 32

personal responsibility, 50*b*
Personal Responsibility and Work Opportunity Act (PRWORA, Welfare Reform Act), 95
personhood movement, 103
"person in environment" concept, 52–54
pharmaceutical companies ("Big Pharma"), 8, 16–18, 18*f*, 183, 194–96
Philadelphia, Pennsylvania, 20
physical health, 24–25
pill mills, 17–18, 18*f*, 20
pill presses, 183
Pizzagate, 114*b*–15*b*
Plan Colombia, 154, 155
planning
　case plans, 88*b*
　permanency, 88–89
Podsnap, Mr. (character), 59
Polaris Project, 108–9, 112, 114*b*
polarization, 51–55
policy, 1–13, 213
　case study, 28–34
　definition of, 2–3
　homeless population (case study), 28–34
　poverty-related issues that get overlooked by policymakers, 76
　rationale for study of, 1–2
　recommended initiatives to reduce overdose deaths, 176–77
political discourse, 40–41
political radicalism, 35*b*
political spectrum, 41*f*, 41–49
political violence, 37–40
politics, 37–58, 208
polysubstance use, 125, 139
　co-use of methamphetamine, 177–81
　definition of, 10*b*
Portland, Oregon, 34*b*, 35*f*
Portman, Rob, 49
Portsmouth, Ohio, 20
post-traumatic stress disorder (PTSD), 93*b*–94, 112, 142–43
poverty, 24, 26, 31
　absolute, 61
　children in, 73
　concept of, 60–62
　cultural, 60–61
　culture of, 60–61
　deep, 73
　Federal Poverty Line (FPL), 61
　Great Depression, 2, 34*b*, 36, 52
　Great Recession, 62
　macaroni-and-cheese issues, 80*b*
　macro issues, 80*b*
　new poor, 62
　portrayals of, 69
　punishing effects of, 59–80
　related issues that get overlooked by policymakers, 76
　relative, 61
　spiritual, 61
　stigma of, 79
　time, 60
　War on Poverty, 77*b*
　"white trash," 65–66
Poverty Bill of Rights, 73–76
pregnancy
　criminalization of, 100*f*, 100–4
　unintended, 100
Prescription Drug Monitoring Program (PDMP), 18–19
prescription drugs. *See also* opioid crisis
　off-label use, 181
　risk factors for abuse, 132
preventive services, 25
Prince, 183
prison
　COVID-19 and, 173
　drug use and treatment in prisons/jails, 158–59
　mass incarceration, 12, 150–53, 156*b*–57*b*, 160–61, 162–65
　private prisons, 151
　women in, 119–22, 149*b*
prison-industrial complex, 151
Prison Policy Initiative, 157
prison reform, 165
private prisons, 151
Prohibition Act, 153–54
Proposition 184 ("Three Strikes and You're Out Law"), 151
Proud Boys, 39, 45
PRWORA (Personal Responsibility and Work Opportunity Act, Welfare Reform Act), 95
pseudo-addiction, 16–17

PTSD (posttraumatic stress disorder), 93b–94, 142–45
public housing, 164
public opinion, 49. *See also* stigma
    anti-immigrant attitudes, 131
    attitudes about SUD, 48
    attitudes toward the poor, 59
    racism, 59, 107–8
    stereotypes, 136
Purdue Pharmaceuticals, 16, 18, 197

QAnon, 45, 114b–15b

race (concept), 188
race/ethnicity, 23, 31
    and child welfare system, 84–86
    and human trafficking, 117
    racism, 59, 107–8
    and sentencing, 168b
race relations, 62–64, 65f, 66
racial cleansing, 151
radicals, 42–43, 51–55
rapid release programs, 173
Rave Act (Illicit Drug Anti-Proliferation Act), 185–86
Reagan, Ronald, 3, 42, 44, 77b, 95, 154, 193–94
REBUILD (Rebuilding Urban Inner Cities is Long Overdue Act), 80b
recovery
    parents in, 86–87
    teens in, 92b
recovery high schools (sober high schools), 92b, 92
re-entry programs, 173
Regnery Publishing, 156
rejection sensitivity, 60
reproductive justice, 104
Republican National Committee, 40
Republican Party, 40, 49
research, 195, 208
responsibility, 50b
Rise Above Movement, 45
Roosevelt, Franklin D., 53
Rosen, Hy, 41–42
Route 33 ("Heroin Highway"), x–xi, 20
Rules for Radicals (Alinsky), 51, 52, 53
Ryan White Act, 3–5

safe harbor laws, 116–17
safe injection sites, 209–10
Safety Recommendations for First Responders (DEA), 187
Sanders, Bernie, 48
San Francisco General Hospital One, 178
Save Our Adolescents from Prostitution (SOAP) project, 106–7
Scanlan, Steven, suboxoneC1P32
school counselors, 92b
schools
    recovery high schools (sober high schools), 92b, 92
    responses to the opioid crisis, 91b
Seattle, Washington
    Bread of Life Mission, 29, 30f
    homeless population (case study), 28–34
    Hoovervilles, 35b–36b
    Navigation Team program, 33
    overdose deaths, 133
    steps to fight the homeless crisis, 32
Second Amendment Foundation, 41
secondary trauma, 4b
Second Look Act, 167
second look laws, 166–70
self-determination, 25
self-inflicted harm, 105b
self-reflection, 15
self-stigma, 26–27
Sentencing Project, 169
SES (socioeconomic status), 24, 161
sex trafficking, 107–9, 110b, 112, 115b, 116–17
    case study, 118b
    Save Our Adolescents from Prostitution (SOAP) project, 106–7
sexual activity, 178
    hypersexualized women, 109
    transactional sex, 179
sexual minority persons, 123
sex workers, 107–8, 109, 111, 112, 115–16
    case study, 118b
    incarcerated women, 121
Shappley, Kai, 147
Shared Hope International, 117
Sinaloa Cartel, 184
Sinclair Broadcasting, 30

Sister Song, 104
1619 Project, 123
slavery, 55–58, 64, 65f, 66
Smarter Sentencing Act, 168b
Smoking Opium Exclusion Act, 153–54
SNAP (Supplemental Nutrition Assistance Program), 94–95, 162
SOAP (Save Our Adolescents from Prostitution) project, 106–7
sober high schools (recovery high schools), 92b, 92
sober housing, 211–12
social constructionism, 187–90, 191–92
Social Contract theory, 44
Social Determinants of Health, 27–28
social disorganization, 52–54
social hierarchy, 62–68
social isolation, 171, 175f
social justice, 2–3, 68b–69b, 164b
Social Security, 39–40, 90, 140
social workers, x, 34
sociodemographic factors, 23–24
socioeconomic status (SES), 24, 161
South Africa, 188
South Dakota, 133
special populations, 123–47
speedballs, 177
Sperling, Gene, 78
spiritual poverty, 61
squatters, 65–66
State Children's Health Insurance Program, 46
"Stay Safe Ohio" program, 39
stereotypes, 136
stigma, 3–5, 35b, 64
  ACTS script for, 106
  advocacy against, 195
  definition of, 189
  of foster care, 94
  of HIV/AIDS, 179
  of poverty, 79
  punishing effects of, 9, 60, 111–12, 115–16
  self-stigma, 26–27
  of SUD, 98, 180, 187–92
stimulants, 113
Stoll, Steven, 70
storytelling, 200b

street drugs, 10b, 15–16, 111–12, 138–39, 209–10. *See also* substance use disorder (SUD); *specific drugs*,
stress, 24
structural unemployment, 151
suboxone, 8, 49, 126, 159, 172
Substance Abuse and Mental Health Services Administration (SAMHSA), x, 12b, 13, 82, 124
substance use disorder (SUD), ix–x, 5, 14, 91. *See also* opioid use disorder (OUD)
  ACEs and, 96
  barriers to recovery, 131
  barriers to services, 103, 132–33
  as brain disease, 211
  case studies, 6b, 72b, 118b
  child welfare and, 82–83
  co-use of methamphetamine, 177–81
  COVID-19 complications, 171, 172, 174
  definition of, 10b, 188–89
  Hillbilly Elegy (2018), 68b
  homelessness and, 28, 204–6
  human trafficking and, 111–12, 113–15, 116
  jailcare for, 121
  medical-social framework, 15
  moral framework, 15
  newly released prisoners and, 173
  older adults and, 139, 140–41
  personal costs of, 72b
  pregnancy and, 103
  preventive services, 25
  protective factors, 131–32
  public's attitudes about, 48
  racial and ethnic aspects, 84–86
  risk factors, 115–16, 131–32
  as social construct, 192
  stigma of, 187–92
  women and, 99–100, 103, 104
successful aging, 137f, 137–41
SUD. *See* substance use disorder
supervised (or safe) injection sites, 209–10
Supplemental Nutrition Assistance Program (SNAP), 94–95, 162
SUPPORT (Substance Use-Disorder Prevention that Promotes Opioid Recovery and Treatment) for Patients and Communities Act, 87
Swain, Carol, 201

Taylor, Breonna, 154, 200*b*
TBI (traumatic brain injury), 144–45
teachers, 91*b*–92
teamwork, 195
teens in recovery, 92*b*
televisits, 172
temporary housing, 205, 206
Tennessee, 102, 146
terminology, 5, 10*b*, 19, 63, 208
    "Caucasian" term, 84
    for child welfare, 81
    LGBTIA+ acronym, 190
    social constructionism, 187–90, 191–92
    for transgender/nonbinary persons, 145–46
Tess (case study), 72*b*
Texas, 103
Therapeutic Arts Program (Ohio), 93*b*
thoughtful activism, 49–51
"Three Strikes and You're Out Law" (Proposition 184), 151
time poverty, 60
tiny home villages, 32, 205
traditional medicine, 132
"trailer trash," 65–66
Trail of Tears, 71
Trainspotting (1996), 198
transactional sex, 179
transgender persons, 145–47, 190
transparency, 195
trauma
    childhood, 15
    exposure to, 24
    secondary, 4*b*
trauma-informed care, 211–12
traumatic brain injury (TBI), 144–45
TRHT (United States Commission on Truth, Racial Healing, and Transformation), 76
Tribal Healing to Wellness Courts, 134–36
Trump, Donald, 19, 37, 38, 40, 44
Truth Social, 115*b*
twelve-step meetings, 158–59

UNAIDS, 155
Unbelievable, 94
unemployment, 151
United Nations Children's Fund (UNICEF), 110*b*
United Nations Convention on the Rights of Children, 81
United States
    Biden administration, 49
    child welfare system, 82–87
    Civil War, 57
    drug-induced homicide laws, 202
    Federal Poverty Line (FPL), 61
    fentanyl routes of entry, 183–84
    Great Depression, 34*b*
    incarcerated population, 153
    January 6, 2021 attack on the U.S. Capitol, 37–38, 45
    mass incarceration, 150–53
    Obama administration, 64
    opioid crisis, 15–16, 22
    overdose deaths, 15–16, 172
    poverty rates, 24, 73–74
    public opinion, 49
    race relations, 62–64, 65*f*, 66
    slavery system, 188
    social hierarchy, 62–68
    suggestions for cooperation with China, 185
    Trump administration, 40, 54, 84–85
    voter turnout, 39–40
United States Commission on Truth, Racial Healing, and Transformation (TRHT), 76
United States Department of Defense, 141–42
United States Department of Homeland Security (DHS), 42
United States Department of Housing, 76
University of Chicago, 51
"untouchables," 63
Uzbekistan, 110*b*

Valium, 19
Value of Integrity, 197
Value of Service, 197
Vance, J.D., 70
Vermont, 199
veterans, 141–45, 143*f*
Veterans' Health Administration, 141–42, 145
Vicodin, 183
"video ho" meme, 109
Vietnam veterans, 143

Vietnam Veterans Against War, 144
Vietnam War, 154
violence, 35*b*, 37–40
Vivitrol, 72*b*, 158–59, 180
Volkow, Nora, 174
Voting Rights Act Extension, 46

Walker, Frank X., 69*b*
Walker, Scott, 48
War on Drugs, 151, 152, 153–58
    and drug-induced homicide policy, 202
    and harm reduction, 209–10
    and mass incarceration, 12
    opposition to, 48
    social costs, 125, 160
    and women in prison, 121, 122
War on Poverty, 77*b*
Warren, Elizabeth, 48
Washington, DC, 11–12, 128–29
Washington State, 28–34
welfare queens, 95
Welfare Reform Act (Personal Responsibility and Work Opportunity Act, PRWORA), 95
West Virginia, 18, 104, 194, 195
White, Ryan, 3–5
whites
    in criminal justice system, 168*b*
    human trafficking, 117
    incarcerated women, 119
    myth of whiteness, 68*b*
    overdose deaths, 130, 133
    poverty rates, 24, 73–74
    sentences for drug crimes, 168*b*
    sex trafficking, 108–9
    terminology, 84
white supremacy, 45, 68*b*–69, 84
"white trash," 65–66, 67*f*
Wilberforce, William, 57–58
Williams, Robin, 67–68
women, 99–122
    "baby mama drama," 94
    forced labor of, 110*b*
    human trafficking of, 99–100
    hypersexualized, 109
    incarcerated, 119–22, 149*b*
    marginalized, 104
    mothers in treatment, 203*b*
    as nurturers, 91
    pregnant, 100*f*, 100–4
    social costs of mass incarceration, 160–61
    welfare queens, 95
Women and Prison website, 120
Women of African Descent for Reproductive Justice, 104
Working Partners, 211
World War II, 2, 6–7
wraparound services, 32

Xanax, 176, 183

Yang, Andrew, 49
Young, Whitney M., Jr., 213
YouTube, 147
Yvette (case study), 162

Zoom, 171